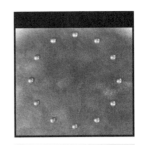

Understanding Policy-Based Networking

Dave Kosiur

Wiley Computer Publishing

John Wiley & Sons, Inc.

NEW YORK · CHICHESTER · WEINHEIM · BRISBANE · SINGAPORE · TORONTO

Publisher: Robert Ipsen

Editor: Carol A. Long

Managing Editor: Angela M. Smith

Text Design & Composition: North Market Street Graphics

Designations used by companies to distinguish their products are often claimed as trademarks. In all instances where John Wiley & Sons, Inc., is aware of a claim, the product names appear in initial capital or ALL CAPITAL LETTERS. Readers, however, should contact the appropriate companies for more complete information regarding trademarks and registration.

This book is printed on acid-free paper.

This publication is designed to provide accurate and authoritative information in regard to the subject matter covered. It is sold with the understanding that the publisher is not engaged in professional services. If professional advice or other expert assistance is required, the services of a competent professional person should be sought.

Library of Congress Cataloging-in-Publication Data:

Kosiur, David R.
    Understanding policy-based networking / Dave Kosiur.
      p. cm. — (Wiley Networking Council series)
    Includes bibliographical references and index.
    ISBN 0-471-38804-1 (pbk. : alk. paper)
    1. Business networks. I. Title. II. Series.

  HD69.S8 K67 2001
  658'.0546—dc21

                                00-050979

Printed in the United States of America.

10 9 8 7 6 5 4 3 2 1

Wiley Networking Council Series

Series Editors:

Scott Bradner
Senior Technical Consultant, Harvard University

Vinton Cerf
Senior Vice President, MCIWorldCom

Lyman Chapin
Chief Scientist, BBN/GTE

Books in series:

- *ISP Survival Guide: Strategies for Running a Competitive ISP*
  Geoff Huston
  ISBN: 0-471-31499-4

- *Implementing IPsec: Making Security Work on VPN's, Intranets, and Extranets*
  Elizabeth Kaufman, Andrew Newman
  ISBN: 0-471-34467-2

- *Internet Performance Survival Guide: QoS Strategies for Multiservice Networks*
  Geoff Huston
  ISBN: 0-471-37808-9

- *ISP Liability Survival Guide: Strategies for Managing Copyright, Spam, Cache, and Privacy Regulations*
  Tim Casey
  ISBN: 0-471-37748-1

- *VPN Applications Guide: Real Solutions for Enterprise Networks*
  Dave McDysan
  ISBN: 0-471-37175-0

- *Converged Networks and Services: Internetworking IP and the PSTN*
  Igor Faynberg, Hui-Lan Lu, and Lawrence Gabuzda
  ISBN: 0-471-35644-1

Contents

Networking Council Foreword

The Networking Council Series was created in 1998 within Wiley's Computer Publishing group to fill an important gap in networking literature. Many current technical books are long on details but short on understanding. They do not give the reader a sense of where, in the universe of practical and theoretical knowledge, the technology might be useful in a particular organization. The Networking Council Series is concerned more with how to think clearly about networking issues than with promoting the virtues of a particular technology—how to relate new information to the rest of what the reader knows and needs, so the reader can develop a customized strategy for vendor and product selection, outsourcing, and design.

In *Understanding Policy-Based Networking* by Dave Kosiur, you'll see the hallmarks of Networking Council books—examination of the advantages and disadvantages, strengths and weaknesses of market-ready technology, useful ways to think about options pragmatically, and direct links to business practices and needs. Disclosure of pertinent background issues needed to understand who supports a technology and how it was developed is another goal of all Networking Council books.

The Networking Council Series is aimed at satisfying the need for perspective in an evolving data and telecommunications world filled with hyperbole, speculation, and unearned optimism. In *Understanding Policy-Based Networking*, you'll get clear information from experienced practitioners.

We hope you enjoy the read. Let us know what you think. Feel free to visit the Networking Council web site at www.wiley.com/networkingcouncil.

Scott Bradner
Senior Technical Consultant, Harvard University

Vinton Cerf
Senior Vice President, MCIWorldCom

Lyman Chapin
Chief Scientist, BBN/GTE

Acknowledgments

The writing of this book has followed a long, though not necessarily tortuous, path to completion since I first started writing about policy-based networking back in 1997. Along the way, I have had the help of many people.

First, I owe a lot to my wife, Sue, for her understanding and patience as I undertook yet another book project. I also have her to thank for once again being my graphics artist for this book, turning my sketches and ideas into concrete figures.

I owe Scott Bradner a sincere thank you for keeping me on an even keel when it came to comparing the proposed protocols and technologies surrounding policy-based networking.

Various members of The Burton Group contributed to this book in one fashion or another. Jamie Lewis and Mary Petrosky were the ones who initially discussed directory-enabled networking, the DEN Initiative, and the details of policy-based networking with me. Phil Schacter helped with some of the issues surrounding security policy and Ray Keneipp brought in some of the issues of regular network management and the capabilities of today's networking equipment.

Rick Roeling, Jeff Scheaffer, and Hugh Mahon of Hewlett-Packard's Open-View Network Management Division reviewed parts of this book and provided valuable information on some of the case studies. Richard Muirhead of Orchestream Ltd. and Tom Hussey of Nortel Networks also helped me with a few of the case studies presented in this book.

Although Carol Long, now executive editor of Wiley Computer Publishing, originally suggested that I write a book on policy-based networking (at a time when I wasn't prepared to do any writing), Shai Herzog of IP Highway was the one who finally got me "roped into" this book.

Last, there are our two cats, Agate and Dusty, who continually tried to add their "two cents worth" to the text by scampering across my keyboard while I was working. Maybe they do know something about policy, but I haven't found out what … yet.

Introduction

Policy-based networking (or policy-based network management, as it's often called) is becoming increasingly important for today's networks. Not only are enterprises and service providers looking to provide new services on today's IP networks, such as quality of service and virtual private networks, but the devices on networks have become more numerous and more complicated to configure. Network management today faces numerous challenges, ones that older ways of doing things cannot solve.

By offering a system-wide view of the network and its services, and shifting the emphasis of network management away from devices and interfaces to users and applications, abstracting the details of device configuration, and centralizing the creation and storage of network policies, policy-based networking offers a solution to many of the pressing network management problems.

Policy-based networking is in its relative infancy, yet the basic framework, components, and protocols are already reasonably well defined and available for use with a number of management applications by enterprises and service providers. The application of policy-based networking requires not only an understanding of new software components and protocols, but also a shift in the way you view the network and its services. The view shifts from one of dealing with the network as a loose collection of separate elements, where each element is often individually configured and monitored, to a more holistic view of the network, where element configurations are performed in a more cooperative, or collective, fashion.

The aim of this book is to provide you, the reader, with an appreciation of both of these aspects of policy-based networking. Not only do we delve into the details of the components of policy-based networking in this book, but we also focus on the change in paradigm from the old element-based view of network management to the newer, holistic view that policy-based networking enables.

How This Book Is Organized

This book is divided into three parts:

- A New Network Management Paradigm
- The Components of Policy-Based Networking
- Applications of Policy-Based Networking

Part One: A New Network Management Paradigm

Part One covers the philosophy behind policy-based networking, including many of the reasons for the growing interest in policy-based networking. It also presents a brief overview of what policy-based networking is and its general framework, setting the stage for the rest of the book.

Chapter 1: New Services, New Requirements

In the first chapter, you'll get an introduction to policy-based networking and learn about the philosophy and terminology behind policy-based networking. Then we'll give you a brief overview of the framework of policy-based networking systems, one that we'll continue to expand upon in the rest of this book.

Chapter 2: Introduction to Policy-Based Networking

This chapter traces the development of policy-based networking, pointing out the main requirements for policy-based networking. This chapter introduces you to the basic components and architecture of policy-based networking systems that we will discuss throughout this book.

Part Two: The Components of Policy-Based Networking

Part Two comprises the bulk of the book, covering each component of the framework for policy-based networking in detail. We start out by defining *policies*, move on to the architectures for policy-based networking, and then to the individual processes—policy creation, policy storage, policy translations and distributions, and finally policy enforcement. This part of the book closes with an example of all the steps in creating and distributing policies and a discussion of some of the standards involved in policy-based networking.

Chapter 3: What Are Policies?

As a first step in understanding policy-based networking, we describe the structure and types of policies, showing how they can be abstracted at various levels within a policy-based networking framework. We discuss some of the methods that have been proposed for representing policies within PBN systems.

Chapter 4: Architectures for Policy-Based Networking

Policy-based networking systems can be built out of the following components: policy console, policy management tool, policy repository, policy decision points, and policy enforcement points, which each get their own chapter in this part of the book. As we start to delve into the details of what these components do and how they communicate with each other, you'll see that a policy-based networking system can be designed in a few different ways. The main difference among these architectures is where the functions of policy-based networking are located.

Chapter 5: Creating and Managing Policies

This chapter is the first in a series of four that deal with the functions of and issues surrounding the main components of a policy-based networking system. Chapter 5 covers the policy console and policy management tool. We start out discussing the basic functions of these components, then move on to other, extended functions (including a feature wish list). The latter half of the chapter covers the details of some of the main issues surrounding the design and use of the policy console and the policy management tool before we wrap up the discussion with our list of the main requirements for a usable component using today's technology.

Chapter 6: The Policy Repository

This chapter takes us one level deeper into the policy-based networking framework, to the policy repository. In Chapter 6, we discuss the advantages and disadvantages of using directories and databases to store policies and other data that's important to policy-based networking. This chapter presents some of the basic features of both directories and relational databases so you could see how they can be used as policy repositories.

Chapter 7: The Policy Decision Point

Chapter 7 covers the procedures and protocols surrounding the policy decision points (PDPs). This chapter focuses not only on the policy decision point itself, but also on the way that a PDP interacts with policy enforcement points (PEPs, the subject of Chapter 8). Much of this chapter focuses on the protocols that have been proposed for the distribution of policy-based device configurations from PDPs to PEPs. We present the pros and cons of COPS, COPS-PR, SNMP, and SNMPCONF in particular, and those of CORBA and telnet/CLI to a lesser degree. The later part of this chapter covers some of the important issues of PDPs and policy distribution, such as scalability, security, and handling of non-policy-aware devices.

Chapter 8: Policy Enforcement Points

This chapter takes us to the lowest layer in our model of policy-based networking, the policy enforcement points (PEPs). Here we discuss the types of PEPs that developers and vendors are considering deploying in policy-based networking and what some of their major requirements are. Chapter 8 examines how many different classes of devices—routers, switches, firewalls, VPN gateways, Web switches, traffic shapers, remote access servers, and even end-user hosts—can serve as policy enforcement devices. This is the last chapter in our series describing the components of the policy-based networking architecture.

Chapter 9: Monitoring Network Behavior and Policies

In this chapter we cover a related—but important—feature, that of monitoring network behavior. Network managers and policy-based networking systems require input from service and application-level monitors in addition to the information garnered from element monitors in order to determine whether policies are producing the desired results. We review the basics of network monitoring, pointing out how monitoring is being extended to include measurements of services. Then we discuss service-level agreements and their importance for verifying services before we talk about how network monitoring can be integrated with policy-based networking.

Chapter 10: An Example of Policy Processing

To close our discussion of the components and their functions, we show how you can use policy to do something useful in managing a network. Chapter 10 presents a detailed example of how policies are generated and distributed within a policy-based networking system all the way from the network manager to the policy enforcement points.

Chapter 11: The Role of Standards in Policy-Based Networking

This chapter attempts to show how the power of policy-based networking is increased by the use of standards. Standards can prove particularly useful when sharing policies among organizations, such as between an enterprise and its service provider; sharing policies among policy domains, such as between network and security managers; coordinating PDPs from different vendors; and supporting multivendor networks. Some of the important protocols that impact these uses are LDAP, SNMP, CORBA, COPS, and XML, as well as the Common Information Model with its DEN extensions.

Chapter 12: Directory-Enabled Networks Initiative

One of the more important developments in policy-based networking has been the work of the DEN Ad Hoc Working Group and the Distributed Management Task Force (DMTF) in what's often referred to as DEN, or Directory-Enabled Networking. These two groups have focused their efforts on the development of an information model that's suitable for use in policy-based networking, among other areas. Chapter 12 covers the evolution of the DEN specification and shows how some of DEN's components can be used in policy-based networking.

Part Three: Applications of Policy-Based Networking

Part Three starts out by covering the two main areas of applying policy-based networking, quality of service (QoS) and security. Then we move on to a more detailed look at how enterprises and service providers can use policy-based networking, including discussions of a few case studies.

Chapter 13: An Introduction to Quality of Service

Policy-based networking systems are needed because QoS capabilities, while desirable, are often too difficult to implement. But before we can describe how you can apply policy-based networking for the control of QoS on a network, we need to provide some background on QoS. This chapter is an overview of the two main methods that have been proposed for QoS on IP networks: Integrated Services (IntServ) and Differentiated Services (DiffServ).

Chapter 14: Policies for Quality of Service

Chapter 14 investigates how policies can be applied to the two main frameworks for QoS—IntServ and DiffServ—showing how they differ. We discuss how, in the IntServ model using RSVP, a device proactively seeks decisions from the decision maker in response to incoming requests for resources, while, in the DiffServ model, policy-based decisions are pushed downward to the devices in response to the creation of higher-level policies, prior to receipt of traffic requiring a QoS treatment.

Chapter 15: Policies for Network Security

This chapter covers how policy-based networking can be applied to security. Before we discuss how security policies can be applied to various devices to enforce security, we describe the components of a security framework that should form the basis of any organization's security policy. In our coverage of the application of security policies using policy-based networking, we focus on two major areas of security: access control and virtual private networks (VPNs).

Chapter 16: Policy-Based Networking for Enterprises

In this chapter, we discuss some of the ways that enterprises have used policy-based networking for their networks, pointing out some of the questions you should answer as you plan your own deployment of policy-based networking. First, we start by reviewing the reasons why you might choose to deploy policy-based networking, and then we discuss some of the common challenges you may face during deployment. We close the chapter by using two case studies to illustrate how some of the early adopters of policy-based networking have accomplished their goals and what they've learned.

Chapter 17: Policy-Based Networking for Service Providers

Chapter 17 talks about some of the reasons service providers have for using policy-based networking, pointing out some of the unique problems they face on their networks. We also discuss some of the deployment issues they have to take into account, and close with a few case studies that show what ISPs are already doing with policy-based networking. As the case studies show, some service providers have already started to use policy-based networking to offer new services to their customers.

Chapter 18: Deploying Policy-Based Networking Systems

In this, the book's final chapter, we recap the important steps to deploying policy-based networking.

Who Should Read This Book

This book is aimed at business and IT managers, system administrators, and network managers who are looking for better ways to manage their networks and tie networks to business uses. Policy-based networking offers one avenue to this goal, and our goal is to provide the reader with enough background to understand the concepts, protocols, and systems associated with policy-based networking. With this background, readers and enterprises should be able to decide whether they want to deploy policy-based networking, for what applications they would use such systems, and what the expected benefits will be.

PART

One

A New Network Management Paradigm

Today's networks are complex connections of resources that often are difficult, if not impossible, to manage. Network managers are still struggling with the configuration of individual devices while their users are concerned with the end-to-end performance of their applications. What's needed is a more holistic view of the network, one that allows network managers to see how their network is performing at a higher level, that of services rather than just throughput.

Policy-based networking provides just such a paradigm shift, shielding network managers from some of the tedium of individual device configuration, allowing them to concentrate on the health of the entire network and how the network is meeting business needs.

New Services, New Requirements

Today's data networks have become such an integral part of business and communications that we often overlook all the effort that's required to maintain and manage these networks. Businesses today are increasingly reliant on IP networks, whether they form an intranet within a business or connect a number of businesses over the public Internet.

The commercialization of the Internet and widespread adoption of Web-based technologies are having a profound impact on how businesses operate. Many industries are moving rapidly to embrace electronic commerce and exploiting the Internet to tap new online markets. At the same time, they are creating intranets and extranets to link employees, customers, suppliers, and business partners. Many enterprises have found that by moving traditional business applications to intranets and extranets they can improve information access, boost productivity, and speed product delivery. For many enterprises, IP networks have become central to their operations, and their networks' importance to the bottom line continues to increase.

To support these new business uses of networks, information technology (IT) managers find themselves continually challenged to meet the demands for new applications and services such as virtual private networks, packetized voice, and streaming media without overtaxing network capacity or compromising security. At the same, IT managers must protect the performance of mission-critical applications even as new, often bandwidth intensive, applications are rolled out. Furthermore, they must ensure that their network is scalable, secure, and reliable.

But the old paradigm of point-based network management—managing each network device as a separate entity—leads to costly inefficiencies on large networks. Furthermore, the old methods do not help the IT manager obtain a holistic, system-wide view of the network, a fundamental necessity for providing the new end-to-end services that network service providers and enterprises are anxious to deploy and use.

A newer paradigm for managing networks is needed, one that provides a better network-wide view than previous approaches. The new approach must add more intelligence to network management, relieving network managers of mundane, repetitive, and error-prone tasks, allowing them to concentrate on the health of the entire network and how the network is meeting business needs. That new approach is called policy-based networking, the subject of this book.

There are a number of reasons why policy-based networking is becoming increasingly important for today's networks. For instance, not only have the devices on networks become more numerous, they have also become more complicated to configure as new services are added. Finding qualified personnel to configure many of these new devices, which incorporate new algorithms and techniques few have extensive experience with, poses another difficulty in managing today's networks. Add to that the need to set and maintain access and security policies that are consistent across the enterprise, and network management today faces numerous challenges, ones that older ways of doing things cannot solve.

By shifting the emphasis of network management away from devices and interfaces to users and applications, abstracting the details of device configuration, and centralizing the creation and storage of network policies, policy-based networking offers a solution to many of the pressing network management problems that we've outlined. Policy-based networking is not a panacea, but it is a step in the right direction, one that's likely to bear fruit for some time. In this chapter, we'll discuss the ways business networks are evolving and the impact that evolution has on network management before we go on to briefly introduce you to policy-based networking. The details of how policy-based networking works and how it can be used will be presented in the rest of the chapters that make up this book.

Business Quality Networks

In order to run their businesses over IP networks, particularly the Internet, corporations expect those networks to be secure and reliable and that their traffic will make it from site to site with a minimum amount of interruption. In the past, corporations would install private networks, often using leased lines between offices, for the transmission of their crucial business traffic. Unlike the Internet, these private networks did not suffer from interruptions due to competition with traffic from other customers. On the Internet, the story is a bit different, since all traffic is transmitted in a best effort manner, that is, each person's traffic has as much chance of making it across a network as the next person's traffic.

Service providers (SPs) face the challenge of supporting IP networks that not only are secure and reliable but also provide the necessary bandwidth and network response for their customers' business-critical applications. Plus, as companies respond faster than ever before to new applications and changes in business, the service providers and their networks must be able to respond quickly to the needs of their customers and their traffic (see Figure 1.1).

Demands on bandwidth are increasing as more users and more applications are added almost daily, increasing the load on networks. In addition, both branch offices and telecommuters have newer, higher bandwidth access to the Internet, enabling them to make more use of these newer network applications. The trend away from dial-up modems to cable modems and digital subscriber line (DSL) services not only places greater demands on bandwidth, but also places new restrictions on address and security management for service providers and businesses. The cost to enterprises to add bandwidth in the wide area network (WAN), while declining, is still prohibitive and provides no guarantee that mission-critical applications will receive priority service.

Today, Internet engineers are working to provide quality of service, or QoS, methods for prioritizing different types of IP traffic over the Internet. QoS

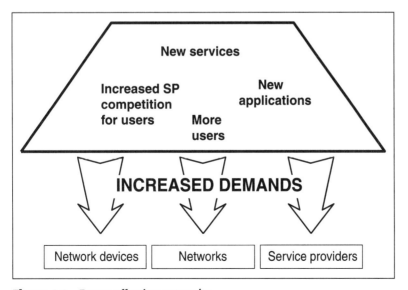

Figure 1.1 Forces affecting networks.

insures that the various types of network traffic (for example, telephony, interactive video, transaction processing, bulk file transfers, Web browsing, and so on) can each obtain network service with the characteristics that they require. This includes bandwidth, delay or latency, error rate, jitter, and packet loss.

While QoS features are useful, enterprises still have to figure out when and how to apply all of these capabilities in their networks. In particular, network managers have to determine which QoS features should be turned on in each network node, so that the resulting flow of traffic meets enterprise needs. Using the usual airline travel analogy, managers should be able to specify which traffic should travel in the typical coach class (everyone gets the same best-effort treatment) or gets upgraded to either first class or business class on the network, and which traffic gets bumped when there is not enough capacity or when cancellations (network outages) occur, all based on business or organizational needs.

Network managers may need policy control over bandwidth-hungry applications, which consume bandwidth at the expense of performance and drive up the cost of expensive wide-area resources. If the network manager plans to use policy-based networking, then he or she also needs to be able to map business requirements into specific policies that link the business needs with the desired network behavior. For example, if an organization is running an enterprise resource planning (ERP) application for strategic competitive advantage, the network manager can create a policy that gives ERP traffic priority to network resources. The business policy is automatically translated into network behavior, such as QoS mechanisms, to prioritize ERP traffic ahead of other traffic.

Policy-based networking systems are needed because QoS capabilities, while desirable, are often too difficult to implement. Some of the issues include the complex and difficult learning curves for switches and routers, the workload associated with configuring QoS parameters and a large enterprise network, and the lack of the system-wide view. Policy-based networking helps hide the complexity QoS controls bring to network management. In addition, policy-based networking helps network managers by providing the following features: centralized network configuration, management of the network as a system, nontechnical definitions of policy, and ease of use.

New applications may also place certain constraints on network performance, including not only bandwidth requirements but also minimal delays, or latencies, in transmission, requiring QoS, further increasing the need for policy-based management of the network. Some of these new applications include voice over data networks, streaming media, and webcasting. Another application that's gaining in importance, IP telephony, requires specific latency and jitter guarantees to deliver a voice quality comparable to that delivered on traditional telephone lines. Videoconferencing can impose similar constraints on the processing of multimedia traffic.

We also mentioned that business networks must be secure. As enterprise networks open up for external access and more business-critical resources become available on the network, security becomes a more critical component of daily operations. Administrators must not only control who has what level of access to what resources, but must also audit the network to guarantee security policy enforcement. Security management includes not only configuring firewalls and servers, but also managing virtual private network (VPN) gateways and a public key infrastructure, each of which has its own parameters and complexity.

Rather than force the network manager to set security policies for individual devices, policy-based management systems can consolidate and synchronize access control lists and related policy information to promote a consistent security policy across the enterprise, regardless of the types or number of devices involved.

Furthermore, instead of treating each policy domain—such as QoS and security—as separate responsibilities with their own data sources, policy-based networking allows managers to manage networks together, using common resources.

Providing Scalable, Manageable Networks

We've already mentioned that the use of the Internet by businesses and individuals alike has been skyrocketing. More users mean more network devices to configure and manage. More uses means more services to manage. The networks of both service providers and enterprises are growing in size, adding to the strain of managing each device on the network.

In the past, you might have thought that many new network services would be restricted to corporate sites that had plenty of bandwidth for their users. But now, with the advent of cheaper, higher bandwidth links such as cable modems and DSL for individuals as well as small businesses and branch offices, you can see how quickly the number of users, devices, and services that need to be configured on a network multiplies. Dealing with these ever-increasing numbers of clients (and their new services) is an impossible task when done manually.

Another factor driving the need for policy-based networking and automatic configuration of both network devices and session setup is the proliferation of more types of mobile devices, such as laptop PCs, cellular phones, and personal digital assistants (PDAs). Now, with a business network supporting all of these different types of devices, the type and quality of the data being transmitted to the user depends on the type of device that he or she is using. And it's highly likely that any single user will have access to more than one type of device, which means that the network has to be smart enough to maintain multiple user profiles for each user and react based on the type of device that the user is using. Obviously this is not the type of task that can be handled manually by a network manager for each user's session.

The problem arises when you consider that most networks are made up of a large number of devices and that these devices must be configured with an increasingly large number of parameters in order to perform the new tasks associated with QoS and VPNs. For any network of appreciable size, such as those found in any medium-sized business, large business, or service provider, it is humanly impossible to configure all the necessary devices within a reasonable time frame. The magnitude of the task is further increased by the need to change these configurations whenever needed, which may be on an hourly, daily, or weekly basis. If it takes longer to configure these devices than the time period for which the configuration is valid, then you can see this as a no-win situation. For instance, it would be a difficult task for a service provider to change the way hundreds of routers prioritize a customer's traffic at the end of each business day if this had to be done manually.

Policy-based networking offers a solution to this dilemma (see Figure 1.2). Rather than expect network managers to configure every individual device on the network, a company using policy-based networking can create policies that are tied to network performance and other services at a high level and have the system translate these policies into configurations for the devices. The policy-based networking system then distributes these configurations to

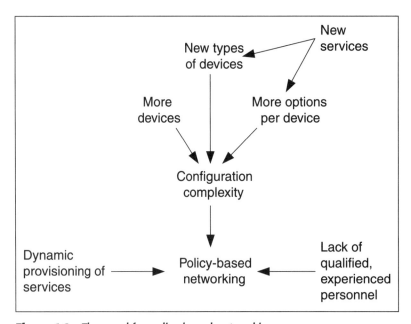

Figure 1.2   The need for policy-based networking.

the appropriate network devices automatically. Plus the policies can change dynamically as network conditions change.

Networks don't run on their own; they must always be monitored and tweaked, which requires skilled personnel. Finding experienced personnel to manage IP networks is a difficult enough task these days, but the difficulty is also compounded by the fact that many of the services supported by new network devices and software are so new that it's difficult for network staff to gain the experience in the short time since the devices were introduced. Policy-based networking can shield network managers from needing to know all the fine details of element management and the myriad number of configuration parameters that many new technologies require. In turn, this may let the enterprise get away with using less highly trained (i.e., cheaper) personnel for some network management tasks.

Shifting from Network Access to Services

We've already mentioned some of the more important network services that businesses expect to use on the Internet, such as security via VPNs and prioritized forwarding of application and user traffic via QoS. But providing these services is not as simple as throwing a switch in a network control center somewhere. This is a fundamental shift in viewing the way networks are used. No longer are we looking at merely buying or selling access, that is, bandwidth, to the Internet. Now we're more concerned with what services the network can offer, especially if those services can help businesses run better.

Services, not just bandwidth or traffic forwarding, are what is now important. And, even as services become more important, the term itself is undergoing a change. Historically, many services—such as telephony and Web services—have not been viewed as part of the network. The network was simply used to deliver those services. Even to today's network manager, *services* usually means things such as Domain Name Service (DNS) and Dynamic Host Configuration Protocol (DHCP).

But there's another way of looking at the network and services. Consider that a network is defined by the services that constitute it. Plus, rather than being specific to a given operating system or hardware platform, as they often have been in the past, these services are interoperable across software and hardware platforms. The availability of a set of interoperable, interchangeable services is becoming a prerequisite for globally scalable networks.

Let's delve into this services-based network a bit more. We can define a series of core network services, such as network-layer services as well as file, print, directory, security, messaging, Web, and object management services (see Figure 1.3). These core services constitute a working network. The services that network managers are most familiar with are the network-layer

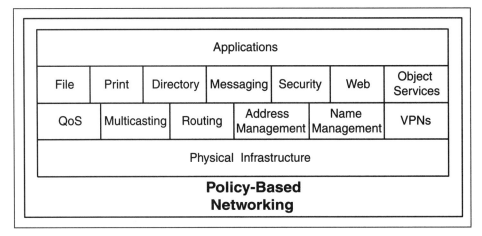

Figure 1.3   The network services model.

services, which include such services as TCP/IP, address management, multicasting, QoS, and virtual private networks. Combining these network-layer services with the other core services puts more of a focus on the application and the user than previously.

This shift to a services-based infrastructure model can have a significant impact on how networks are used and managed. For example, as directory services evolve to support network objects such as switches, routers, addresses, connectivity services, and their attributes, they become a key tool for managing the physical infrastructure, as we'll discuss later in this book. In particular, the availability of interoperable directory, security, and QoS services enables a new management model based on policies. Rather than managing a collection of devices by IP and media access control (MAC) addresses, network managers and service providers can manage users and their associated resources and services via a policy-based networking system.

The services that comprise a network bring with them some intriguing and useful new opportunities for businesses. Primary among these is the opportunity to customize services. This can include customization according to the type of application or the user, the group or organization the user belongs to, the user's role (for example, is the user the CEO or an engineer?), or the time of day or time of month (for example, is it time to do the monthly payroll?).

In order to provide these new services, service providers and enterprises face a number of challenges, including balancing per application state against the complexity and fragility of the network, configuring a wider variety of network equipment on a more dynamic basis than previously, and evolving from an element-based view of networks to one that's a more holistic view, including a focus on end-to-end services. Furthermore, the IP services that service providers wish to offer tend to consist of a complex layering of composite services that span multiple layers of the network model, including the network layer, the presentation layer, and the application layer.

For the most part, data networks are "dumb." The devices themselves may be intelligent, but each device on a network largely acts on its own; there is little cooperation between devices to implement a service on behalf of a client. The model of decentralized control combined with endpoint control (or the "end-to-end argument," as it is known) underlies the design philosophy of the Internet. The idea is that reliable data transfer must be provided by protocols operating at the endpoints, not in the network. Thus the network can be slow, "dumb," or broken, but intelligence in the endpoints should compensate for this. This approach is exactly the opposite of the design philosophy of the telephone network, where endpoints are assumed to be "dumb" and all the intelligence is provided by telephone company equipment.

Whereas networks based on the end-to-end argument are relatively simple and robust, networks designed to support services customized for different applications and users can be expected to be more complex and fragile. What's needed as we move forward is a blending of the two approaches, where the end-to-end argument provides the appropriate simplicity and robustness for a network's core while a controlled degree of complexity is applied at the network's edge. One way of controlling some of the complexity is by means of policy-based networking. (There's another reason for treating the core and edge differently. Many technologies proposed for application- and user-specific services don't scale well and need to be kept out of, or at least aggregated within, the core of a network.)

Accompanying the shift from devices and interfaces to applications and users, network management must also shift from configuring and monitoring network devices to configuring and managing the network services. Since the services are often offered on an end-to-end basis, network management now must include methods for tracking performance from end-to-end as well as determining how the devices are working together to deliver the desired service. Not all devices will work the same way to provide a given service like QoS. Different vendors use different algorithms for queuing, prioritizing, and forwarding traffic, for example. On a given network, even routers from the same vendor may be running different versions of their operating system, forcing the routers to use different QoS techniques and forcing network managers to maintain different configuration options for each router. This point-by-point configuration method isn't conducive to providing end-to-end services on a routine basis.

An added complication is the need for personalizing these services for customers. If everyone gets premium-quality QoS, then it's no different from the times when everyone sent their traffic using best-effort techniques. (QoS implies that someone will always get better service than others will.) In the new services market, some customers will pay for preferred forwarding of their traffic;

others may pay for preferred forwarding of traffic from specific applications or users. In either case, network management needs to be able to configure devices to preferentially treat some traffic, and do so dynamically, that is, whenever the traffic is generated.

Many of these requirements are largely incompatible with the current methods for managing networks.

Managing Network Elements

Until recently, the primary aim of network management was configuring network devices and obtaining network statistics. While these are necessary steps for maintaining a network, the philosophy behind device configuration was rather restrictive—each device had its own unique configuration. Even on those occasions when you had more than one of the same devices performing identical functions on the network, you had to configure each one individually.

Consider how difficult it is to manage a network to provide many of the personalized services we described earlier. In order to provide an end-to-end service, say QoS, the traditional approach would be to individually configure each device in the network's path between the two end users. If some of the routers use a different queuing algorithm to provide the required level of QoS, then the network manager has to be aware of that difference and program those routers accordingly. If he or she does it incorrectly, then the entire QoS setup may be negated.

Another difficulty with today's approach to network management is that, typically, there is no centralized repository for the configurations or rules used to run the networks. Different management consoles are often used to configure or monitor different devices. And different departments are usually responsible for different types of policies. For example, security managers usually control the configuration of firewalls controlling access to enterprise resources, while network managers configure the enterprise's routers and switches. Yet all of these configurations and policies have an immediate impact on each user and each application, so they need to be coordinated.

As we'll see shortly, one of the advantages of policy-based networking is that policies of all kinds can be centrally stored and then distributed as needed to the devices that must enforce them, leading to corporate-wide policies that can be applied in a consistent fashion.

Solving the system and service management challenges of today's networks demands a new generation of network management systems featuring a tighter linkage between network, system, and application-level management information. Effective allocation of network resources requires that network elements understand the profiles governing the performance and business-critical nature of the applications and users on the network. Management information for computing and network elements and resources, whether for configuration, troubleshooting, or performance management, resides in enterprise management applications that should be able to share this information.

However, information describing users and binding them to application services and computing resources is more often the province of enterprise directory systems, not network management systems. Since directories already hold some of this data because of the role that they play in locating systems, mailboxes, Web pages, and application processes, it's become more important than ever to integrate directory, policy, and lower-level network and systems resource data. Although directories play little, if any role, in legacy network management systems, we'll see shortly that directories form an important component of policy-based networking systems.

Now that we've introduced you to many of the crucial reasons for using policy-based network management, let's take a brief look at how policy-based network management differs from the traditional approaches to network management.

Policy-Based Networking: Managing Networks as Systems

Policy-based networking is a shift in the way that networks are managed and network resources are allocated. Instead of emphasizing devices and interfaces, a policy management system focuses on users and applications. It does this by hiding the user to device mapping from the network administrator and relying on a set of network authorities to provide dynamic associations between users of the network and traffic they generate.

Policy-based networking complements and extends current management methods, and offers many benefits. For example, it allows network operators to better match network resources with business needs, ensuring predictable performance for mission-critical applications. It also simplifies network operations ranging from device configuration to the provisioning of new services, making network operators more productive. And by providing centralized control of network resources and services, policy-based networking ensures that security, traffic priority, and other services are applied consistently across the entire network.

In essence, policy-based networking allows network operators to express business goals as a set of rules, or policies, which are then enforced throughout the network. Policy-based networking systems allow such rules to be defined centrally but enforced in a distributed fashion. This type of architecture makes it possible to apply rules either enterprise-wide or within domains, such as specific user groups or geographic areas.

In addition, policy-based networking systems can automate many tasks that network operators have had to perform manually, such as configuring switches and routers to prioritize specific applications. As a result of this automation, policy-based networking systems enable organizations to use services such as QoS that may be too configuration-intensive to deploy otherwise.

Through their integration with directory services, policy-based networking systems can correlate information about users, applications, and network characteristics to ensure that rules are applied appropriately. The combination of policy-based networking and directory services also allows device configuration, inventory control, and other management functions to be automated.

Policy-based networking thus offers a network manager the ability to manage the network in a holistic and dynamic fashion, rather than treat each device individually. This is an important paradigm shift for network management. In the past, network managers were more concerned with the configuration and performance of individual devices, not the end-to-end performance and services that the network could deliver to the users.

What Are Policies?

A *policy* is a set of rules and instructions that determine the network's operation. Policies express management's view of how the corporate network should be used by employees, applications, suppliers, business partners, Web site visitors, and so on. Policies can encompass many areas of network operations. For example, network operators can define security rules regarding access to network resources, such as application servers and Internet access links. Likewise, network operators can define traffic prioritization rules that protect mission-critical applications from noncritical applications.

The word *policy* is not new to either network managers or security administrators; many of them are already using policies in some form to manage their resources. For instance, network managers often set policies for assigning IP addresses to specific classes of machines, typically using DHCP. Similarly, security administrators define policies regarding what types of traffic a firewall passes or rejects. Although administrators can define policies at a high level—for example, no SAP application traffic should pass beyond the WAN router—implementing policies has been onerous.

The basic building block of a policy is a policy rule, which is a simple declarative statement associating a policy object with a value. For example a policy rule can define a destination, such as destination = AccountingServer, or it can define an action, such as Priority=Gold. Policy rules define either conditions or actions. Each policy includes one or more conditions and one or more actions. The conditions define when the policy rule is applicable.

Simple policies contain a set of conditions and a set of actions, as this example shows:

```
if (((trafficToOrFrom AccountingSubnet) and
     (dayOfMonth is last10days))
then
       priority = high
endif
```

In this example, the two rules between the "if" and "then" are the conditions of the policy, while the then statement (priority = high) is the action rule.

But policies don't have to stop there. Policies might also include a sophisticated user logon policy that sets up application access, security, and reconfigures network connections based on a combination of user identity, network location, logon method, and time of day. We'll have more to say about policies in Chapter 3, "What Are Policies?"

What's Needed for Policy-Based Networking?

Now that we've briefly looked at the basics of policies, let's look at the components of policy tools. A policy-based networking system consists of tools for accomplishing certain tasks:

- Creating rules and policies
- Checking for policy conflicts
- Storing policies
- Distributing policies
- Converting policies into commands that network devices understand
- Distributing those commands to the network devices
- Verifying policy distribution

The general architectural model for accomplishing these tasks consists of a policy management console, the policy repository, policy decision points, and policy enforcement points (see Figure 1.4).

The policy console serves as the interface between the network manager and the rest of the policy system. For example, a network manager would use the policy console to author and edit policies and monitor the status of the network. To simplify the use of the system, the rules are usually created at a high level of abstraction, using English-like commands. The policy console

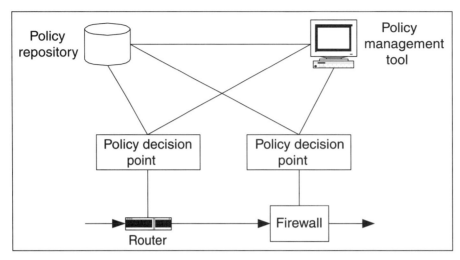

Figure 1.4 Architecture for a policy-based networking system.

also translates the rules that managers create in the editor into entries that match a predefined schema for storage within the policy repository.

Turning to the policy repository, a directory or database stores the rules and policies required by the system. But network devices need other data in order to enforce policies. This data includes mappings between user names and IP addresses (from DHCP and DNS servers, for example) so that the English-like policies that network managers enter at a policy console to control user traffic can be converted to policy data based on IP addresses and port numbers that network devices require to process traffic. Many enterprises will already have some of this stored electronically in a flat file, a database, or a directory. The policy-based management system needs to integrate, or at least link, this data with the data stored in the policy repository.

The next component in the architecture, the policy decision point (PDP) or policy server, is responsible for accessing the policy data stored in the repository and making decisions based on those policies. The PDP is software that may either run on one of the network hosts or be incorporated into a switch or router.

PDPs base their decisions on requests from network devices or applications, policies stored in the central repository, and changes in network conditions. PDPs may have to include a translator module to convert policy decisions into commands understandable to older devices that are not policy-aware. These translation modules most commonly use protocols such as the Simple Network Management Protocol (SNMP) or the device's specific Command Line Interpreter (CLI) to convert policy decisions into device configurations.

The remaining components of the architecture—the policy enforcement points, or PEPs—are the network devices that actually implement the decisions that the policy decision points have passed to them. PEPs include devices such as routers, VPN security gateways, and firewalls.

What Policy-Based Networking Can Offer

Throughout the chapter, we've already pointed out many of the ways that policy-based networking can help make the new services expected of today's networks a reality. Now, as a summary, let's quickly run through two scenarios showing how policy-based networking can be used for two important network services—QoS and VPNs.

Quality of Service

Many of the first policy-based management systems on the market provide a way for network managers to automate the administration of QoS facilities on the network. Using such a system, a network manager can create policies for prioritizing traffic from different users and applications. The system then converts these policies into configurations of the appropriate network devices. If the network manager has defined three classes of traffic priorities, for example, then the system distributes configuration files to the routers that describe the way that the routers should process these three classes of traffic. Since different routers may be running different versions of routing code or may have different queue sizes and traffic-processing algorithms, each configuration file may be different. The point is that the network manager doesn't have to configure each router individually. The policy-based management system takes care of the configuration based on information that it stores about the capabilities of each network device and the high-level policies that the network manager has defined.

Virtual Private Networks

Currently, different devices implement different parts of security policy. Devices at the edge of the corporate network, such as firewalls, routers, remote access servers, and VPN security gateways, allow wholesale access. Devices such as proxy servers handle access from within the network to the outside world. And within the network, individual servers and workstations have access controls such as Windows NT logins and Kerberos tickets. Generally, vendors haven't implemented these controls in a way that allows managers to apply high-level security policies across product boundaries. Different devices may offer the same user different levels of access, eliminating any chance of deploying an effective security policy if network managers must configure security parameters on a device-by-device basis.

Rather than force the network manager to set security policies for individual devices, policy-based management systems can consolidate and synchronize access control lists and related policy information to promote a consistent security policy across the enterprise, regardless of the types or number of devices involved.

Using VPNs as an example, a network manager can use a policy-based management system to set policies for selection of tunneling protocols and client addressing preferences according to the type of user connection (dial-in versus LAN, for example). Managers can also configure the policy-based management system to update client VPN software or configurations instead of configuring each security device and each user's workstation individually, making the management of the VPN system more scalable.

Not only are there many ways to apply policy-based networking, but there are many places on IP networks that policy-based networking can be applied, by network service providers, application service providers, and enterprises alike (see Figure 1.5).

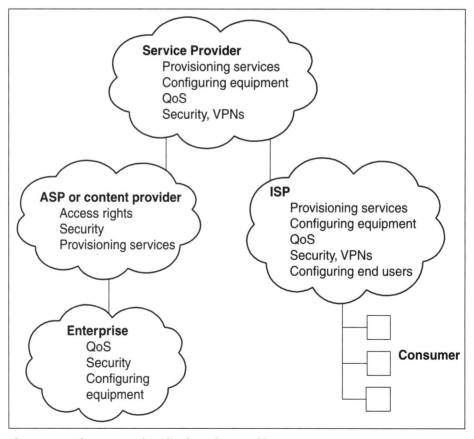

Figure 1.5 Places to apply policy-based networking.

Summary

Policy-based networking is becoming increasingly important for today's networks for a number of reasons. Much of this is driven by the push to provide new services, such as QoS and VPNs, on today's IP networks. Not only have the devices on networks become more numerous, they have also become more complicated to configure as new services are added. Finding qualified personnel to configure many of these new devices poses another difficulty in managing today's networks. Add to that the need to set and maintain access and security policies that are consistent across the enterprise, and network management today faces numerous challenges, ones that older ways of doing things cannot solve.

By shifting the emphasis of network management away from devices and interfaces to users and applications, abstracting the details of device configuration, and centralizing the creation and storage of network policies, policy-based networking offers a solution to many of the pressing network management problems that we discuss in this chapter. This chapter also presents a brief overview of the framework of policy-based networking systems, one that we'll continue to expand upon in the rest of this book.

In the following chapter, you'll get an introduction to policy-based networking and learn about the philosophy and terminology behind policy-based networking. Then we'll give you an overview of the components of policy-based networking before we describe the details of, and issues surrounding, each of the components in following chapters.

Introduction to Policy-Based Networking

We've already explained how policy-based networking has an integral role to play in the management of today's networks. By offering network managers a system-wide view of their networks, translating business policies into device configurations to provide new services, and promoting the use of centralized policies, policy-based networking offers a much-needed new paradigm for the management of today's evolving networks. But policy-based networking is a young technology, one that's relatively unproven and still evolving. Before we get into the details of all the components of policy-based networking (which is the purpose of most of this book), let's take a look at how policy-based networking came to be, and what's needed to put together a policy-based networking system.

In this chapter, we'll set the stage for much of the rest of this book, particularly the following 10 chapters. As an introduction to policy-based networking, this chapter will not only discuss the philosophy behind policy-based networking, but also describe the requirements for, and terminology behind, policy-based networking. Then we'll give you an overview of the components of policy-based networking before we describe the details of, and issues surrounding, each of the components in following chapters.

The Philosophy behind Policy-Based Networking

Rather than force a network manager to manage the network by dealing with each device individually, policy-based networking offers a network manager the ability to manage the network in a holistic and dynamic fashion. This is an important paradigm shift for network management. In the past, network managers were more concerned with the configuration and performance of individual devices, not the end-to-end performance and services that the network could deliver to the users.

Policy-based networking is a shift in the way that networks are managed and network resources are allocated. Instead of emphasizing devices and interfaces, a policy management system focuses on users and applications. It does this by hiding the user to device mapping from the network manager and relying on a set of network entities to provide dynamic associations between users of the network and traffic they generate.

In essence, policy-based networking allows network managers to express business goals as a set of rules, or policies, which are then enforced throughout the network. Policy-based networking systems allow such rules to be defined centrally but enforced in a distributed fashion. This architecture makes it possible to apply rules either enterprise-wide or within domains, such as specific user groups or geographic areas.

In addition, policy-based networking systems can automate many tasks that network managers have had to perform manually in the past, such as configuring switches and routers to prioritize traffic from specific applications. As a result of this automation, policy-based networking systems enable organizations to use services such as QoS that would otherwise be too configuration-intensive to deploy.

To sum up, policy-based networking aims to provide a network-wide view of performance and services by centralizing policies and building on the intelligence of network devices to make decisions for processing traffic based on those policies.

Another term that's been closely linked to policy-based networking is directory-enabled networking. In fact, for some, directory-enabled networking and policy-based networking are synonymous. However, there are some fine distinctions between the two terms, ones worth bearing in mind as we work our way through this book. As the term implies, *directory-enabled computing* focuses on the use of directories for storing policies. In the case of policy-based networking, developers are more pragmatic about how policies are stored, using either directories or databases. Since we're concerned with not only the theoretical concepts behind policy-based networking, but also the pragmatic issues and real-life deployment of policy-based networking, we'll continue to use the term *policy-based networking* to describe the focus of this book, and use *directory-enabled networking* when we describe systems that are specifically tied to directories. As you'll see throughout the book, directories do provide certain advantages for storing certain types of data, but many vendors of policy-based networking systems have chosen to use databases rather than directories for storing policies.

Directory-enabled computing also has some broader objectives than policy-based networking, looking to enable all types of applications to leverage the power of the network via information stored in directories. In these cases, directories are central because they integrate information about users, applications, and the network infrastructure. For example, the use of directory services can also facilitate the automation of device configuration, inventory control, and other management functions.

A Bit of History

While policy-based networking has been on the minds of many networking engineers for at least the last few years, it wasn't until some of the leading vendors looked to apply the capabilities of directories to managing networks that interest in policy-based networking became noticeable. In May 1997, Microsoft and Cisco announced their Directory Enabled Networks (DEN) initiative, aimed at integrating networks and directory services for the purposes of providing advanced management of network elements and services. To encourage industry input into the development of the specification, Microsoft and Cisco held an open design preview in November 1997. Representatives from a broad spectrum of networking and directory service vendors as well as corporate and academic customers attended. This initial design preview followed an announcement of the Directory Enabled Networks Initiative that September.

Many of the vendors who attended the design preview formed the DEN Ad Hoc Working Group (AHWG) for the express purpose of drafting a DEN specification. The goal of the AHWG was the specification of a directory services information model and schemas to facilitate the interoperability of distributed applications, management tools, and network elements. To ensure that the specification included customer input, the AHWG also formed a Customer Advisory Board, which included representatives from Fortune 500 companies such as Texaco, Charles Schwab, Sprint, and the University of Washington.

In fall of 1998, the DEN Ad Hoc Working Group's Customer Advisory Board submitted its final draft of the DEN specification to the Distributed Management Task Force (DMTF). Although much of the original DEN specification was already based on the concepts of the DMTF's Common Information Model (CIM), the DMTF now committed its resources to incorporate the DEN specification into the CIM specifications.

We now have two major standards-setting organizations working on standards that relate to policy-based networking—the DMTF and the Internet Engineering Task Force (IETF). The DMTF is continuing the work on defining the information model originally started by Microsoft and Cisco and the DEN Initiative, while the IETF is focusing on mapping the DEN information model to Lightweight Directory Access Protocol (LDAP) and defining auxiliary protocols for distributing policies on networks.

The IETF is responsible for developing many of the standard protocols used on the Internet. This includes work on LDAP as well as protocols for QoS, such as Resource Reservation Protocol (RSVP) and Differentiated Services (DiffServ), and network management (the Simple Network Management Protocol, for example). In 1999, the IETF created a new working group, the Policy Framework Working Group, for the express purpose of coordinating other IETF groups' work on directory-enabled networking and defining the relationships between CIM and the work done within the IETF. The Policy Framework WG thus focuses on the architecture and data model of DEN; its work on the data model includes defining the mapping of CIM's DEN-related schemas into LDAP.

There are other IETF working groups that are either developing protocols or schemas for use in policy-based networking. For example, the Dynamic Host Configuration Working Group is working on the schemas for address management using the Dynamic Host Configuration Protocol (DHCP), making it easier to map IP addresses to users. The Resource Admission Policy (RAP) Working Group developed the Common Open Policy Service (COPS) protocol for distributing policies between policy decision points and policy enforcement points. The DiffServ Working Group has been working on the appropriate information model and directory mappings for QoS. On the security front, the IP Security (IPSec) Working Group is developing schemas for security policies for VPNs.

What's Required for Policy-Based Networking?

If you're going to use policy to control your networks and networked applications, a policy-based networking system should meet the following four requirements:

An extensible information model for network elements, network services, networks, and clients of the network

A policy specification language that can represent business requirements and functions in a vendor- and device-independent manner

A scalable framework for policy administration, management, conflict resolution, and distribution

A scalable means to translate from device- and vendor-independent policy
specification to vendor- and device-specific configuration commands

Let's look at each of these requirements in a little more detail.

First, what is an information model? An information model is a representation of the entities that make up your managed environment and the way
they interact with each other. In other words, the information model is
where you formally describe the types of devices and services that make up
your network, what the components of each device and service are, and how
the devices relate to the services (and vice versa). The best-known (and
most extensive) information model for policy-based networking is the DEN
model we mentioned earlier, which has become part of the DMTF's Common
Information Model. The information model makes it easier to build interoperable applications and systems because it provides a common description
of network entities.

It's one thing to define objects in an information model; it's quite another to
have a common language for those objects that can be shared among applications. It's not a question of data access—if the information model were mapped
to an LDAP-compatible directory, for example, then LDAP can be used as the
data access protocol. It's a question of how the data is described. Sticking with
our directory example, directories from different vendors may store data differently and the data from these directories cannot be exchanged directly.
Instead, if two directories are sharing data, one directory would have to discover how the other's storing data (for example, is a user's name stored as last
name, first name or first name, last name or just a single field with the full
name?) and then transform the data to mesh with its own way of storing the
same data. (For those of you interested in specific terms, the first part of this
process is called *schema discovery*.)

As we've mentioned before, one of the difficulties facing network managers
today is that they must manage ever-increasing numbers of network devices,
with ever-increasing numbers of configuration options. Since it's doubtful that
networks will get smaller in the future, this is an issue that we'll have to deal
with for some time. Any system designed for policy-based networking must
therefore be able to scale upward to the largest conceivable networks. This
includes such issues as policy representation and storage, as well as policy
retrieval methods and policy distribution protocols. We'll discuss these issues
where appropriate in the following chapters.

The framework, or architecture, for policy-based networking can affect a
system's scalability, but the performance of each of the protocols and devices
also has an impact. We'll see in later chapters, especially Chapters 6 to 8, how

the different components of policy-based networking systems affect the system's scalability and what's being done to improve scalability.

Internet engineers and vendors are still working on meeting the four requirements listed previously. Of the four requirements, the one that's probably seen the least progress is that of defining a policy description language, although it's quite likely that Extensible Markup Language (XML) will be used as the foundation for such a language.

Although we hadn't stated it earlier as a requirement, we expect that a policy-based networking system will be interoperable with similar systems, whether they are policy-based networking systems from other vendors or other types of network management systems. The architecture of policy-based networking, which we'll discuss later in this chapter, supports interoperability at different levels within the system.

At the highest level in the architecture, policy-based networking systems can be interoperable with each other. This is important when policies must cross domain boundaries and the two domains are using systems from different vendors, say, between an enterprise customer and a service provider, or between two service providers. In order for the systems to be interoperable, the systems should be built upon the same information model (here's where the DEN work of the DMTF becomes especially valuable) and have a common language, a policy description language, for describing the policies that need to be shared.

At an intermediate level in the architecture, policy-based networking systems can be interoperable by sharing policy repositories. This could be the situation when managers with two different areas of responsibility—say, a network manager handling QoS and an IT manager handling security—are using different consoles, or even different vendors' products for setting policies. Again, sharing the same information model is important but so is sharing the same mapping of the information model to the data model. (In other words, using a data store with the same mappings.) Some vendors already offer different consoles for different areas of responsibility, but no vendors yet claim that their products are interoperable at the data store level.

At the lowest level in the architecture, policy-based networking systems need to work with network devices from more than one vendor. It's rare to find a network of any appreciable size that's built out of products from only one vendor. One way that policy-based networking systems deal with a multi-vendor network is to use standard protocols, such as SNMP, CLI (a command line interpreter), and COPS, to distribute policies. However, even when standard protocols are used, each vendor of a policy-based system must create its own set of rules for translating policies into configuration commands for network devices from other vendors.

While system-wide interoperability is an admirable goal—one that allows you to select best-of-breed components for your management system—you'll find that most currently available policy-based networking systems use proprietary methods somewhere in their architecture, limiting their interoperability. That may change as DEN evolves and is more widely adopted than it is today.

Policies versus Decisions

While we've pointed out that policy-based networking systems hide the details of device configurations from network managers, allowing the managers to create network-wide policies that define and control services, there are a number of important steps that must be followed to turn those high-level policies into information that the network devices can act upon.

At the higher levels in a policy-based networking system, policies may be represented at various levels of abstraction. As these policies percolate down through the system, they have to be translated into forms that can be understood by the devices that act on them. As we get deeper into the system, some of the devices will have to make decisions based on the policies they receive and act on those decisions to configure other devices to enforce the decisions.

Before we move on to the next section, which describes the different devices that make up a policy-based networking system, let's quickly review what policies and decisions are, at least within the framework of policy-based networking.

The basic building block of a policy is a *policy rule*, which is a simple declarative statement associating a policy object with a value. For example, a policy rule can define a destination, such as destination = R&D or destIPaddr = 192.168.72.12, or it can define an action, such as Priority = Gold. Policy rules define either conditions or actions (see Figure 2.1). Each policy then includes

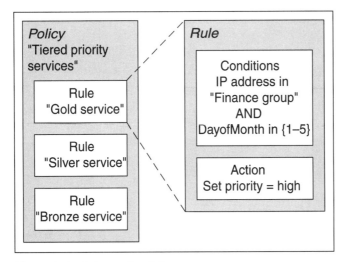

Figure 2.1 Rules and policies.

one or more conditions and one or more actions. The *conditions* define when the policy rule is applicable; if the conditions in a policy aren't met, then the actions comprising that policy are not enacted.

It's important to note that policies can contain other policies in an inheritance model. This notion of inheritance is crucial for efficient and scalable use of policy-based networking, since it enables network managers to build complex policies from a set of simpler policies. Inheritance also simplifies the management of policies, since an entire policy doesn't need rewriting when a manager redefines a rule. For example, if a manager changes a policy rule defining the Accounting Subnet (AccountingSubnet = 192.168.72.0) to a new subnet (say, 206.168.71.0), then he or she doesn't have to rewrite any policies using the AccountingSubnet.

Policies trigger a number of translation steps in a policy-based networking system. Let's walk through the sequence of events in Figure 2.2 to see how policies can be translated.

First, there's the translation of policies from a user-friendly English-like syntax to forms compatible with the policy repository; the actual format of the

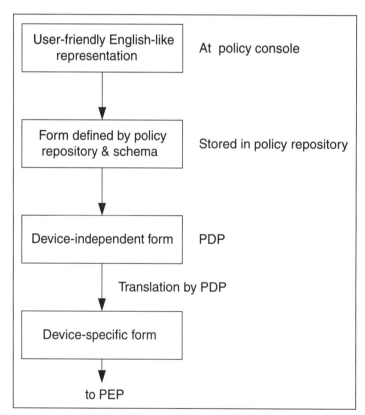

Figure 2.2 Distributing policies, decisions, and configurations.

result depends on the schema defined for the data storage device. The next step is to translate a policy from a form that does not specify how to configure any devices to one that does include device configuration data, but in a device-independent form. This device-independent form is useful for describing a network service (in our case, marking traffic for differentiated services) so that different devices can each play their part in enforcing the policy.

A subsequent translation is from this device-independent form to a device-specific form. This may be necessary for a variety of reasons. For example, not all devices have the same capabilities, so some mapping is necessary to accommodate the limitations of the device. Also, not all devices can implement a function the same way; some devices use the same general type of algorithm, such as weighted fair queuing, but have different resource requirements.

Let's leave our example showing the different ways that policies can be abstracted and add one more complicating factor. Since networks and the traffic they carry are always changing, a policy-based networking system needs to be able to respond to the dynamics of the network. That means that there must be decision-making points throughout the system, either to interpret the results of combining policies or reinterpreting policies when network conditions change.

As an example, the software converting device-independent policies to device-dependent policies may have to stop implementing a policy and notify the system administrator that a given policy is not enforceable. This might occur if one or more of the devices that it's responsible for couldn't support the action required by the policy. (A router might not have enough queues to support the number of traffic classes required in the policy.) If the original conditions of policy are not met, it's possible to include fallback rules so that the decision-making software can implement a slightly different form of the policy, say, using two traffic classes instead of four. Similarly, if a VPN gateway is inoperative, the decision-making software may have to reject any traffic coming from the CEO when he or she is off-site because there's no way to set up an encrypted VPN tunnel.

The Components of Policy-Based Networking Systems

Now that we've looked at the basics of policies and their enforcement, let's look at the components of policy-based networking tools.

Although many descriptions of policy-based network management still use the original component names—console, repository, policy decision point, and policy enforcement point—the terminology is in a state of flux. Policy-based management involves more than one technology—network management, device configuration, signaled QoS using RSVP, and provisioned QoS using DiffServ, for example—and some terms have different meanings to each of the groups involved in the development of these technologies. See Table 2.1 for a list of synonymous terms.

Table 2.1   Terms for Components in Policy-Based Networking

BOOK TERMINOLOGY	SYNONYMOUS TERMS
Policy console	User interface
Policy management tool	Policy manager
Policy repository	Master archive
Policy decision point	Policy server Remote decision point Local decision point Policy consumer Policy advisor
Policy enforcement point	Policy target Enforcement device

As you might expect, policy-based networking systems have a large number of tasks to perform in order to manage today's complex networks. Much like today's window-based operating systems, a great deal of processing underlies the simplified interface that's presented to the user or, in this case, the network manager. The more important tasks include policy storage, policy translation, policy distribution, and policy enforcement. The general architectural model developed by the DMTF and the IETF to accomplish these tasks consists of a policy console, the policy repository, policy decision points, and policy enforcement points as shown in Figure 2.3. This is the model that we'll use to describe policy-based networking and compare other management systems throughout this book.

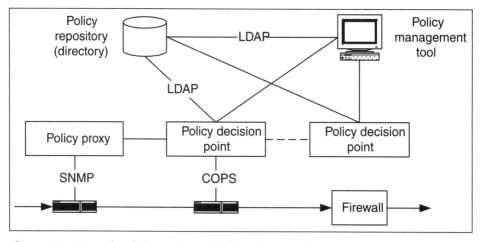

Figure 2.3   General architecture for policy-based networking.

The policy console serves as the interface between the system and the network manager. A network manager can use the policy console to author and edit policies and monitor the status of the network, for example. To simplify using of the system, the rules are usually created at a high level of abstraction, using English-like commands. For example, network managers can group users according to department such as Accounting, Engineering, or Sales, and can classify routers as backbone versus edge routers.

The policy management tool works in conjunction with the policy console to provide the first level of validation for the rules, checking semantics and data types and making sure that rules don't conflict with each other when they're combined into policies. For example, the policy management tool would flag two policies if the first set the priority of all R&D traffic to a value of 6 and the second policy set the priority of all File Transfer Protocol (FTP) traffic to a priority of 5, since a conflict would occur for any R&D FTP traffic. The policy management tool also translates the rules that managers create in the editor into entries that match predefined schemas for storage within the policy repository and can issue alerts to other parts of the system, notifying that policies affecting them have changed.

Turning to the policy repository, either a directory or a database can store the rules and policies required by the system. The repository also may store user data, such as authentication and access rights, user profiles, IP infrastructure data (such as startup files for routers), and address and name server data. Policy-based management systems can leverage the inheritance of the underlying directory, giving managers the ability to aggregate policies based on a whole company, specific organizations within a company, and specific users.

The primary purpose of the policy repository is to store the policy rules that the network manager creates for the policy-based networking system. In order for the policy-based networking system to meet the goals we described earlier, policies need to be related to information about users, such as their current IP address and access rights. If a directory is the policy repository, then it can also be used to store other policy-related information, such as user IDs, attributes, access control information, and pointers to device or network information. On the other hand, if a database is used to store policies, the system must include some link between the database and the data store for user information, which is usually a directory. In most instances, the common protocol for accessing data from a directory is LDAP.

Although the DMTF-IETF architecture allows for various policy repositories, directory services are the preferred repository by the standards groups. LDAP is specifically referenced as the access protocol and schemas used to store the policy rules. In LDAP, the policy rules are represented as a set of object entries that include, among others, object classes for policy rules, conditions, and actions. Many vendors of policy-based networking systems use databases rather than directories for storing policies, however. We'll discuss some of the reasons for these implementation differences later, in Chapter 6, "The Policy Repository."

The next component in the architecture, the policy decision point (PDP), is responsible for accessing the policies stored in the repository and making decisions based on those policies. (Some vendors and IETF documents refer to the policy decision point as either a policy server or a policy consumer.) PDPs base their decisions on requests from network devices or applications, policies stored in the central repository, and changes in network conditions. For instance, the priority of the Accounting group's traffic may change from Gold to Silver at 5 P.M. every Friday. A PDP would monitor the system clock and reassign the Accounting group's traffic to the lower priority, perhaps by reassigning the traffic from the Accounting group's subnet to a lower priority queue on all routers and switches, at 5 P.M. every Friday.

Two different models for implementing policies between PDPs and policy enforcement points (PEPs) have been proposed—the outsourced model and the provisioned model. PDPs may support either one, or both. In the outsourced policy model, some components of the policy framework rely upon other components of that same framework to perform policy-related decisions. This model locates the policy decision-making function in a component separate from the device where the policy is executed. In the architecture outlined previously, a PEP would outsource the policy decision-making function to a PDP; this might occur, for example, if a router is processing RSVP requests.

In the provisioned policy model, devices that execute policy are configured prior to the events that will prompt decisions. Configuration is pushed to the device, for example, based on time of day or at the initial booting of the device. In this model, routers would obtain their DiffServ Code Points (DSCPs) from a PDP upon booting.

The PDP also resolves any policy conflicts, such as two policies that each request 100 Kbps bandwidth on the same 128 Kbps line, and then distributes its decisions to the policy enforcement points (PEPs). Before it can distribute decisions to PEPs, a PDP must translate the decisions into device-specific mechanisms, such as a traffic filter or an instance of a traffic policer.

A PDP may have to use more than one protocol to communicate policy information to network devices. A PDP can use telnet along with a Command Line Interpreter (CLI) or SNMP to communicate with network devices. However, the IETF has also defined a new protocol, the Common Open Policy Service (COPS) protocol, which provides a more interactive link between PDPs and PEPs for exchanging policy decision information and device state information. We'll discuss the different approaches to policy-based networking using COPS, SNMP, CLIs, and other methods in Chapter 7, "The Policy Decision Point."

The PDP also logs events from network devices and monitors network usage. The PDP can use this information about the network to invoke new policy-based decisions. It might also aggregate information about the state of network devices and forward that information to the policy console for display to a network manager.

The remaining components of the architecture, the policy enforcement points, are the network devices that actually implement the decisions that the policy decision points pass to them. (Some IETF documents refer to PEPs as policy targets.) This is where the rubber meets the road. Policy enforcement points include devices such as routers, VPN security gateways, and firewalls. If a PEP does not already have a policy for processing specific traffic, then it will request an appropriate decision from a PDP (using COPS, for example). But in many cases, the PEP will have received a series of policies from the PDP upon startup, and those policies will be cached within the device. The PEP may also relay events to a PDP to keep the PDP informed of changes in network or device conditions.

The policy enforcement point uses the commands it receives from a PDP to process network traffic. How a PEP actually processes the traffic is entirely up to the device's type; that is, whether it's a switch, router, remote access server, firewall, VPN gateway, or host. Processing the traffic also depends on the device's capabilities, such as whether a layer 3 switch has two or four queues and what queuing algorithms are supported.

As we mentioned previously, a policy-based networking system cannot work in a vacuum. The system also may need to store or access user profiles and user data, such as authentication and access rights, as well as IP infrastructure data (such as startup files for routers) and address and name server data. Furthermore, to be an effective tool in network management, the system needs an idea of the network topology and how the network is performing. Monitoring network traffic, for example, provides important feedback to network managers about the efficacy of the policies they've created.

Summary

Policy-based networking is a shift in the way that networks are managed and network resources are allocated. Instead of emphasizing devices and interfaces, a policy-based networking system focuses on users and applications. It does this by hiding the user to device mapping from the network manager and relying on a set of network entities to provide dynamic associations between users of the network and traffic they generate.

In addition to tracing the development of policy-based networking, this chapter points out the main requirements for policy-based networking: an extensible information model, a policy specification language that can represent business requirements and functions in a vendor- and device-independent manner, and a scalable framework for policy administration and policy translation.

We also discussed the different levels of abstraction of policies as they change from policies we humans deal with to ones that network devices must understand to process network traffic. Last, this chapter introduces the architecture of policy-based networking systems—which are composed of policy console, policy repository, policy decisions points, and policy enforcement points—that we will use throughout this book.

In the next chapter, we'll delve into more of the details of rules and policies, discussing their structure, how they can be represented, and presenting more details on their levels of abstraction within policy-based networking systems.

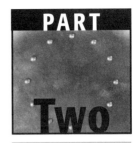

PART

Two

The Components of Policy-Based Networking

Network managers need to understand what we mean by *policy* as well as how the policies are translated and distributed throughout the management system. More than one type of policy can be involved in network management: quality of service (QoS) may be one of the most visible, but don't forget security, including access control as well as VPN setup.

   A typical policy-based networking system consists of a number of components: policy console, policy repository, policy servers, and policy enforcement points. Each of these components has it own strengths and weaknesses; the way the components are integrated into an architecture also affects the functionality of the system.

What Are Policies?

Two of the more important advantages of policy-based networking (PBN) are the mapping of business goals to network resource usage and PBN's ability to hide many of the details of network element configuration from the network manager. But, in order to accomplish these goals, the system needs a series of standard representations for policies, ones that make sense to the network manager as well as the equipment being configured. As we'll see in this chapter, we need more than one representation of policy because the system needs to work our way through different amounts of detail in different policies, plus we want the policies to be scalable across the policy-based networking system. It's not enough to simply represent a device's configuration in an English-like language if network managers still have to use that language to deal with each individual device; they haven't really gained much efficiency in the process. We want network managers to be able to define larger, network-wide entities within policies so that devices or services can be grouped and managed together. That means that the translation process for policies has to understand the composition of these groups and new policies must be written as needed in different parts of the policy-based networking system in order to convert high-level abstractions to device-dependent configurations when needed, with minimal human intervention. Proper policy representations are an essential component enabling this process.

   As a first step in understanding policy-based networking, we'll describe the structure and types of policies, showing how they can be abstracted at various levels within a policy-based networking framework. We'll also discuss some of the methods that have been proposed for representing policies within PBN systems.

Policy Structure

In basic terms, policies consist of conditions and corresponding actions. Following the lead of the IETF and the DMTF, the basic building block of a policy is a *policy rule* (or simply, rule), which is a simple declarative statement associating a policy object with a value. For example a policy rule can define a destination, such as destination address = Sales Server, or it can define an action, such as Priority = Gold. Policy rules define either conditions or actions. Each policy includes one or more conditions and one or more actions, as shown in Figure 3.1. The conditions define when the policy rule is applicable.

Policy conditions could be items such as a user, a user's organization, an application, the time of day, the computer used, or a subnet. Some example rules describing conditions for a policy are shown in Table 3.1.

The other type of rule, the policy action, describes what the network, device, or similar entity should do, as shown in Table 3.2.

Another use of policy actions can be the installation or removal of a device configuration.

When we combine rules together to form policies, we end up with policies that fall into one of two classes—simple or complex.

Simple policies contain a set of conditions and a set of actions, as this example shows:

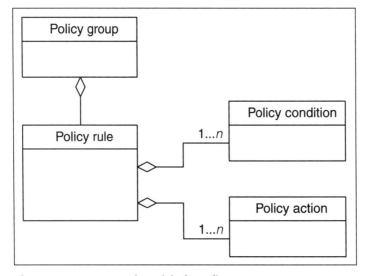

Figure 3.1   Conceptual model of a policy.

Table 3.1 Sample Condition Rules

CONDITION	EXAMPLE
Select a destination	(destination address = HR Server)
Select a user	(user = dkosiur@tbg.com)
Specify a time	(Day of Week = Tuesday) (Time of day = 9 A.M. to 5 P.M.)
Specify a network condition	(network congestion = high)
Select a traffic type	(traffic = http)
Specify an application	(application = NetMeeting)
Specify a network device	(target = edge router)
Select a subnet	(subnet = Accounting subnet)

```
 if (((trafficToOrFrom AccountingSubnet) and
(dayOfMonth in last10days))
or
((trafficToOrFrom AccountingSubnet) and
(monthIn [April, July, October, January]) and
(dayOfMonth in [1-15])))
     then
             priority = high
     endif
```

Which the system would translate into something like the following to configure network devices:

```
if (srcIPaddr = 192.167.34.2)
     then
             priority=5
     else if (destIPaddr = 192.167.72.12)
     then
             priority=6
```

Table 3.2 Sample Action Rules

ACTION	EXAMPLE
Set a relative priority for traffic	(Priority = 7)
Allow or deny access	(Allow through firewall)
Mark traffic for specific handling	(Mark = EF)[*]
Choose an encryption algorithm	(encryption = 3DES)

*EF = Expedited forwarding, a QoS setting defined in DiffServ.

```
else if (destIPsubnet = 192.167.72.0/21)
then
        priority=7
endif
```

Even when there is a large number of conditions and actions, the policy is still considered to be a simple policy. Complex policies are built from simple policies but also include interactions between objects. For example, a complex policy might include a sophisticated user logon policy that sets up application access, security, and reconfigures network connections based on a combination of user identity, network location, logon method, and the time of day.

One of the important properties of policies within the policy-based networking framework is their use of inheritance. *Inheritance* is a mechanism that allows an object or class of objects to be defined as a special case of a more general class of objects (see Figure 3.2). The newly defined object or class is said to inherit the characteristics of another, parent object or class. This notion of inheritance is crucial for our use of policies, since it enables network managers to reuse existing policies and build complex policies from a set of simpler policies. Inheritance also simplifies the management of policies, since an entire policy doesn't need rewriting when a manager redefines a rule. For example, if a manager changes a policy rule defining the Accounting Subnet (AccountingSubnet = 192.167.72.0/16) to a new subnet (say, 206.167.71.0/16), then he or she doesn't have to rewrite our earlier English-style example using the AccountingSubnet. Plus, hosts get moved around and networks get reconfigured on a frequent basis, so using the term AccountingSubnet to refer to a series of hosts makes it easier to deal with changes, adds, and moves.

We've mentioned before that a key value of policy-based networking is that the policies are stored centrally and can be shared by a variety of management applications. This implies that some standard method exists for storing these policies. The main approach is to define the schema for the basic building blocks of the policies, such as the conditions and actions that make up policies, so the policy objects can be mapped to a data store. Within the information model defined as part of DEN, for example, the schemas define attributes that have a system-wide meaning, along with common object classes that represent system-wide objects in the same way. (We'll discuss some of these details in Chapter 12, "Directory-Enabled Networks.") Many vendors have designed their own schemas, following the general principles described by the DEN specifications. Since each vendor has pretty much followed its own course in this first generation of schemas, the products are not interoperable. Interoperability between data stores and policy-based networking systems from different vendors will improve when the vendors adopt the DMTF's final version of DEN. We'll say more about DEN and policy schema later in this chapter as well as in Chapter 6, "The Policy Repository," and Chapter 12.

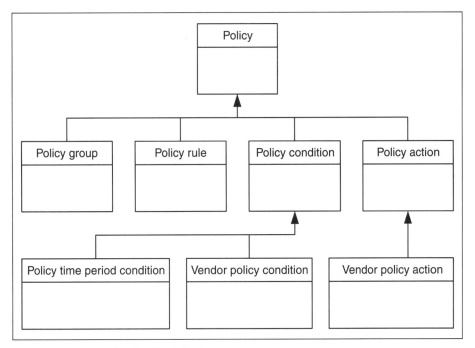

Figure 3.2   Example of policy inheritance.

Types of Policies

Policies are not unique to policy-based networking, nor is the word *policy* new to either network managers or security administrators; many of them are already using policies in some form to manage their resources. For instance, network managers often set policies for assigning IP addresses to specific classes of machines, typically using the Dynamic Host Configuration Protocol (DHCP). Similarly, security administrators define policies regarding what types of traffic a firewall passes or rejects. Furthermore, we operate in a world where some policies are implicit while others are explicit. For example, nctwork address translators (NATs) include implied policies—mapping private IP addresses to the assigned pool of available addresses on the Internet. On the other hand, blocking specific URLs using Domain Name Services (DNS) is set explicitly.

Whatever the type of policy, the majority of policies are currently set either for specific devices or for servers and not in an enterprise-wide fashion, which is one of the capabilities of policy-based networking. Although administrators can define policies at a high level—for example, no SAP traffic should pass beyond the WAN router—implementing policies has been onerous in the absence of policy-based networking systems. Table 3.3 summarizes many of the policies already used on networks and their functions.

To better understand the many uses of policy within policy-based networking, the architects of policy-based networking systems have found it useful to categorize policies into five classes according to their purpose and intent: motivational policies, installation policies, error and event policies, security policies, and service policies.

Motivational policies are targeted at whether a policy's goal is accomplished or how a policy's goal is accomplished. Configuration and usage policies are specific kinds of motivational policies. *Configuration policies* define the default (or generic) setup of a managed entity (for example, a network service). *Usage policies* control the selection and configuration of network entities based on specific usage data. Examples of usage policies include upgrading network forwarding services after a user is verified to be a member of a "gold" service group, or reconfiguring a printer to be able to handle the next job in its queue.

Installation policies define what can and cannot be put on a system or component, as well as the configuration of the mechanisms that perform the installation. Installation policies typically represent specific administrative permissions, and can also represent dependencies between different components (e.g., to complete the installation of a component, components B and C must be successfully installed beforehand).

Error and event policies define what actions should be taken when a device or network goes down or is malfunctioning. For example, if a device fails between 8 A.M. and 9 P.M., call the system administrator, otherwise call the Help Desk.

Security policies deal with verifying that the client is actually who the client purports to be, permitting or denying access to resources, selecting and applying appropriate authentication mechanisms, and performing accounting and auditing of resources.

Service policies characterize network, and other, services. For example, a service policy might read "all wide-area backbone interfaces shall use a specific type of queuing." Service policies are not designed to use the actual services, that's left for the usage policies, as we described earlier. Service policies describe services available in the network while usage policies describe the particular binding of a client of the network to services available in the network.

Policy Abstraction

We mentioned earlier that a policy-based networking system will most likely use more than one kind of policy representation to promote scalability and represent the differing amounts of detail that may be required by different components. We'll refer to these different kinds of representations as different

Table 3.3 Types of Policies and Their Functions*

PRIVATE NETWORK		INTERNET/ IP SERVICE NETWORK	
Function	**Policies**	**Function**	**Policies**
NAT	IP policy: keep IP addresses private	Web caching	Performance policy: which to cache, refresh rate
DNS	DNS policy: host name visibility, naming conventions	URL blocking	URL policy: blocking
Firewall	Access policy: by services or network source	Remote access VPN	Remote access policy: who, where
Authentication	Zones of control (privileges)	Extranet VPN	Extranet policy
		Authentication	Zones of control (privileges) extend to partners, vendors, other divisions, customers
		Bandwidth management	Policies to monitor and enforce band-width allocation by users or services
		E-mail	Policies to monitor and block messages from specific sites, block specific content (viruses)

*(Modified from *Infonetics*, 1998)

levels of abstractions. In general, architects of policy-based networking systems define three levels of policy abstraction—administrator-defined, device-independent, and device-dependent. In order for the proper information to pass from one abstraction to another, the policies at one level must be translated to policies at the next level.

An *administrator-defined policy* is a policy that is expressed in human-oriented terms using rules which convey organizational or operational goals. An administrator-defined policy is independent of any of the details of how or where the policy will be implemented. For example, the Sales Department runs a different set of applications compared to the Engineering Department, and an administrator would define policies selecting different conditioning of their traffic compared to that of the Engineering Department.

A *device-independent policy* is a policy that is expressed in terms of rules that describe conditions and actions to be taken by a device in a generic or implementation-independent fashion. Multiple device-dependent policies can be derived from a single device-independent policy. For example, a single device-independent policy could designate various Differentiated Services Code Points (DSCPs) to distinguish different traffic conditioning for different service classes.

Administrator-defined policies must be translated to a device-independent form so that different devices can each play their part in the enforcing of the policy. For example, a policy stating "permit no more than 30 percent of the core bandwidth to be used for video conferencing" would be translated into a policy specifying a particular DSCP to use.

A *device-dependent policy* is a policy that describes the conditions and actions to be taken by a specific device using terms that are particular to a given implementation. Continuing the preceding example, a set of device-dependent policies would be defined to express how different devices are configured to express the conditioning defined in the single device-independent policy. Some network devices might support weighted fair queuing (WFQ) with two queues, while another router might use class-based queuing (CBQ) with three queues. In this case, at least two device-dependent policies would be created, one for the WFQ devices, the other for the router running CBQ.

The next translation is from the device-independent form to a device-specific form. This may be necessary for a variety of reasons. For example, not all devices have the same capabilities, so some mapping must be done to accommodate the limitations of the device (e.g., we want to provision four classes of service, but the device only has two queues—we need to map which service goes to which queue). As another example, not all devices can implement a function the same way; some devices use the same general type of algorithm (e.g., weighted fair queuing) but have different resource requirements.

Let's walk through the example shown in Figure 3.3, where we want to insure that the traffic from the R&D Department will always get though the network. For the purposes of this example, we'll suppose that the network has been engineered to provide three classes of service through appropriate queue definitions on all the network's routers. The network manager must ensure that any routers processing traffic from the R&D Department have a Per-hop behavior (PHB) defined for the assigned DSCPs; these configurations would be handled by another set of policies, which we won't show here for the sake of simplicity. (For more details on the DiffServ architecture, see Chapter 13, "An Introduction to Quality of Service," and Geoff Huston, *Internet Performance Survival Guide: QoS Strategies for Multiservice Networks*, Wiley, 2000.)

Using DiffServ Code Points, we plan to set up the following actions for different network conditions, as shown in Table 3.4.

Now let's see how the policies could be set and translated for the three different network conditions. We'll need three sets of policies to satisfy the business goal, as follows and in Figure 3.3.

The first set of policies (set A), to be applied only under normal conditions, is:

Policy 1a:

If   (Source = "R&D Department" or Destination = "R&D Department")

Then   (DSCP = high priority)

Policy 2a:

If   (Application = "E-mail")

Then   (DSCP = medium priority)

Policy 3a:

If   (Application = "Telnet")

Then   (DSCP = low priority)

The second set of policies (set B), to be applied only under degraded conditions, is:

Policy 1b:

If   (Source = "R&D Department" or Destination = "R&D Department")

Then   (DSCP = high priority)

Policy 2b:

If   (Application = "E-mail")

Then   (DSCP = low priority)

Policy 3b:

If   (Application = "Telnet")

Then   (drop)

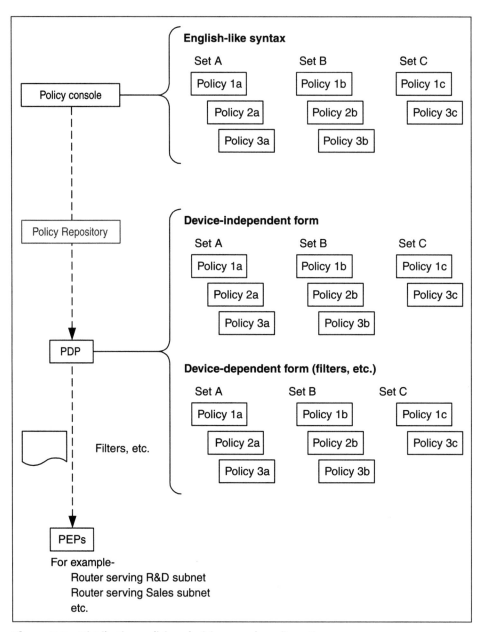

Figure 3.3 Distributing policies, decisions, and configurations.

Table 3.4 DiffServ Actions for Different Network Conditions

NETWORK CONDITION	R&D DEPT. TRAFFIC	E-MAIL TRAFFIC	TELNET TRAFFIC
Normal	DSCP = high priority	DSCP = medium priority	DSCP = low priority
Degraded	DSCP = high priority	DSCP = low priority	DROP
Catastrophic	DSCP = high priority	DROP	DROP

Finally, the third set of policies (set C), to be applied only under catastrophic conditions, is:

Policy 1c:

If   (Source = "R&D Department" or Destination = "R&D Department")

Then   (DSCP = high priority)

Policy 2c:

If   (Application = "E-mail")

Then   (drop)

Policy 3c:

If   (Application = "Telnet")

Then   (drop)

First, there's the translation of policies from this English-like syntax to forms compatible with the policy repository; the actual format depends on the schema defined for the data storage device. Since schema may vary from one type of repository to another, we'll not illustrate that here.

The next step, which is transparent to the network manager, is for a software module to translate a policy from a form that does not specify how to configure any devices to a device-independent form. Let's look only at the first set of policies, set A, to see what the translation might be:

Policy 1a:

SrcSubnet == "192.167.72.1/32" or DestSubnet == "192.167.72.1/32" —>
    DSCP = 6

Policy 2a:

SrcPort == "25" or DestPort == "25" —> DSCP = 4

Policy 3a:

SrcPort == "23" or DestPort == "23" —> DSCP = 2

In this translation, a subnet's IP address range was substituted for the named organizational unit—R&D Department—and well-known port numbers were substituted for the two application protocols—SMTP (for e-mail) and telnet.

The subsequent translation would be from the device-independent form to a device-specific form. This would most likely take place at the policy decision point, taking into account the capabilities of the policy enforcement points that it controls.

In this case, the PDP would most likely create a series of filters that each PEP can use to classify traffic. For instance, one filter would be as follows:

```
Filter2:
    Type:                 IPv4-6-tuple
    IPv4DestAddrValue: 0
    IPv4DestAddrMask:  0.0.0.0
    IPv4SrcAddrValue:  0
    IPv4SrcAddrMask:   0.0.0.0
    IPv4DSCP:          0
    IPv4Protocol:      6
    IPv4DestL4PortMin: 0
    IPv4DestL4PortMax: 65535
    IPv4SrcL4PortMin:  25
    IPv4SrcL4PortMax:  25
```

This sample filter would filter any traffic meant for port 25, the well-known port for SMTP, regardless of source or destination address. As part of the configuration, the PEP would be instructed to assign a DSCP of 4 to any packets that passed this filter (when set A of the example policies is in effect).

Roles

Some policies are global—they apply everywhere in the network. Other policies are location-specific—they apply at one and only one specific location. But those are only two endpoints in a range of applicability. In order to deal with different groupings of devices on the network, such as all core routers or all edge switches on the third floor of building A, we need more granularity than these two endpoints provide. The concept of roles provides this intermediate level of granularity.

A *role* is a means of grouping together a set of objects, so that one or more policies can be specified as being applied to the entire group of objects. This idea is not new; for example, it has been used to assign multiple users to a group, and to attach user profiles, privileges, and permissions to the group, so that each user in the group gets those profiles, privileges, and permissions. It has also been used extensively in database management systems. For policy data, the idea is applied by assigning policies to roles and assigning roles to network components (devices, interfaces, etc.).

The concept of role is an important one in the framework for policy-based networking. Roles provide a way to bind policy to interfaces without having to explicitly identify interfaces in a consistent manner across all network devices. Rather than configuring hundreds or thousands of resources in a network, and then later having to update the configuration of each of these resources, a network manager assigns each resource to one or more roles, and then specifies the policies for each of these roles. The policy-based networking system is then responsible for configuring each of the resources associated with a role in such a way that it behaves according to the policies specified for that role. When network behavior must be changed, the network manager can perform a single update to the policy for a role, and the policy-based networking system will ensure that the necessary configuration updates are performed on all the resources playing that role.

Here are some of the advantages of using roles in policy-based networking:

- New policies are specified for a role, instead of having to specify them for each and every individual network component to which they apply.

- The modification of existing policies is specified within a role, instead of having to modify them for each and every individual network component to which they apply.

- Existing policies are applied to a newly installed network component by assigning the relevant roles to the new component, rather than copying policies from existing components to the new component.

- Operators are encouraged to generate network-wide policies rather than having to remember all the individual components to which they should be applied.

- Neither the permanently stored policy data, nor the policy service, needs to have intimate knowledge of each and every device (let alone each and every device interface) in the network; rather, each device can inform the policy service of the roles for which it needs policy data.

- Policy management and communication traffic is greatly minimized, since the same policy can be distributed and applied to a number of components.

Roles and role combinations are especially useful in selecting which policies are applicable to a particular set of entities or components when the policy repository can store thousands or hundreds of thousands of policies. This use emphasizes the ability of the role (or role combination) to select the small subset of policies that are applicable from a huge set of policies that are available. It's also possible to define role combinations to further delimit where policies are applicable.

Suppose an installation has three roles defined for interfaces: "Ethernet," "Campus," and "WAN." In the policy repository, some policy rules could be associated with the role "Ethernet"; these rules would apply to all Ethernet interfaces, regardless of whether they were on the campus side or the WAN side. Other rules could be associated with the role combination "Campus"+"Ethernet"; these rules would apply to the campus-side Ethernet interfaces, but not to those on the WAN side. Finally, a third set of rules could be associated with the role combination "Ethernet"+"WAN"; these rules would apply to the WAN-side Ethernet interfaces, but not to those on the campus side.

If we have a specific interface A that's associated with the role combination "Ethernet"+"WAN," we see that it should have three categories of policy rules applied to it: those for the "Ethernet" role, those for the "WAN" role, and those for the role combination "Ethernet"+"WAN." Going one step further, if interface B is associated with the role combination "branch-office"+"Ethernet"+ "WAN," then B should have seven categories of policy rules applied to it— those associated with the following role combinations: "branch-office," "Ethernet," "WAN," "branch-office"+"Ethernet," "branch-office"+"WAN," "Ethernet"+"WAN," and "branch-office"+"Ethernet"+"WAN."

In order to get all of the right policy rules for a resource like interface B, a policy decision point must expand the single role combination it receives for B into the list of seven role combinations, and then retrieve from the policy repository the corresponding seven sets of policy rules. Bear in mind that this example is unusually complicated: A normal case would probably involve expanding a two-role combination into three values identifying three sets of policy rules.

Representing Policies

It should be obvious that, as policies are created and translated at various levels of a policy-based networking system, the policies will be represented in different ways. While the central repository of administrator-defined policies is likely to be a directory or database, other components, such as policy servers and policy enforcement points, will store their policies in formats that differ from those a directory or database would use.

At the highest level in our framework for policy-based networking, that of the policy repository, the policy representations are defined by schema, either for a directory or a database. Vendors of policy-based networking products have created their own schema for storing policies, usually in databases. At the same time, the DMTF and IETF have been formulating standard mappings from the Common Information Model and the DEN extensions into schema that can be used by LDAP-compatible directories. For policy-based networking, much of the schema mappings have been organized by the Policy Framework Working Group of the IETF. These efforts have been divided into mappings of core schema and QoS schema. Two other IETF working groups, the Dynamic Host Configuration (DHC) Working Group and the IP Security (IPSec) Working Group, have also been defining schema for address management and VPN tunnels, respectively.

Specifically, the Policy Core Information Model developed by the Policy Framework Working Group defines the generic structure of a policy and provides a framework for describing specific conditions and actions that are used to construct application and domain-specific policies. The QoS Policy Information model then refines this information to describe policy rules, conditions, and actions, as well as other data, that are needed to represent network QoS policies. Using another way of putting it, the QoS Policy schema is a middle layer in a three-level hierarchy of schemata:

Core Policy Schema is extended by

QoS Policy Schema is extended by

Implementation-specific schemata

The core schema correspond to the core information model developed by the DMTF and the Policy Framework Working Group. The LDAP schema for the core information model consists of six very general classes: policy, policyGroup, policyRule, policyConditionAuxClass, policyTimePeriodConditionAuxClass, and policyActionAuxClass. The schema also contains two less general classes: vendorPolicyConditionAuxClass and two auxiliary classes: policyGroupContainmentAuxClass and policyRuleContainmentAuxClass. Five other classes are required to distinguish between rule-specific and reusable policy conditions and policy actions: policyRuleConditionAssociation, policyRuleActionAssociation, policyConditionInstance, policyActionInstance, and policyRepository. Finally, the schema includes two classes, policySubtreesPtrAuxClass and policyElementAuxClass, for optimizing LDAP retrievals. See Chapter 12 for more details.

Once we enter the world of network components like routers, switches and firewalls, we need other representations of policies, ones that the devices will understand. There's already one way of representing policy data at this level, at least as far as individual device configurations are concerned—that's the Simple Network Management Protocol (SNMP) and its Management Information Base (MIB). In addition, another method, one tied more closely to the development of policy-based networking, has been proposed as a way of representing policy at this lower level in the framework. It's called the PIB, or Policy Information Base, and started out as part of the development of the COPS protocol.

In the world of network management using SNMP, MIB modules define the management information that is maintained by the instrumentation in managed nodes, and made remotely accessible by management agents, for manipulation by management applications.

Managed objects are accessed via a virtual information store, termed the Management Information Base, or MIB. MIB modules usually contain object definitions, definitions of event notifications, and sometimes include compliance statements specified in terms of appropriate object and event notification groups. These MIB modules are defined according to the rules defined in the Structure of Management Information (SMIv2) and related documents. The SMI defines fundamental data types, an object model, and the rules for writing and revising MIB modules.

Objects in the MIB are defined using the subset of Abstract Syntax Notation One (ASN.1) defined in the SMI. The objects are arranged into the following groups: System, Interfaces, Address Translation, IP, ICMP, TCP, UDP, EGP, Transmission, SNMP.

In particular, each object has a name, a syntax, and an encoding. The name is an object identifier which specifies an object type. The object type together with an object instance serves to uniquely identify a specific instantiation of the object. The encoding of an object type is simply how that object type is represented using the object type's syntax. Implicitly tied to the notion of an object type's syntax and encoding is how the object type is represented when being transmitted on the network.

A PIB is also a data definition, much like a MIB. In the case of the PIB, they're designed for communications between a PDP and a PEP. The PEP uses the PIB to report device capabilities to the PDP responsible for controlling it. The PDP uses the PIB to provide configuration information and updates to the PEP.

The proposals to extend the COPS protocol to handle provisioned QoS include the definition of a PIB that's similar to SNMP management information bases (MIBs) but focuses on policy decisions. By using PIBs in conjunction with COPS, a PEP can inform a PDP of its capabilities, thus providing the PDP with information that it needs to properly translate policies into device-specific configurations. New PIBs can be defined as needed to extend the usage of COPS-PR to new data items without changing the protocol. This is the same approach the IETF took with MIBs and SNMP.

The PIB can be described as a conceptual tree data structure where the branches of the tree represent types of rules or Policy Rule Classes (PRCs), while the leaves represent the contents of Policy Rule Instances (PRIs). There may be multiple instances of rules (PRIs) for any given rule type (PRC). For example, if one wanted to install multiple access control filters, the PRC might represent a generic access control filter type and each PRI might represent an individual access control filter to be applied. The tree might be represented as shown in Figure 3.4.

The design of PIBs has purposely been defined to leverage as many SNMP mechanisms as are appropriate. Some examples include the following:

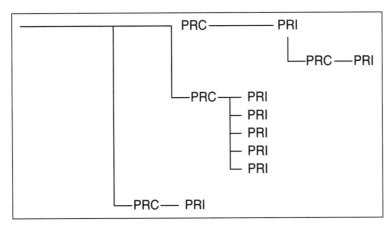

Figure 3.4 The PIB tree.

- PIBs are defined by means of a variant of SNMP's Structure of Management Information (SMI) used to define MIBs. The differences in the rules for defining a PIB are those needed for use with the COPS protocol and network-wide policies/configuration.

- PIBs define a "policy rule class," equivalent to a row definition in a MIB table, and a "policy rule instance," equivalent to a particular row in a MIB table.

- PIBs use Object IDs (OIDs) to name policy rule classes, which is the same naming mechanism used in MIBs.

PIBs differ from MIBs in the way they treat device interfaces. All interface-related policies in the PIB are defined, not per individual interface, but on a per-role basis. In contrast, an SNMP MIB is aimed at device-specific configuration and monitoring. While it's possible to use a PIB to apply the same policies to two similar (but not identical) interfaces having the same role, the MIB must allow each interface to have a different status, different statistics, and different low-level configuration. The use of roles gives COPS greater efficiency over today's SNMP and CLI configuration methods. For example, COPS can load network-wide policies into a device and have those policies apply to multiple components of the device.

Much like SNMP calls for a structure of management information and a management information base of concrete management objects, COPS for provisioning calls for a Structure of Policy Provisioning Information (SPPI) and a Policy Information Base of concrete policy objects. SPPI and PIBs are intentionally like SMI and MIBs, in order to leverage knowledge of and experience with MIBs, but with a few intentional differences. PIBs are aimed at the definition of "higher-level" policy, for example, network-wide policy, rather than the device-specific configuration and monitoring at which MIBs are aimed. PIBs are optimized for bulk configuration of multiattribute objects.

PIBs are a little simpler than MIBs, because they do not need to include multimanager synchronization objects or objects for deleting one or more rows in a MIB table, nor do they need to specify procedures for how these additional objects are used. Since one and only one PDP controls a device (for a specific set of PIBs) at any one time, this exclusive access avoids SNMP's need to provide synchronization mechanisms to protect against multiple SNMP managers trying to access the same MIB objects at the same time. In addition, PIBs do not need other mechanisms to prevent overwriting data which are included in some MIBs. This not only makes a PIB simpler, but it also reduces the complexity of the PDP's code as compared to a SNMP manager.

There's a lot more to translating policies and configuring devices than defining MIBs and PIBs and transmitting them using either SNMP or COPS. Since we're focusing on the representation of policies in this chapter, we're going to leave the remaining details of SNMP, COPS, and related configuration mechanisms to Chapter 8, "Policy Enforcement Points."

Summary

In order for policies to be created and stored in a centralized fashion, a policy-based framework requires that the policies be represented in some standard way. Policies consist of rules defining conditions and rules defining actions; when the conditions are fulfilled, the policy can be applied.

But creating and storing policies in a standardized way is only part of the story. Policies written in an English-like representation aren't recognized by other components of a policy-based networking system, so they need to be translated by the system to other forms of policies that are understood by the other devices (such as policy decision points and policy enforcement points). This usually happens in two steps, first forming a device-independent policy that describes generic conditions and actions, and then forming a device-dependent policy where the configuration accounts for the parameters and capabilities of a particular device. These translation steps allow policy-based networking to provide a scalable means of creating policies for the network manager and make policy distribution more scalable.

Roles provide a way to bind policy to interfaces without having to explicitly identify interfaces in a consistent manner across all network devices. Roles can serve a very important function in policy-based networking by providing a more scalable method of assigning rules to multiple network resources.

Policies need to be represented in a number of ways in a policy-based networking system because different components require different details. At the highest level in the system, policies are represented as schema in a policy repository, while at lower levels they may be represented as filters, for example.

In the following chapter, we'll show how the different components of a policy-based network system fit together and communicate with each other, and the effect that the combinations of these components into different architectures can have on a system's scalability. Chapter 4, "Architectures for Policy-Based Networking," sets the stage for Chapters 5 through 8, which cover each of the components of a policy-based networking system in more detail.

Architectures for Policy-Based Networking

In Chapter 2, "Introduction to Policy-Based Networking," we introduced the main components of policy-based networking—the policy console, policy management tool, policy repository, policy decision point, and policy enforcement point. As we start to delve into the details of what these components do and how they communicate with each other, you'll see that a policy-based networking system can be designed in a few different ways. The main differences among these architectures are where the functions of policy-based networking are located.

The location of policy-based networking functions, such as policy storage and policy-based decision-making, significantly impact the scalability of a system. After we describe the details of the architectural components and how they communicate, we'll discuss what are the major issues affecting system scalability in these architectures.

A policy-based networking system cannot work in a vacuum. To be effective, the system also needs an idea of the network topology and how the network is performing. Monitoring network traffic provides important feedback to network managers about the efficacy of the policies they've created, for example.

Functional Building Blocks

Although many descriptions of policy-based networking still use the original components names—policy console, policy management tool, policy repository, policy decision point, and policy enforcement point—the terminology is in a state of flux. Policy-based networking involves more than one technology—network management, device configuration, signaled QoS using RSVP, and provisioned QoS using DiffServ, for example—and some terms have different meanings to each of the groups involved in the development of these technologies. To alleviate any confusion, we will continue to use the original terms, but see Table 4.1 for a list of synonymous terms.

Each component in a policy-based networking system has a particular set of functions that it must perform, as we outlined in Chapter 2. These functions determine what data needs to be transferred between the components. Both the functionality and data formats depend on the protocols used to describe and transfer the data between components. (See Figure 4.1.)

Policy Console

As we've said before, the policy console serves as the interface between the human network manager and the rest of the policy management system. Most policy system vendors use a graphical user interface and English-like formatting for presenting and combining policy rules at the console.

The policy console works with the policy management tool to translate the policy rules that a network manager creates or edits into a form that's compatible with the schema and storage requirements of the policy repository.

For large enterprises, it's likely there will be more than one policy console for a policy management system. A large enterprise may assign different

Table 4.1 Terms for Components in Policy Management Architectures

BOOK TERMINOLOGY	SYNONYMOUS TERMS
Policy console	User interface Policy admin console
Policy management tool	Policy manager
Policy repository	Master archive
Policy decision point	Policy server Remote decision point Local decision point Policy consumer Policy advisor
Policy proxy	Policy translator
Policy enforcement point	Policy target Enforcement device

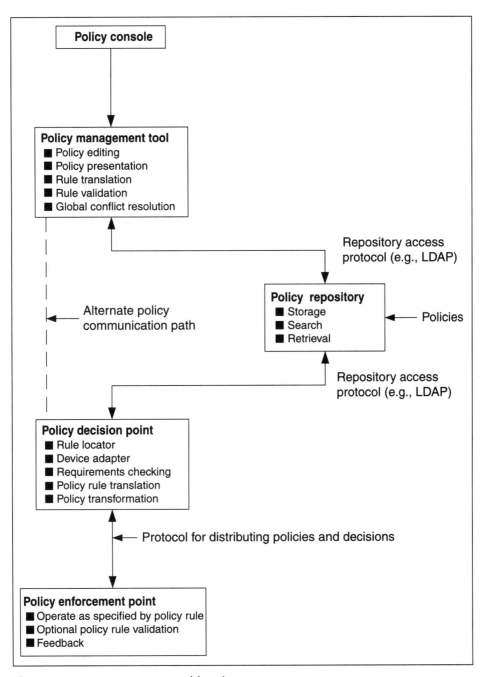

Figure 4.1 PBN components and functions.

types of policy setting to different network managers, each requiring their own consoles—one for QoS and one for security, each with a different user interface that best matches the managers' functions and resources they control, for example. Or an enterprise may choose to set up a distributed hierarchical management structure where managers are assigned responsibilities for local policies, such as for a department or geographic location. When more than one network manager is involved in setting policies, the system must also compare policies set by different managers to ensure consistency among the policies.

Even more details on the policy console, typical user interfaces, and distributed management are presented in Chapter 5, "Creating and Managing Policies."

Policy Management Tool

Much of the functionality of the policy management tool is driven by the policy console. For instance, the management tool translates the policies created at the console and handles communications with the policy repository on behalf of the console. The management tool also has the responsibility of notifying PDPs (and perhaps even PEPs) of changes in policies.

The policy management tool performs the first checks of policies for conflicts. For example, the policy management tool would flag two policies if the first policy set the priority of all R&D traffic to Gold and the second policy set the priority of all FTP traffic to Brass, since a conflict would occur for any R&D FTP traffic. Since the management tool must check for conflicts with existing policies, it may have to generate a large number of queries to obtain all pertinent policies and then process the results of these queries, which can impact how quickly policies can be checked for conflicts.

Although PDPs primarily obtain policies and policy updates from the policy repository, it's also possible to send policy updates directly to a PDP using the management tool. Thus, we have two sequences of events for distributing policies to PDPs, as shown in Figure 4.2.

In the first scenario, the policy management tool stores new or edited policies in the repository and a PDP can retrieve policies from the repository as needed. A PDP might be programmed to query the repository at regular intervals or it might initiate a query to a network event, such as a request from a PEP, or an alert from the policy management tool.

In the second scenario, the policy management tool would transmit new or edited policies to the PDP either at the same time as or before the policies are stored in the repository. This sequence eliminates the need for the management tool to alert the PDP that it needs to retrieve new policies and speeds up the response of the system, but it also raises issues about the coordination of policies (i.e., those stored in the repository and those distributed to the PDPs).

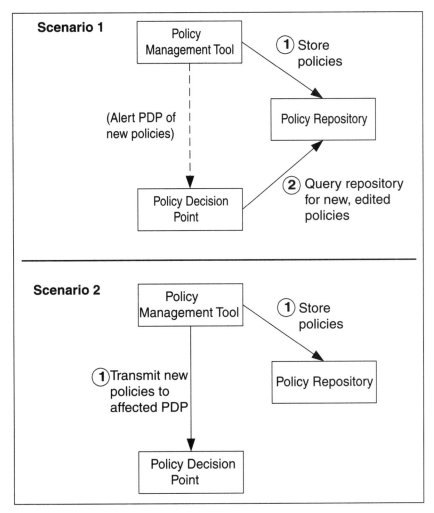

Figure 4.2   Alert and policy distribution to PDPs.

Policy Repository

The primary purpose of the policy repository is to store the policy rules that are created for the policy management system. In order for the policy-based network management system to meet the goals set forth in our previous document, policies need to be related to information about users, such as their current IP address, and access control lists (ACLs). If a directory is the policy repository, then it can also be used to store other policy-related information, such as user IDs, access control lists, and pointers to device or network information. On the other hand, if a database is used to store policy, the system must include some link between the database and the data stores where user information is located, which is usually a directory. In most instances, the common protocol for accessing data from a directory is LDAP.

Many of the first generation of policy-based management products use a database as a policy repository. Some vendors have expressed their intent to switch to directories as policy repositories in the near future, mainly to promote interoperability between different data stores and policy-based networking systems. We expect more vendors to adopt directories as policy repositories when the DMTF releases its final version of DEN and LDAP mappings for the schema although, as we'll see in Chapter 6, "The Policy Repository," LDAP directories still lack some features that would make them an ideal policy repository.

Whether the repository is a directory or a database, the structure of the data stored in the repository is determined by the schema developed for the system. A number of vendors of policy-based networking systems have designed their own schemas, following the general principles described by the DEN specifications. Since each vendor has pretty much followed its own course in this first generation of schemas, the products are not interoperable.

Policy Decision Point

The policy decision point converts administrator-defined and device-independent policies into device-dependent policies that the policy enforcement points understand. The PDP must therefore maintain a list of the PEPs for which it is responsible and be able to retrieve policies that pertain to its PEPs.

The PDP also plays a role in resolving conflicts in policies, such as two policies that each request 100 Kbps bandwidth on the same 128-Kbps line. PDPs may also have to exchange information among themselves, to notify PDPs either when a particular policy could not be enforced (due to lack of support for certain features by the PEPs, for example) or when a policy was not successfully loaded on a PEP (due to problems with the PEP), forcing a rollback to a previous policy.

The PDP may also serve a role in aggregating network information as it's sent upstream to the policy console or a related network monitor. While this role isn't a requirement for policy-based networking systems, it can improve the scalability of such systems. By acting as intermediate aggregators of data, the PDPs can relieve the policy console and/or network monitor of some of the processing overhead required to collect and interpret network statistics. This functionality is not offered as part of the first generation of policy-based networking products, but should appear in following generations as vendors seek to integrate their other network management and monitoring systems with policy-based networking products.

In order to translate network policies into device-specific configurations, a PDP may have to configure different interfaces on the same device differently. The architects of DEN have proposed that interfaces be grouped according to what they call *roles*, which are labels that abstract interface capabilities (see Chapter 3, "What Are Policies?"). For example, edge routers connecting corporate LANs to a WAN would contain an interface to the WAN (say, a T1 interface) which might be assigned a role called "WAN-interface". All the T1 interfaces identified as "WAN-interface" would receive the same configuration information from the PDPs. Roles are useful for aggregating device interfaces to apply a common set of changes without having to name specific device interfaces.

Policy Proxy

Most of today's networking devices are ignorant of policies as we've described them in this book. In most cases, network devices process traffic based on the configurations they receive from a management console and they are not able to proactively request new instructions from a management console or PDP. In addition, few products support COPS, the latest protocol for distributing policies.

Therefore, some additional translator module must intervene between the PDP and most of today's network devices—that's the role of the policy proxy. The policy proxy is responsible for converting policies generated by a PDP to configuration files that non-policy-aware PEPs can understand. That usually means that the proxy will translate policies into CLI or SNMP commands. Furthermore, unlike COPS, which is a stateful protocol that can maintain a connection between a PDP and a PEP, the proxy is stateless and merely sends the configuration data to the PEPs. There's no return of information from the PEP that's being configured unless the proxy requests it.

Policy Enforcement Point

The policy enforcement point utilizes the commands it receives from a PDP (directly or via a policy proxy) to process network traffic. How a PEP actually processes the traffic is entirely up to the device's type, that is, whether it's a switch, router, firewall, VPN gateway, or host. Processing the traffic also depends on the device's capabilities, such as whether a layer 3 switch has two or four queues and the type of queuing algorithms supported.

Very few devices currently installed in networks support protocols such as COPS or LDAP that have been proposed for disseminating policies. While this lack of policy awareness does not prevent a device from enforcing a policy, it makes it more difficult for a PEP to notify a PDP or policy console of changing network conditions or device conditions. We'll discuss the current prominent issues about policy-based communications between PDPs and PEPs in later sections.

Many of today's policy-based networking products focus on devices that are located either in the network core or at the network's edge, that is, the LAN-WAN boundary. Thus, the devices they're primarily concerned with are fire-walls, VPN gateways, remote access servers, routers, and switches. But these products may not prove to be scalable solutions when network managers create increasingly finer-grained policies that are based on users and their applications. Some vendors have already started to incorporate software agents that reside on servers and end-user hosts to enforce policy at the point where the packets are generated. We'll get into more of the details in Chapter 8, "Policy Enforcement Points," but locating policy-based classification and enforcement of traffic at the host is also needed when the traffic is encrypted by the host, as in IPSec.

Intercomponent Communications

Now that we've described the functions of each component in more detail than we gave in Chapter 2, let's turn our attention to the communications that take place between these components.

Console-Repository Communications

Since the policy repository is a passive repository, the policy management tool acts on behalf of the console to initiate any communications between the policy console and the repository. In some cases, the network manager will use the policy console to retrieve existing policies or policy rules in order to edit them. In other cases, the network manager will create new policies and will want to store them in the repository. Retrieval and storage of policies therefore would use the protocols defined for use with the database (such as SQL) or with the directory (such as LDAP) that's used as the repository.

Console-PDP Communications

While a PDP is a more active participant in the policy system than the repository, the architects of policy-based networking systems do not anticipate that the PDP will actively poll the policy console or policy management tool for information. Rather, most vendors expect network managers to push specific policies to the PDP if immediate notification is required, side-stepping the usual chain of events—that is, storage in the repository and acquisition of the policies from the repository by the PDP.

If we look at communications in the other direction, from PDP to the policy console, PDPs may proactively communicate with the policy console to transmit network events or related information to the console so that it can be brought to the attention of the network manager.

PDP-Repository Communications

A standard method of applying policy to a system is for the PDP to acquire policies from the policy repository. This can be accomplished via either a *push* process or a *pull* process. Most systems currently use a pull process, where the PDP may detect changes in policy rules by periodically polling the policy repository. The PDP may also request policies or policy updates from the repository when it receives an alert from the policy management tool or network conditions change.

In the push process, the repository would directly notify the PDP when policies change. At this time, a system using an LDAP-based directory would have to use proprietary notification methods, since the IETF has yet to develop a standard for an event notification mechanism for LDAP. It's also possible to use other notification methods, such as the Common Object Request Broker Architecture (CORBA), with either databases or directories.

PDP-PEP Communications

Communications between a PDP and a PEP are perhaps the most complex and varied of any within a policy system. That's because there's a wide variety of PEPs (including both policy-aware and non-policy-aware devices) and the PDP and the PEP must exchange information in a timely manner in order to respond to changing network conditions. Also, the system must ensure that all PEPs receive the proper configuration for a consistent end-to-end application of policy.

The PDP has to translate policies into configuration parameters for any PEP it controls. But, in order to do so, the PDP must also learn the capabilities of the PEP. This could be accomplished by pre-loading PEP capabilities into a data store on the PDP or by having the PEP inform the PDP of its capabilities. The latter choice is preferred, since a PDP's capabilities may change dynamically. At the same time, the PEP must keep the PDP informed of changing network and device conditions, so that the PEP can either enforce new policies or inform the network manager at the policy console of the changes.

Many of the protocols already used for network management, such as telnet/CLI, SNMP, HTTP, and CORBA, can be used to distribute policy-based device configurations to PEPs. Another protocol, Common Open Policy Service (COPS) protocol, has also been proposed for exchanging information between PDP and PEP.

The selection of protocols for exchanging policy-based data between PDPs and PEPs is still in a state of flux. Established methods for configuring devices, such as telnet/CLI (and SNMP, to a lesser extent), require significant overhead if the state of the device needs to be maintained and changes must be made dynamically, which is the case for many QoS applications. Such protocols as

LDAP, which are good at distributing information and therefore suited to accessing stored policy data, weren't designed to query clients and maintain session states, either. What's needed for effective policy-based network management is a protocol that can maintain state between PDPs and PEPs, dynamically update device configurations, and, perhaps most importantly, do so in a network-wide fashion; that's why a protocol like COPS (and proposed extensions to COPS) was invented.

Flavors of Policy Systems

As we've mentioned throughout the book, the use of policies is not new to network and security administrators. Policy-based networking has its origins in the simpler systems that were designed for configuration of individual devices. We'll call this the single-tiered architecture. Of more interest are the two-tiered and three-tiered architectures for policy-based networking, ones in which a central repository is used to store policies and the policy decision points can be distributed throughout the network. We'll cover the details of each of these architectures and then discuss how the architectures can affect the scalability and functionality of policy-based systems.

First, let's take a brief look at the single-tiered architecture. In this setup, network managers create and store policies on their workstations and download them to the devices they want to configure. This method has been around for a long time, for firewalls, routers, and so on. It's not really a policy-based networking system as we've defined it in this book, since the system does little to use any network intelligence to distribute policies, convert business rules into configuration data, or change configurations dynamically.

One variant of this approach does get a little closer to our idea of a policy-based networking system, though. Many products for managing VPN gateways and load-balancing switches now include the capability to centrally store and reuse the same configuration data for multiple devices. This affords network managers some semblance of consistency in their policies and configurations even if the distribution of these policies is still initiated only by the network manager. This approach may suffice for a limited number of situations, where the number of devices is relatively small, and only a few types of devices need to be managed.

Both the two-tiered and three-tiered architectures for policy-based networking systems provide network managers with more flexibility, more dynamic responses, and better scalability than the single-tiered architecture. In fact, we've included the single-tiered architecture here only for the sake of completeness. We do not consider it a true policy-based networking system in the sense used throughout this book, nor do we see it providing many of the advantages attributed to policy-based networking. But some readers may be using these single-tiered systems and will need to integrate their control with a true policy-based networking system; we'll discuss some of those issues in later chapters.

While most vendors of policy-based management systems are implementing the components we just described in their systems, the systems vary according to how PDPs and PEPs are combined and what protocols are used for distributing policies. Although these systems cannot be classified into just two architectures, it's still convenient to use two architectures as endpoints for comparison and discussion. These two architectures are the three-tiered architecture and the two-tiered architecture. In a three-tiered architecture, PDPs and PEPs are physically separate devices, which requires the use of another protocol, such as COPS or SNMP, for communication between them. In a two-tiered architecture, a PDP resides on the same device as the PEP, eliminating the need for an intermediary communications protocol such as COPS.

In a two-tiered policy management architecture, the upper tier is the same as that of the three-tiered architecture; that is, it consists of the policy console and the policy repository. However, the middle tier is eliminated by locating the policy decision point and the policy enforcement point on the same physical device, as illustrated in Figure 4.3.

This architecture eliminates the need for a protocol, such as COPS, for exchanges between the PDP and the PEP since the link between the PDP and PEP can be entirely proprietary and custom-written for that particular device.

In a three-tiered policy management architecture, illustrated in Figure 4.4, the upper tier consists of the policy console and the policy repository. Policy decision points comprise the middle tier, while the lower tier consists of the policy enforcement points.

One of the strengths of the three-tiered architecture is that it simplifies management of legacy devices that are not policy-aware. With this architecture, a policy translator or proxy can be used with the PDP in the middle tier to convert policy decisions into information, say using SNMP commands or a CLI, that a legacy device can understand.

Of the two architectures, more products are related to the three-tiered model than to the two-tiered architecture. 3Com, Cisco, IP Highway, Lucent, Nortel Networks, and Orchestream, among other vendors, are all offering policy-based networking systems that are designed using the three-tiered architecture. Some examples of two-tiered policy-based systems are the products offered by Alcatel, Fore Systems (now a part of Marconi plc), and IBM.

Since the intelligence of a PDP must be added to a PEP in the two-tiered architecture, only a few policy-aware network devices are currently available for use in two-tiered systems. It's also more difficult to control legacy network devices, since they don't include a PDP. To solve these problems, vendors such as Marconi extend the two-tier model to one similar to the three-tier model, where a Marconi switch containing both the PDP and the PEP can serve as the PDP for other PEPs as well.

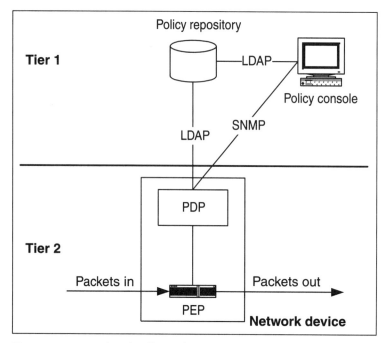

Figure 4.3 Two-tiered policy architecture.

Outsourcing versus Provisioning

Although policy-based networking can be applied to a number of network services, one of its major applications currently is the control of QoS. There are two main approaches to providing QoS on IP networks—Integrated Services (IntServ) and Differentiated Services (DiffServ), which we'll describe in more detail in Chapter 13, "An Introduction to Quality of Service." Each of these methods requires different responses from PEPs providing QoS, which in turn, requires different responses on the part of the PDPs.

Part of the IntServ architecture is the Resource Reservation Protocol (RSVP), which is used as a QoS signaling protocol. When RSVP is used, each router participating in the signaling can independently allocate local resources to an individual RSVP session, or reject a request when local resources are exhausted. But local information is insufficient to make a decision based on network-wide policy. In a policy-based networking system, a PEP processing an RSVP request can outsource its decision to its controlling PDP, that is, it will forward a request to the PDP for a decision on how to treat the RSVP request.

DiffServ, on the other hand, does not use a signaling protocol to operate. Instead, each packet gets marked with a DiffServ Code Point (DSCP) and it is the DSCP which then determines which QoS treatment a packet receives. In this

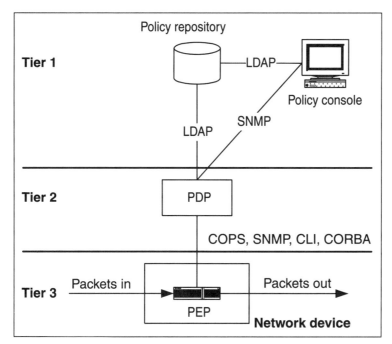

Figure 4.4   Three-tiered policy architecture.

situation, a router does not have the opportunity to ask a PDP for an applicable policy. The PDP should therefore transmit the policy for treating defined DSCPs to the router before the router is expected to receive the traffic. This is called provisioning the router.

Policy-based systems need to push policies to PEPs when network devices need to be provisioned, either with QoS policies using DiffServ as we just outlined, or with access control filters. On the other hand, PEPs request policies from a PDP when a network device encounters a new situation that's not covered by its set of cached decisions (such as a new user logging in to a remote access server requiring RADIUS [Remote Authentication Dial-In User Service] authentication), or when devices handle signaled QoS using the RSVP.

To support the dynamic nature of networks, it's important that a policy-based networking system support both outsourcing and provisioning mechanisms for distributing policies. While LDAP readily supports acquiring policies by client request (either from PDPs as policy servers or as components of a PDP/PEP colocated on a network device), it does not have a method for pushing policies to the affected servers or devices. SNMP and CLI are good for device-specific configurations; network managers can therefore use them as the final step in distributing policy-based configuration to PEPs. However, neither of these methods includes a way for PEPs to notify a PDP that they need new configuration data, for example, in response to network events arising from RSVP or RADIUS.

COPS, on the other hand, supports both push and pull methods for distributing QoS-related policies (or will shortly, when COPS for provisioning [called COPS-PR] is approved as a standard). Likewise, CORBA's event service can be used to push and pull policy data as required. The current situation of enterprise networks—where networks have few, if any, COPS-capable devices—requires continued support of older configuration methods and protocols such as CLI and SNMP. But we expect this to change over the next few years as COPS becomes an important protocol for distributing policy-based configuration data to network devices.

Scaling, Redundancy, and Fault Tolerance

Since policy-based networking systems may have to control the configuration of hundreds of network devices, these systems need to scale across large internetworks. Each of the components of a policy-based networking architecture can affect the scalability and performance of the system. We'll discuss some of the important ways that the components can affect a system's scalability. (Some more details will also pop up in the following chapters when we discuss each component in even more detail than we have here.)

The factors affecting the scalability and performance of a policy repository differ according to whether the repository is a directory or a database. For instance, databases are better than directories at handling queries involving relations between multiple objects. Such queries are exactly what one would expect when a PDP has to compare a new policy with existing policies for possible conflicts; the PDP would have to issue repeated queries for policies related to the devices it manages in order to process all pertinent policies. This problem would be further exacerbated in the two-tier architecture since the number of PDPs querying the repository for possible conflicts would be greater than in the three-tier architecture.

As we pointed out previously, in the absence of some repository-based event notification method, PDPs must poll the repositories to obtain policies. Systems using LDAP-based repositories would therefore experience more network traffic and processing overhead since LDAP directories do not include an event notification method. On the other hand, when CORBA is used, communications is simplified since policies need to be distributed only when they're changed and this can be triggered using standard CORBA services on either the server or the client (that is, the policy repository or the PDP).

Proponents of the three-tiered model argue that the use of the PDPs in a middle tier provides a more scalable solution than the two-tiered model.

That's because each PDP can control a number of network devices and aggregate information from these devices before passing it on to the policy console or repository. In contrast, in the two-tiered architecture, each PDP/PEP device has to poll the repository for policies. Also, each PDP/PEP device has to send its status and statistics to the network monitor individually rather than in an aggregated form (which the PDP does in the three-tiered architecture).

The number of PEPs that a single PDP can serve is still a matter of trial and error. In our conversations with vendors of policy-based management systems, vendors have suggested that a PDP can control on the order of a hundred or more PEPs. Vendors of two-tiered systems have suggested that a single repository can serve about 10 network devices. Thus, in order to expand a policy-based management system or improve its performance, a network manager has to either add more PDPs (in the case of the three-tiered system) or add more directories (in the case of the two-tiered system). In either approach, you'll have to pay close attention to how the PDPs or directories replicate data among themselves. There are a few standard methods for replicating data among directories or databases, but coordinating data among PDPs has not been standardized.

The scalability of policy-based systems and the performance of the PEPs are also intertwined. The PEPs can hold a limited amount of information, so the number of policy-based decisions and the size of the resulting configuration files must be optimized in some way so as not to overload the PEP. This will most likely change over time as the industry begins designing policy-aware devices and not just trying to bolt policy support onto existing equipment. Furthermore, tests performed by trade periodicals in the past year indicate that the performance of many network devices is seriously impacted by the number of access control lists and filters. If PEPs are expected to cache a large number of filters in order to enforce policies, their performance would also degrade.

The use of end-user hosts as enforcement points poses a scalability problem of its own. The number of hosts connected to any network is significantly larger than the number of routers or firewalls on that network. A policy-based networking system distributing policies to the hosts must therefore scale to even larger sizes in order to be able to distribute policies to all the end users. Some of the vendors working on host-based enforcement have suggested using another, intermediate, layer of policy servers between the policy servers in layer 2 of our three-tiered architecture and the PEPs in layer 3. Others are looking at multicasting as a way to distribute policies to end users, while still others are investigating the use of DHCP tied to user network logins to distribute policies to the hosts. At this point, nothing's been standardized and there isn't sufficient field experience with the different techniques to determine which methods, if any, will improve the scalability of policy-based networking when applied to hosts.

Since one aim of policy-based management systems is to manage business-critical network services, the system controlling these functions should be as reliable as possible. For policy-based products, reliability revolves mainly around repository and PDP redundancy and data replication.

In a policy-based network management system, two different servers require redundancy: the policy repository and the PDP. Large policy-based systems are likely to use distributed data stores for efficiency and reliability. The policy repository must therefore include some type of replication or synchronization mechanism for the various data stores that make up the repository. The frequency of data replication may affect the distribution of rules to, and interpretation of those rules by, PDPs. For instance, in order to ensure that all PDPs receive the same policies, data between policy repositories must be replicated more frequently than PDPs are updated.

If the repository is directory-based, the system can use a directory's replication features to ensure that crucial data is stored and replicated in more than one location. However the IETF has not approved a replication protocol as a standard for LDAP directories. This situation currently limits directory replication to vendor-specific solutions. Early adopters of policy-based management systems should therefore plan to use a single vendor's directory product for their systems. It's also possible that vendors will turn to Directory Services Markup Language (DSML) as an alternative approach to replication, especially where directory information is exchanged between companies, perhaps involving different directory implementations and vendor products.

Since PDPs are crucial to the distribution of policy decisions to PEPs, a policy system should include backup PDPs. Only a few vendors of policy-based management systems currently provide this capability. Since systems using a two-tiered architecture colocate the PDP and PEP, secondary PDPs are not considered a part of the system.

While server redundancy can ensure that policy-based management systems are available whenever they're needed, the data stored in these servers must also be reliable to ensure the consistency of policies. As we've mentioned earlier, some vendors base their policy-based networking systems on databases, while other vendors have chosen to use directories as a data store. In general, today's databases include more mechanisms for reliably guaranteeing data reliability than do current directories. For example, typical online transaction processing (OLTP) databases include rollback and forward recovery procedures as well as audit logs to ensure the integrity of transactional data. The current generation of directory products does not provide similar capabilities, although directory vendors are committed to correcting this shortcoming. Some vendors of address management products and directory tools have added the necessary functionality to LDAP directories, but there currently is no standard way of doing this.

Summary

Policy-based networking systems can be built out of the following components: policy console, policy management tool, policy repository, one or more policy decision points, policy enforcement points, and a policy proxy (if needed).

Although some vendors may promote a single-tiered architecture for policy-based networking, we feel that the single-tiered architecture is a stretch of the term policy-based networking as we've defined it in this book. More legitimate architectures are the two-tiered and three-tiered architectures, which differ mainly in the location of the PDPs and PEPs. Both the two-tiered and three-tiered architectures for policy-based networking systems provide the network manager with more flexibility, more dynamic responses, and better scalability than the single-tiered architecture. Proponents of the three-tiered model argue that the use of the PDPs in a middle tier provides a more scalable solution than the two-tiered model, although there's too little field evidence at this point to completely write off one architecture in favor of the other. In fact, as policy-based systems grow to include end-user hosts, added layers of intermediate policy servers may be required.

In a policy-based networking system handling RSVP requests for QoS, a PEP processing an RSVP request can outsource its decision to its controlling PDP; that is, it will forward a request to the PDP for a decision on how to treat the RSVP request. Policy-based systems also need to push policies to PEPs when network devices need to be provisioned, either with QoS policies using DiffServ as we just outlined, or access control filters. To support the dynamic nature of networks, it's important that a policy-based networking system support both outsourcing and provisioning mechanisms for distributing policies.

Now that we've gained a better understanding of policies and how the systems can be architected in this and the previous chapter, the next chapter will focus on the details of, and issues surrounding, the policy repository. Following chapters will focus on the other components of policy-based networking.

Creating and Managing Policies

It should be obvious by now that policy-based networking is a top-down management framework, where the network manager integrates business goals with networking policies. Much of the intelligence of the policy-based networking framework occurs at the lower levels of the system, where the abstract, network-wide policies are translated to other policies and configuration files that the enforcement devices understand. But network managers cannot simply create any policies they wish without regard to their network's topology or capabilities. Nor can they start creating contradictory policies. In order for policy creation and management to be as effortless and efficient as possible, a policy-based networking system has to present a well-designed interface to the network manager and inform the network manger of potential conflicts and other errors as quickly as possible.

This chapter is the first in a series of four that deals with the functions of and issues surrounding the main components of a policy-based networking system. This chapter covers the policy console and policy management tool. We've decided to treat the two components as one because many of their functions depend on each other, plus the two components often coexist on the same computer. We'll start out discussing the basic functions of these components, then move on to other, extended functions (including a feature wish list). The latter half of the chapter covers the details of some of the main issues surrounding the design and use of the policy console and the policy management tool before we wrap up the discussion with our list of the main requirements for a usable component using today's technology.

Basic Functions

Let's start out by reviewing the basic functions that the policy console and policy management tool must perform within a policy-based networking framework, as illustrated in Figure 5.1.

Policy Console

The policy console is the basic interface between the network manager and the policy-based networking system. It allows the network manger to create and edit policies and review past policies. It also works with the policy management tool to translate the policy rules that a network manager creates or

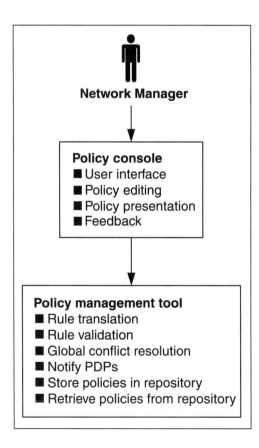

Figure 5.1 Functions of the policy console and policy management tool.

edits into a form that's compatible with the schema and storage requirements of the policy repository.

The policy console should not only guide a network manager through the creation of new rules and policies, perhaps by offering templates, but it should also provide immediate feedback when the network manager uses an improper syntax or enters incorrect data types (IP addresses when priorities are required, for example).

Since the policy console uses a graphical interface for policy entry, editing, and review, it usually includes a hierarchical view of all the policy-related components, including rules, policies, policy domains, services, schedules, and devices (see Figure 5.2). In some cases, the policy console may also allow the network manager to extend the schema of the policy repository.

Since a network manager cannot always be certain what effects new policies will have on the network, the policy console must provide some way of either naming or at least identifying past sets of policies so that the network manager can roll back the system to a previous set if necessary. As we'll see later, this requires versioning support in the policy repository.

The policy console also acts as the first level of security for the network by authenticating each user (i.e., network manager) of the system. At present,

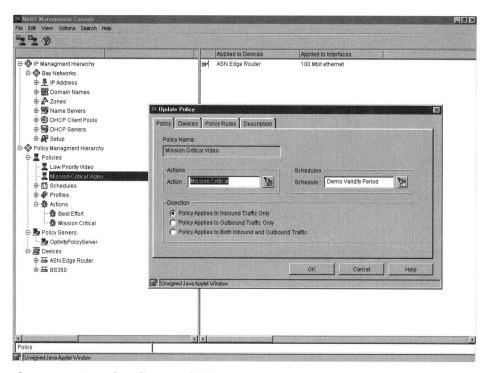

Figure 5.2 Example policy console UI.

policy-based networking systems only authenticate users by means of a user-name and password.

Policy Management Tool

The policy console drives much of the functionality of the policy management tool. For instance, the management tool translates the policies created at the console and handles communications with the policy repository on behalf of the console. In some cases, the network manager will use the policy console to retrieve existing policies or policy rules in order to edit them, so the management tool will have to retrieve the required policies from the repository. In other cases, the network manager will create new policies and will want to store them in the repository. In either case, the management tool would retrieve and store policies using the protocols defined for the database (such as SQL) or the directory (such as LDAP) that's used as the repository.

While the policy console will most likely perform syntax and data-typing checks, the management tool works with the console to check policies for conflicts. The policy management tool performs the first checks of policies for conflicts. The management tool is involved because, in order for it to check for conflicts with existing policies, it has to retrieve all pertinent policies.

Using an example we presented earlier in the book, the console would alert the network manager of a conflict if he attempted to define a policy that first set the priority of all R&D traffic to a value of 6 and a second policy set existed that set the priority of all FTP traffic to a priority of 5, since a conflict would occur for any R&D FTP traffic.

The management tool also has the responsibility of notifying policy decision points (PDPs) and perhaps even policy enforcement points (PEPs) of changes in policies. Some systems store policies in the repository and then send alerts to the PDPs notifying them that new policies affecting them have been created. The PDPs then retrieve the policies from the repository. Another approach is to have the management tool send the appropriate policies directly to the affected PDPs at the same time as the policies are stored in the repository.

Extended Functions

To be an effective tool in network management, the system needs an idea of the network's topology. Before a network manager can create policies, she needs to know the logical topology of the network. Setting policy without knowledge of the network topology can lead to unpredictable results. In the absence of knowledge about the topology, the network manager can define policies without any idea of whether they can actually be implemented in the network until run time. On the other hand, when network topology information is available, the policy console can use it to validate policies when the network manager submits the policy rules (see Figure 5.3).

The majority of the current policy-based networking products require manual entry of the network's logical topology. A few policy-based networking products include procedures for importing network topology data from network management programs or discover devices using SNMP on their own to determine the network topology.

As long as the initial deployment of policy-based networking systems focuses on pilot projects and a limited number of network devices, a single policy console will suffice. However, as the number of devices controlled by policy-based networking increase, more than one network manager will most likely be involved, perhaps at different geographical locations. Full-blown policy-based networking systems therefore need to support not only multiple consoles, but also the definition of policy domains (or areas of responsibility). For large networks, it'll probably even be necessary to support a hierarchy of network managers, where, for example, site managers can create and edit all policies while departmental network managers can only work on policies that apply to their subnets.

For the moment, unfortunately, policy-based networking products are self-contained systems that do not interoperate with similar products from other vendors. Eventually, network managers should be able to share policies between policy consoles from different vendors, but right now, that's not possible, partly

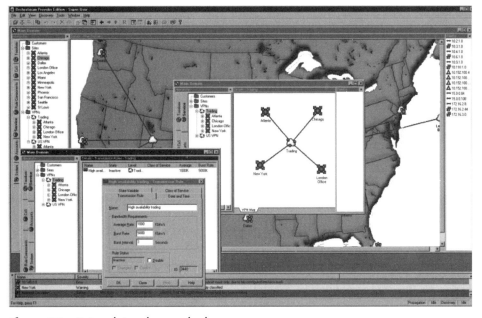

Figure 5.3   Network topology and rules.

because there's no standard policy description language. If you're considering using a policy-based system to control your enterprise network and transfer or map some of those policies to your Internet service provider (ISP), you'll have to use the same vendor's product as your ISP uses, for the moment. There are some possible solutions on the horizon, though; we'll discuss some of them later in this chapter.

Considering the complexity and promises of policy-based networking, it shouldn't surprise anyone that network managers are not just going to write a set of policies for their networks and walk away, trusting the policy-based system to do everything else. Network managers require some assurance that the policies are, in fact, creating the desired configuration policies and controlling network services properly. That requires some type of policy monitoring that is distributed throughout the system. At the level of the policy console and management tool, this monitoring should include information about which current policies are installed on network devices, the status of PDP-PEP links, which policies are active, and which PDPs control which PEPs.

Another option for troubleshooting the system and helping network managers gain trust in policy-based networking is a drill-down feature, which is a way of matching final device configurations with the policies that created them. Since there are different levels of abstraction of policies in a policy-based networking system (see Chapter 3, "What Are Policies?"), there can be a one-to-many correspondence between high-level policies and device configurations. Some network managers will want to see just what configuration policies are created by the high-level policies they create, and a drill-down tool allows them to do that.

Network managers also require some feedback on how their networks are performing in order to gauge the efficacy of their policies and determine whether new ones are needed. There's a wide variety of network monitoring tools available, especially ones using SNMP and RMON for collecting data on device and network performance. Policy-based networking systems aren't designed to assume the performance monitoring roles of these other systems, but need to work alongside them. But the last thing network managers want is yet another console for managing their network! Some vendors of management products have started to integrate policy-based networking with network monitoring, but you should look for better integration of the two functions in future products.

Issues

Since we're somewhat early in the development of policy-based networking products—many products are still first-generation or early second-generation—there are still unresolved issues regarding the capabilities and features of the policy console and the policy management tool. (That's actually the case for all components, but our focus here is the console and the management tool.) When you're considering a policy-based networking system, you should pay attention to the following important issues regarding the policy console and the policy management tool:

- Usability
- Policy interoperability between consoles
- System integration with network management applications
- Management of data from other sources
- Handling of policy conflicts

This section focuses on discussions of each one of these issues. You'll find a similar section in the following chapters as we work our way through the other components of policy-based networking.

Usability

The policy console is the interface between the network manager and the rest of the policy-based networking system. All vendors provide a GUI with their policy console applications. In general, the user interfaces of the current policy management products don't differ significantly from each other. As shown in Figure 5.4, the interface resembles the Windows Explorer interface, with a pane on the left side of the window to display a hierarchy of policies. The right-hand pane in the display then displays configuration details for the item selected in the left-hand pane.

A well-designed graphical user interface (GUI) can simplify some steps in policy-based management, such as defining roles or groups of devices and assigning configuration parameters to them. Using a GUI can also help prevent some errors in creating policies by validating the syntax of each policy as it's created. One issue that has not yet been resolved by policy-based networking vendors is the level of abstraction of the policies presented to the network manager. For instance, most systems still include the models of routers and switches in policies rather than allowing higher-level abstractions, such as edge router or core router. That's partly due to the lack of the full use of the CIM/DEN model to describe managed objects and because most vendors have focused on handling many existing devices by means of CLI commands, which requires knowledge of the actual product being managed. We'd expect a higher-level approach to become more general in the next few years, including more abstract naming terms and the implementation of roles.

In today's policy consoles, a network manager has a variety of ways to create policies. Many products include a set of templates for basic rules and policies, so a network manager can simply fill in the fields in the templates to

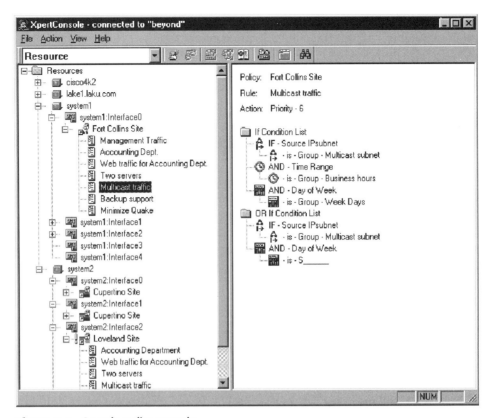

Figure 5.4 Sample policy console.

create his or her own policies. One advantage of using a form fill-out mode is
that the console can immediately ensure that the proper data type is entered
in each field. For instance, it could flag a field requiring a priority class if a
network manager erroneously entered an IP address in that field.

One thing the policy console's interface should do is hide the policy schema
from the network manager, at least for everyday tasks. It's not necessary for
the network manager to know how the schema is structured in order to write
policies. It may be necessary for the policy console/management tool to know
what the schemas are, though, in order to flag erroneous policies and inform
the network manager what the error is and how to correct it. If the schema
can be extended to meet a customer's needs, either the policy console or an
associated schema editor might be used for this task.

While the UI should hide the policy schema from the network manager, it's
wise to allow the network manager to drill down into the system to discover
how a policy is abstracted at different levels of the system. Some network managers want to know exactly what the configuration file looks like, so they

require the ability to see what CLI commands, SNMP commands, or PIBs are generated to configure the devices they control. This capability is also valuable for troubleshooting the network. It can also be valuable for weaning network managers from the old paradigm of point-based configurations to policy-based configurations, since a network manager could see what the effects of the policy are to ensure it meets his requirements before he places his trust in what the policy-based networking system will do for him. Cisco's Quality Policy Manager (QPM), for example, can show the network manager the exact CLI commands that will be sent to a router.

Centralized versus Distributed Management

In enterprises with small networks, a single policy console may suffice for controlling a policy-based networking system. But for large enterprises, it's likely there will be more than one policy console for a policy management system. A large enterprise may assign different types of policy setting to different network managers, each requiring his or her own console; for example, one for QoS and one for security, each with a different user interface that best matches the manager's functions and the resources he or she controls. Or, much like the situation for IP address management using DHCP servers, an enterprise may choose to set up a distributed hierarchical management structure where managers are assigned responsibilities for local policies, such as for a department or geographic location. When more than one network manager is involved in setting policies, the system must also compare policies set by different managers to ensure consistency among the policies.

Multiuser management of policy-based systems places added demands on the policy repository. The repository should support versioning of data and rollback features so that changes can be traced back to administrators, or so that policies can be reset to previous versions in case of an error. As we'll see in the next chapter, databases provide better support for versioning and rollback of data than LDAP-enabled directories. Also, since policy rules are reusable objects within the repository, access to the repository will have to be granted on an object-by-object basis.

Policy Interoperability between Consoles

Although there's been a lot of work, particularly by the DMTF and IETF, to promote interoperable schema and policy definitions at the repository level and lower, we still have some way to go to achieve interoperability at a higher level, such as that of the policy console and management tool. One reason is the lack of a standard language for describing policies. Right now, you're stuck with using single-vendor solutions if you want to install multiple policy consoles in different parts of your network. This lack of interoperability also makes it difficult to link your enterprise policy-based networking system with that of your service provider. Having the capability to exchange policies at a high level of abstraction will become increasingly important in the future as enterprises seek assurances of QoS from their ISPs using service-level agreements (SLAs).

Since the DEN extensions to CIM include definitions of policies as well as services, it's a natural extension to define service-level objects (SLOs) that can be used to create SLAs (see sidebar). The DMTF is still working on the definition of these service-level objects. When the definitions of these SLOs are released, that will solve some of the problems related to communications between enterprise and ISP policy-based systems, but we'll still need some sort of policy description language that will work on systems from different vendors.

There's currently little visible activity on defining a standard policy definition language (PDL), at least within working groups defining policy standards. The original proposal to the Policy Framework Working Group for a PDL was withdrawn over a year ago and a new one has not been put forward. One reason for the delay may be the desire to wait until SLOs are standardized within CIM and the DEN extensions, which should happen sometime in 2001.

SERVICE-LEVEL AGREEMENTS AND POLICY-BASED NETWORKING

Service-level agreements, or SLAs, are meant to ensure that network managers' expectations regarding network performance, maintenance, and problem resolution are met by their ISPs. Three basic items are covered in a SLA: availability, effective throughput, and delay. One of the purposes of SLAs is the documentation of customer expectations and what an ISP is willing to provide in common terms. At the moment, this is done by means of a signed contract.

But as new services are offered by an ISP, monitoring and guaranteeing the services become a greater challenge. And, as we've pointed out before, service providers want to be able to provision these services dynamically as they work to meet the needs of today's e-businesses. That's where the definition of SLOs comes into play. By defining a set of standard objects (the SLOs) for services, performance, and so on, it will be easier to construct a SLA by combining SLOs, especially since SLOs can be arranged in a hierarchy and inherit properties from higher-level objects. Plus, when SLOs are standardized, different parties can agree on what's being monitored as part of a SLA. This will be important not only for enterprise customers dealing with an ISP, but also for arrangements between ISPs.

One likely candidate for a multipurpose policy description language is XML (the eXtensible Markup Language). The DMTF has already created XML mappings for Web-Based Enterprise Management (WBEM), which is aimed at desktop and system management and uses CIM. As the DEN extensions become an integral part of CIM, it's likely that the DMTF will extend its XML mappings of CIM to include DEN.

Integration with Other Management Apps

Although policy-based networking systems can ease the configuration of network devices, they are not substitutes for many of the functions of other network management tools and systems, such as those for monitoring network performance. There is a wide variety of network monitoring tools available and most of these use SNMP and RMON (Remote MONitoring) to collect data on device and network performance. Policy-based networking systems will have to work with network monitoring tools in order to show network managers how networks behave as policies are applied to them.

But the last thing network managers want is yet another console for managing their network! Some vendors of management products have started to integrate policy-based networking with network monitoring, but you should look for better integration of the two functions in future products.

The integration of policy-based systems with other management tools will become increasingly important in the future. When the DMTF standardizes terms for SLAs and includes the relationships between network services and SLAs within CIM, perhaps this year, it'll be possible to relate policies to SLAs and use network-monitoring data to indicate whether SLAs are being complied with.

While incorporating the definition of SLA objects in CIM can help the integration of other management data with the DEN model, network managers face working with other network management applications for at least the next few years. One step in integrating network management data and applications, including policy-based management, is the use of XML to describe management data.

Managing Data from Other Sources

Policy-based networking systems often have to deal with a variety of data or at least base decisions on data from other sources, which may or may not be contained entirely within the repository. Although the policy repository is the focus for storing policies, the same repository might also store user-related and device-related information. But the common situation is that the ancillary data used by a policy-based network management system exists in a variety

XML AND NETWORK MANAGEMENT

Although CIM defines the meta-model for managing objects and services at the desktop and network level, it says nothing about how data is actually instantiated in a management application. It also does not define how data can be moved between management applications.

In order to provide an interoperable management solution, an application first has to be able to represent actual management data (such as the number of errors observed on a port) in a standard way. Second, there must be a protocol capable of carrying the data between applications. XML is an answer to the data-representation problem, while HTTP is an answer to the transport-protocol problem.

Mapping CIM to XML is an important step for management vendors looking to integrate data from a variety of sources. This has already been done for WBEM and desktop management, but we haven't yet reached the same stage for network management. Some vendors have already started to introduce management applications that can exchange and process data that's described via XML.

But representing policies via XML is another story, one that's barely started. We expect the DMTF to again take the lead in such a mapping (of the DEN extensions to CIM), but a few vendors are already using XML to represent services and policies in a proprietary way in their products for service providers.

of sources, such as in network operating system files, DNS and DHCP servers, and so on. Many systems already use directories for storing information about users and will continue to do so, expanding their use to incorporate additional user information such as digital certificates. At the same time, other applications will continue to use data stores; for example, network-monitoring systems using SNMP and RMON will continue to store data in flat files or databases. (The subject of data storage for policy-based networking will be covered in the next chapter.)

Just as network managers don't want added consoles for network management, they shouldn't be forced to use added consoles to manage related data. A full-blown policy-based networking system not only maps policies to network devices, but also needs to map users to their IP addresses and track application types. Some vendors of PBN systems have already started to link their products to DHCP servers to handle the user-to-address mapping issue. In some cases, these vendors combine the management of the DHCP servers with policy management at the policy console. Others obtain user information from logins to a NOS (network operating system) like Netware or Windows NT.

But, even as policy-based networking utilizes data from other sources, maintaining that data is not the responsibility of the network manager or security manager. It's not unusual to see user data scattered across a variety of directories and other data stores in an enterprise, and the integration of all this data, either via meta-directories or just consolidation to a single vendor's directory product, is an important issue in many companies. There probably never will be a master console for managing user and network data in a given environment, but the use of protocols such as LDAP and XML will improve links between applications that need to use the data from these different sources.

Handling Policy Conflicts

As we've mentioned throughout the book so far, the policy-based networking system is responsible for monitoring policies for possible conflicts. The system supposedly has a better knowledge of network devices and applicable policies than the network manager who's creating the policies does. As we've pointed out, conflicts can occur at all levels of a policy-based networking system, which means that policies need to be checked for conflicts at all levels in the system, by a variety of components. In this section, we'll concentrate on the types of conflicts the policy console and policy management tool can monitor.

There are two types of conflicts that we'll always mention throughout this book: global conflicts and local conflicts.

Global conflicts are those based on the properties of the policy and not the specific devices (or their interfaces) to which the policy might apply. Whereas the policy console and policy management tool can check for global policy conflicts, checking for *local policy conflicts* that apply to all network devices that are controlled by its PDP or Policy Proxy is relegated to the PDP or the proxy.

Two policies globally conflict when all their conditions are satisfied, but one or more of the actions of one policy conflict with one or more of the actions of another policy. The conditions of two policies are both satisfied when their criteria are both met simultaneously.

The actions of two policies conflict when they cause different operations to be applied to the same resource. This can happen only if their corresponding conditions are all satisfied. For example, if policy A specifies that traffic should be forwarded for a particular source IP address, but policy B specifies that traffic should be denied for that same source IP address, these policies will conflict if each of their conditions is all satisfied. For example, if packets from Joe are supposed to receive a DSCP of 6, and FTP packets are supposed to get a DSCP of 8, what happens when Joe sends FTP packets?

Within a single policy, it is possible to have more than one policy rule that will evaluate "true" for one circumstance. An oft-cited example is:

Rule 1: If (srcIPaddr == 192.168.2.3) Priority=5

Rule 2: If (srcIPsubnet == 192.168.1/21) Priority=3

In the preceding example, both rule 1 and rule 2 would evaluate true if the source IP address were 192.168.2.3. If these two rules were used in a policy to configure an existing device (e.g., a router), there would be a forced ordering of evaluation, so that the first match would be the action implemented.

One attempt to solve such problems is to associate a priority value with each policy rule, as suggested by the Policy Framework Working Group. This priority is used by the network manager to set which policy rule is to have a higher priority, to determine which policy rule has precedence if more than one policy rule can evaluate as true. Unfortunately, there is no uniqueness to the priority value, so that it is still possible to have multiple rules which could evaluate true and there is no way for the system to determine which has higher priority.

The problem with the priority approach is that since priority values do not have to be unique for a given set of rules, different systems may choose different rules to apply given the same input. Rule evaluation must be deterministic, such that the same policy, encountering the same input conditions, renders the same results wherever the policy is installed. When multiple policies are deployed throughout the network, it is possible that the behavior specified in one location will not be the same as behavior specified in another location.

It's also possible that policies can be inconsistent when applied across a network composed of multiple policy domains, which might be detectable at the policy console. As another example, look at Figure 5.5. In Figure 5.5, there are two network elements—A and B—which are connected together serially, and traffic may pass from LAN alpha through LAN beta to LAN gamma. If a user on LAN alpha expects to have the same QoS when communicating with systems on LAN beta and LAN gamma, then the subset of policy pertaining to the user's traffic (based on address, traffic type, or other characteristic) deployed on the interfaces of network elements A and B must agree.

If all of the LANs are being maintained by one IT department, and the user has contracted for 200 Kbps for traffic to systems on LAN gamma, then the policies deployed on interfaces 1, 2, 3, and 4 must all support at least that much throughput for the user. For instance, if policy deployed to interfaces 2 and 4 allow 200 Kbps for traffic coming from the user's machine, and policy deployed to interfaces 1 and 3 allowed only 150 Kbps of traffic to the user's PC, then the policies deployed to interfaces 1 and 3 could be in conflict with the policies deployed to interfaces 2 and 4.

For policy management, such a conflict should be detected before the user complains about lower than expected performance. The means for such detection would have to be in policy system at a point where the policies are visible. That is, interface 1 cannot determine that its policies are in conflict

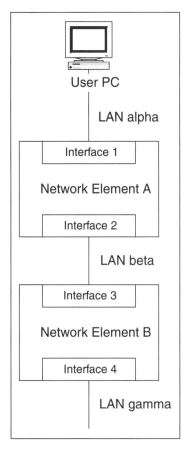

User PC

LAN alpha

Interface 1

Network Element A

Interface 2

LAN beta

Interface 3

Network Element B

Interface 4

LAN gamma

Figure 5.5   Policy conflicts between devices.

with interface 2 unless it has visibility into the policies for interface 2. Network element A cannot determine whether the policies for it are in conflict with the policies for network element B unless it can see the policies for network element B.

It makes sense, then, for the function to determine inconsistencies between policies to be implemented in the policy system before policies are deployed to their targets, namely at the policy console or the policy decision point. Determining inconsistencies such as just described may not be possible with policy information alone. It may be necessary to have a higher-level, or different, set of information which describes the actual service that is to be delivered and probably means that such conflicts need to be monitored at the policy console.

Some conflicts in policies cannot be determined in advance of the policy's distribution. For instance, if a link breaks down and forces unexpected traffic onto a particular path, policies intended for that path may not be appropriate.

Basic Requirements

It will be some time before network managers will be able to assemble policy-based networking systems out of best-of-breed components rather than accept a single vendor's solution. In either case, there are certain minimum requirements they should expect from the product. We'll review these minimum requirements in this and each of the following three chapters, focusing on a particular PBN component in each chapter. Obviously, we'll focus on the policy console and policy management tool here.

The basic requirements for the policy console and policy management tool are the following:

- User-friendly interface
- Appropriate security
- Named policy sets and ownership for multiple managers
- Conflict checking capabilities
- Network topology discovery or import functions

A user-friendly interface can do two things: It can shield the network manager from many of the unnecessary details of policy management. It also allows less-experienced network managers to assume some of the roles of network management that they might not otherwise be able to handle. A user-friendly interface to a policy-based networking system should not merely include graphical representations of policy hierarchies, but also a form fill-out mode and templates for creating or editing policies.

Security is always an important issue in network management, especially considering the increased business-critical nature of today's networks. Network managers should be authenticated at least as well as any other users of important services are.

We mentioned previously that network managers might not always be able to anticipate what effect their policies may have on a network. Network managers should have the ability to experiment with policies but revert to a previous set of policies if the results are not suitable. Being able to name policy sets would be helpful in such cases. Also, some means of associating policies with their creators, either directly or via an audit log, can be helpful when troubleshooting policies and networks, especially when more than one network manager may be involved in running the policy-based networking system.

We've already said enough about checking policies for conflicts, so we'll only emphasize the point that the console and management tool not only needs to check syntax and data typing but also must alert the network manager of global policy conflicts when the policies are created.

Last, network managers need some idea of the logical topology of their networks in order to properly create and apply policies. Most products currently include some way to import network topology data from other tools or to manually create the topology. Look for products that make this task as automatic as possible, either by importing existing data or by discovering the topology themselves.

Summary

Providing a good UI for policy-based networking depends on a balance between providing the network manager with enough information to do his or her job and hiding unneeded details from that same network manager. Using techniques such as form fill-out, policy templates, and drag-and-drop, a policy console can make it easier for any network manager to create and edit policies. The policy console, working in conjunction with the policy management tool, should also act as the first line of defense against incorrect or conflicting policies, not only performing syntax and data type checking, but comparing policies for conflicts.

For the moment, network managers looking for policy-based networking systems are best served by sticking with single-vendor solutions, partly because of lack of interoperability between different vendors' policy consoles. This situation will continue until someone creates a standard language for describing policies at a high level of abstraction, such as that used at the level of the policy console. One possibility is XML. The requirement for a policy description language will become increasingly important as enterprises look to exchange policies with their ISPs to ensure services like end-to-end QoS.

The next chapter takes us one level deeper into the policy-based networking framework, to the data repository. There, we discuss the advantages and disadvantages of using directories and databases to store policies and other data that's important to policy-based networking.

The Policy Repository

Once you've created policies for controlling your network services and configuring network devices, as we described in the previous chapter, you'll need to store those policies somewhere. If policies are only stored locally, say on the workstation you use as a policy console, then your system loses the power of being able to distribute the management tasks while at the same time ensuring consistency of the policies. For that, you need some type of distributed storage technology such as a directory or a database.

In this chapter, we'll focus our attention on the two different approaches to storing policies in a policy-based networking system: directories and databases. We start out by explaining the basic functions required by a policy repository and then discuss the differences between directories and databases as they relate to policy-based networking. The latter half of the chapter goes into detail on some of the more important issues surrounding policy storage, and whether directories or databases are a better answer. (Hint: Neither technology is the perfect answer.) Then we wrap up the chapter with our list of the main requirements for a usable policy repository using today's technology.

Basic Functions

On the face of it, a policy repository has a simple task: It must store policies in such a way that whoever or whatever needs to use those policies can retrieve them. It might be a network manager using a policy console, or it might be a policy decision point requesting policies on behalf of the network devices it controls.

But in order to accomplish this "trivial" task, a policy repository has to provide certain services in order to do the job correctly. For instance, a data repository must maintain the integrity of the data it receives and stores, which means that any transaction that changes data must be complete and verified or else the affected data is restored, or rolled back, to its previous state.

Although our conceptual drawings of architectures for policy-based networking have only shown a single repository (see Chapter 4, "Architectures for Policy-Based Networking"), bear in mind that policy-based networking systems are distributed systems and that more than one instance of the policy repository may exist. Furthermore, even a policy repository that appears as a single logical entity within the system may be distributed across multiple locations to deal with scalability and reliability issues. When you're using a distributed data store for your policies, then the data store should include methods for replicating data among the different locations and ensure that data replication does not affect the distribution of policies within the system. As we'll see later in this chapter, replicating data infrequently may mean that not all parts of a policy-based networking system are distributing the same policies when they should.

The policy repository is also one of the linchpins in ensuring the security of the policy-based networking system. The policy repository should include mechanisms to guard its data against unauthorized access and alterations. As we've pointed out, policies are composed of rules, so the repository may not only store policies, but also individual rules, as distinct objects. Since network managers may have different permission levels for editing policies and reusing rules, the repository's security features may have to support object-level security to ensure that only the right users can use or edit the rules.

Extended Functions

While the policy repository's main task is to store policies, the repository may also serve as a repository for other data that the policy-based networking system requires. Directories are often used to store user profiles and access control lists, for example, so a directory that's relegated to be a policy repository may also store this other data. In some cases, directories may also store IP addresses as part of a DHCP server system, and this data would be used for mapping usernames to addresses.

Even if the policy repository does not store all this added data, it may include pointers to other data stores in the system which do store this data, simplifying the network manager's task of associating this ancillary data with his or her policies.

The two main types of products used for storing policies are directories and databases. In the following sections, we'll cover some of the main points of directories and relational databases as we discuss the advantages and disadvantages of each of these types of data storage products.

A Brief Introduction to Directories

A *directory* is an information repository for data about objects such as users, applications, files, and other resources. Directories help system users and administrators answer questions, find people and resources, identify authorized users, and maintain the integrity and security of the network. But data alone does not make a directory. The information in a directory must be stored within a structure that helps make the information easy to retrieve.

You use a directory client to obtain information from, and to put information into, a directory server. By using standard directory access protocols, such as LDAP, different types of clients can access the data in a directory. As an example, if you are using an LDAP directory server, then any directory client that can use the LDAP protocol can use your directory. This is one of the primary differences between a directory and a local database: The database can communicate only with the local administration server, whereas the LDAP directory server can communicate with any LDAP-capable client. Furthermore, with a directory server, you can manage your information from a single source even if the directory is distributed across multiple locations. You can also configure the directory server to allow your users to retrieve directory information from multiple locations on your network.

Following is a review of the basic architecture of a directory, since it relates directly to policy storage.

An *entry* is the basic unit of information stored in a directory. A directory entry usually describes an object such as a printer, a server, and so on. Entries contain a series of attributes that contain information about the object. Each attribute contains a type and one or more values. A type is associated with a syntax that describes the kinds of values that can be stored.

DIRECTORIES VERSUS DIRECTORY SERVICES

Many developers and consultants make a distinction between directories and directory services. In such cases, *directory* refers to the data repository and a *directory service* refers to the methods, or protocols, used to access the directory. For our purposes, we'll use the single term *directory* to represent both the directory and the directory service.

Directory objects are defined in two ways. First, they belong to specific classes, or categories, of objects. Some common directory object classes, for example, are organization (or company), organizational units, persons, groups, servers, and printers. Second, each object in the directory is defined by the attributes that describe it. The object type person, for example, would have attributes such as last name, employee number, department, postal address, e-mail address, and phone number. The object type file server can have attributes such as server name, serial number, network address, and locality.

As new entries are added to the directory, they automatically inherit the properties of their object class as well as the properties of any superior objects in the directory tree. This combination of common directory objects and a hierarchical naming model exploits the advantage of inheritance and simplifies directory administration and management.

Entries are organized hierarchically in a treelike structure called a Directory Information Tree (DIT). Each entry has a unique identifier called a distinguished name (DN), by which the entry is organized in the DIT. A DN consists of an arrangement of parts called relative distinguished names (RDNs). Figure 6.1 shows a simple Directory Information Tree. In Figure 6.1, each box represents a directory entry. Each entry contains a list of attributes. For example, the entry for the country CAN (c=CAN) could include an attribute called "description" with a value of Canada. The organization of entries in the DIT is restricted by their object class definitions. Entries are named according to their position in the DIT. A distinguished name is made up of a sequence of relative distinguished names. For example, in Figure 6.1 the ou=LDAP Team entry will have a distinguished name of ou=LDAP Team, o=NT c=CAN (o = organization, ou = organizational unit).

We've already mentioned the term schema in prior chapters. A directory schema defines the contents of the directory—the objects and object attributes the directory can contain. Regardless of the physical characteristics of the directory, the schema defines the contents of the directory in such a way that a directory-enabled application can search, add, or modify the contents of the directory. This schema, then, often defines both the directory name space (the actual information in the directory) and the objects the directory can accommodate (users, printers, and so on).

One of the more important directory-related protocols that's been developed in the past few years is the Lightweight Directory Access Protocol (LDAP). LDAP is a communication protocol between a directory client and a directory server (see Figure 6.2). It defines the transport and format of messages that a directory client uses to access a directory. With LDAP, different directory services can communicate with one another, allowing users to create and query directories.

LDAP defines functions for accessing and modifying directory entries such as the following:

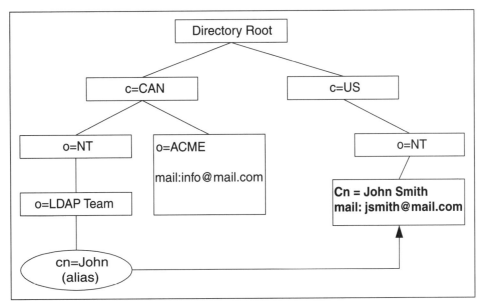

Figure 6.1   Directory information tree.

- Searching for entries that match defined criteria
- Adding entries
- Deleting entries
- Modifying entries
- Modifying the distinguished name (DN) or relative distinguished name (RDN) of an entry
- Comparing entries

LDAP functions can be divided into three categories: query, update, and authentication. A query operation includes the search and compare functions used for retrieving information from a directory. The update operation includes the add, delete, and modify functions used to update information stored in the directory. The authentication operation includes the bind, unbind, and abandon operations used to connect and disconnect to and from the LDAP server. (For more details on LDAP, see T. Howes, *Understanding and Deploying LDAP Directory Services*, Macmillan Technical Publishing, 1999.)

LDAP also defines the format and content of messages that a directory client and server use to communicate with each other. The messages indicate the functions that a client requests (such as search, modify, and delete), the responses from the server, and the format of the data in these messages.

While directories offer many advantages for storing and accessing data, as summarized in Table 6.1, directories are not suited for storing all types of

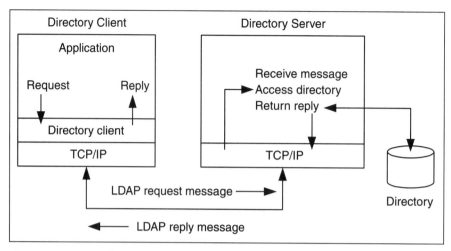

Figure 6.2   LDAP client and server.

data, nor are they optimal solutions for all types of applications. For instance, directories lack object and attribute locking, which makes it harder to ensure data integrity when there's more than one author (or input) of data in the directory. Directories, unlike relational databases, also lack options to maintain referential integrity, that is, rules that control the ability to add and delete records.

Also, directories are not wellsuited to handling transactions, since they have no support for versioning or other features that ensure a transaction is completed (for more, see the next section on relational databases). Application managers won't use a directory to store data for online transaction processing (OLTP) of credit card orders, for instance. Last, directories aren't designed to store data that changes frequently since they're designed to handle mainly write-once (or write infrequently), read-many operations on the data.

Table 6.1   Features of Directories

FEATURES OF DIRECTORIES	FUNCTIONS PERFORMED BY DIRECTORIES
Loosely consistent, distributed, and replicated data stores	Distribution of data for high availability
Independent updates to directory instances	Support of location-independent binding to information
Very fast read operations	Support of fast searches and lookups
Hierarchical data model, with inheritance	Single application of attributes (policy or roles) for organizations, groups, individuals

An Overview of Relational Databases

With that brief introduction to directories in hand, let's take a quick look at relational databases so we can compare the strengths and limitations of both technologies in policy-based networking systems.

A *relational database* is a collection of data items organized as a set of formally described tables from which data can be accessed or reassembled in many different ways without having to reorganize the database tables.

A relational database is a set of tables containing data fitted into predefined categories. Each table (which is sometimes called a *relation*) contains one or more data categories in columns. Each row contains a unique instance of data for the categories defined by the columns. For example, a typical business order entry database would include a table that describes a customer with columns for name, address, phone number, and so forth. Another table would describe an order: product, customer, date, sales price, and so forth. A user of the database could obtain a *view* of the database that fitted the user's needs. For example, a branch office manager might like a view or report on all customers that bought products after a certain date. A financial services manager in the same company could, from the same tables, obtain a report on accounts that needed to be paid.

When creating a relational database, you can define the *domain* of possible values in a data column and further *constraints* that may apply to that data value. For example, a domain of possible customers could allow up to 10 possible customer names but be constrained in one table to allowing only three of these customer names to be specifiable.

The definition of a relational database results in a table of meta-data or formal descriptions of the tables, columns, domains, and constraints.

The standard user and application program interface to a relational database is the *structured query language* (SQL). SQL statements are used both for interactive queries for information from a relational database and for gathering data for reports.

Relational databases provide referential integrity across relational tables and concurrency control with file and record locking. Databases can enable relations between different sets of data, and transactional integrity both within and between data sets, creating powerful tools for building applications. By leveraging these features, relational databases can enforce a very consistent view of data, ensuring both integrity and consistency in multiuser environments. Some of the other advantages of relational databases are summarized in Table 6.2.

In cases where users need information in multiple locations, many relational database products support replication to move the contents of a database, or just its structure and schema, to multiple locations. But when a database is parti-

Table 6.2   Features of Relational Databases

FEATURES OF RELATIONAL DATABASES	FUNCTIONS PERFORMED BY RELATIONAL DATABASES
Relational data model, referential integrity across tables	Consistent view of data
Concurrency control with file and record locking	Integrity and consistency in multiuser environments
Transactional integrity, both within and between data sets	Transactions across databases to enhance relational model
Support for higher ratios of reads to writes	Dynamic data support for high degree of changes

tioned to multiple locations, databases usually encounter many of the same data consistency limitations that directories encounter. And many relational databases don't support location-independent binding to database replicas, which is one of the advantages of directories. While relational databases often require specific applications to connect to specific physical replicas, directory applications can generally access any replica of the data they're authorized to see.

While relational databases are used for a wide variety of applications, they are not well suited for object-oriented designs requiring a hierarchical information model and inheritance, such as the CIM/DEN model for policy-based networking. Also, they lack indexed data stores for highly optimized searches, but use application- and query-specific indices instead. Last, relational databases lack the ability to handle loosely coupled data instances.

Issues

When you're considering a policy-based networking system, you should pay attention to the following important issues regarding the policy repository:

- Data integrity
- Scalability
- Security
- Integration with other data stores
- Schema development

Data Integrity

In a policy-based networking system, the policy repository is one of the two servers that requires redundancy; the PDP is the other. Large policy-based systems are likely to use distributed data stores for efficiency and reliability. The policy repository must therefore include some type of replication or synchronization mechanism for the various data stores that make up the repository.

When data is replicated can pose problems for policy-based networking. The frequency of data replication may affect the distribution of policies to, and interpretation of those policies by, PDPs. For instance, in order to ensure that all PDPs receive the same policies, data between policy repositories must be replicated more frequently than PDPs are updated.

If the repository is directory-based, the system can use a directory's replication features to ensure that crucial data is stored and replicated in more than one location. However, the IETF has not approved a replication protocol as a standard for LDAP directories. This situation currently limits directory replication to vendor-specific solutions. Early adopters of policy-based management systems should therefore plan to use a single vendor's directory product for their systems. It's also possible that vendors will turn to Directory Services Markup Language (DSML) as an alternative approach to replication, especially where directory information is exchanged between companies, perhaps involving different directory implementations and vendor products.

When it comes to data and transactional integrity, databases provide better support for versioning and rollback of data than LDAP-enabled directories. While the DMTF's selection of LDAP for mapping CIM and DEN will go a long way toward assuring interoperable data access in policy-based networking systems, at least in the long term, the current LDAP standards are not sufficient to ensure data integrity. One particular deficiency in LDAP is a hindrance to ensuring data integrity—that's a lack of transactional integrity.

Transactional integrity is the ability of the repository to ensure that a set of related operations are completed as a set. A lack of transactional integrity will result in interoperability problems, since vendor implementations may update objects in different orders. This could cause data repository corruption.

A standard solution will eventually come from efforts within the IETF LDAP working groups, but in the meantime some vendors have added their own layer of software LDAP directories to provide a form of transactional integrity for LDAP transactions. As you might expect, the vendors' solutions are not interoperable.

DIRECTORY SERVICES MARKUP LANGUAGE

DSML is an XML document type for schema and data interchange. DSML provides a format for directory interoperability across various Internet protocols, including HTTP and Simple Mail Transfer Protocol (SMTP), not just LDAP. In this way, DSML helps directory vendors to expose their schemas and entries to Internet-oriented applications through multiple protocols, using XML as the common denominator.

Scalability

Scalability can easily become an issue for policy repositories. The initial deployment of policy-based networking systems may not strain policy repositories because the number of policies and the number of roles and devices that need to be stored are relatively small. When policies are written for individual applications and users and policies must be distributed to end-user hosts (even if the hosts are grouped into workgroups or departments), the number of policy objects that must be stored increases greatly.

The factors affecting the scalability and performance of a policy repository differ according to whether the repository is a directory or a database. For instance, databases are better than directories at handling a high ratio of writes to reads, and in situations in which many changes to the data must be instantly available to all clients. Directories, on the other hand, provide fast read operations, making them ideal for applications that must find resources or publish data to large numbers of PDPs in many different locations.

One of the ways to deal with scalability problems is to distribute the data among multiple data stores, which is one of the features readily supported by directories. But the design of the repository's topology, that is, where the different data stores are located, has a significant impact on the performance of the system. For instance, the topology should most likely be a two-tier hierarchy, with a global master store at the top level and local masters at the second level (see Figure 6.3). If necessary, each of these masters can replicate data to other data stores at each level. While the global master store may store all the policies, the local masters need only store the policies that pertain to the domain in which they're located. If you have a hierarchy of network managers, for instance, with some handling enterprise-wide policies and other relegated to handling departmental policies, then the data stores for the departmental policies could be local masters. Similarly, networks located at different geographical sites could each have their own local or global master stores depending on the complexity of the network at each site.

A key requirement for the design of the repository's topology is how many concurrent reads and writes will occur in each data store. Performance will suffer if too many reads or writes can overwhelm the repository; at that point, it's best to split the data store into two or more stores and rely on replication to insure that the data in each repository is up to date. At the same time, you need to take into account how much data needs to be replicated between data stores since that can affect both network and repository performance if a great deal of data must be exchanged between replicas. As part of the planning, the repository designer must balance user requirements for data availability and server workload.

The design of a policy repository's topology is not something vendors of policy-based networking have directly addressed. Partly because it's antici-

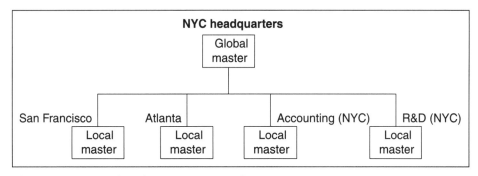

Figure 6.3   A sample policy repository topology.

pated that most early adopters of policy-based networking will want to control a relatively small number of devices, the vendors expect that a single directory or database will be able to handle the storage needs of their customers. But this will become more of an issue as policy-based systems are deployed at multiple sites within an enterprise. The issue will also arise when network managers expand their policy-based networking systems to include end-user hosts, which will significantly increase the number of devices that need to be managed.

The policy repository's performance is more of an issue when dealing with requests from PDPs than from the policy console. As we pointed out in Chapter 4, PDPs must poll the repositories to obtain policies either based on a polling schedule or in response to alerts. That's because policy repositories are passive; if a more active repository were available, such as a database supporting CORBA's notification methods, then polling could be decreased (or done away with entirely) and network traffic for management decreased. Since standard LDAP directories do not include an event notification method, systems using LDAP-based repositories are likely to increase network traffic and processing overhead. On the other hand, using CORBA simplifies communications since policies need to be distributed only when they're changed. This distribution can be triggered using standard CORBA services on either the server or the client (that is, the policy repository or the PDP). CORBA has seen a lot of use in service management systems, such as those utilizing the TMN (Telecommunication Management Network) framework many carriers use. The few commercial systems using CORBA for policy-based networking do not use all of CORBA's features, especially the notification services, which means that the policy management tool must still notify PDPs of policy changes and the repository remains a passive source of data.

Security

It's crucial that the policy-based networking system be secure against unauthorized use. This security includes ensuring that only authorized users can create or modify policies as well as ensuring secure storage and exchange of data. This means that devices (PDPs and PEPs, for instance) as well as users need to be authenticated. It also means that some form of encryption is necessary for data transmissions.

Each console and network manager must be an authorized user of the system, with proper authority to access information within the repository. Current systems use simple user name–password methods for authenticating users.

The repository must control access to the stored policies, allowing only authorized devices and users to access or alter the policies. For directory-based repositories, LDAP currently supports mechanisms for the authentication of clients and for ensuring the privacy of data transported across a network. LDAP authentication can be performed by means of either HTTP Digest Authentication or Secure Sockets Layer (SSL). Also, since policy rules are reusable objects within the repository, access to the repository will have to be granted on an object-by-object basis. The IETF standards for LDAP-enabled directories now support object-based access, but vendors of LDAPv3 directories have not uniformly implemented this feature.

On the other hand, the IETF has not yet standardized the management of access control information and access control lists for LDAP directories. The IETF's proposed access control model defines rights for information stored within the directory itself, as well as for network resources to which the directory points. These rights can be applied to objects in the directory (such as rules and policies), to the attributes of objects in the directory, or to objects that the directory references (other network resources). Although the directory standards bodies continue to work on standard access control information mechanisms, that work is progressing slowly and directory vendors are employing proprietary methods for access control.

Integration with Other Data Sources

Policy-based networking systems often have to deal with a variety of data, which may or may not be contained entirely within the repository. Although the policy repository is the focus for storing policies, the same repository might also store user-related and device-related information. But the common situation is that the ancillary data used by a policy-based networking system exists in a variety of sources.

The integration of policy-based networking systems with other data therefore raises two crucial issues: (1) what is the latency of the data—that is, how frequently does it change? and (2) how can the policy system access the data?

There are three types of data that the systems have to deal with:

Static data, which changes much slower than the replication frequency of the directory.

Low-latency data, which changes somewhat faster than the replication frequency of the directory and/or which requires on-demand replication, within some latency period, instead of scheduled replication.

Transient data, which changes much faster than the replication frequency of the directory and/or which is so voluminous that it doesn't make sense to store it.

For example, IP addresses leased using DHCP, especially for a large Internet service provider, constitute transient data that will change faster than the replication frequency of the directory in general. Similarly, network statistics collected through SNMP or RMON are also transient data that should be stored somewhere other than a directory. Directories can manage devices and applications as long as the system administrator takes care to manage just the static aspects of devices and applications.

Turning to the second issue—that of accessing data that's not necessarily part of the policy-based networking system—we've already commented on some of the issues surrounding the use of either directories or databases for storing the information that policy-based networking systems need. But so far we've concentrated on the policies themselves; other data may be required as well, such as user profiles, access rights, IP address lease information, and device status. Many systems already use directories for storing information about users and will continue to do so, expanding their use to incorporate additional user information such as digital certificates. At the same time, other applications will continue to use data stores; for example, network monitoring systems using SNMP and RMON will continue to store data in flat files or databases.

Since a network manager has to create and validate network policies within the context of the state of the network and user requirements, policy-based networking systems may need to factor in data from these other sources. Furthermore, since it's unlikely that storage of these other types of information will change significantly in the near future, policy-based networking systems need to link to them in their current form. Nor should you expect that all the pertinent data would be stored in a single directory or database. Furthermore, these data stores will not solely be either directories or databases; viewed as a whole, the system providing information for policy-based networking will be a hybrid one.

Although policy-based networking systems depend on data from many different sources, it's unlikely that the network managers responsible for maintaining the policy-based networking system will also have the responsibility or authority to maintain all of the other systems as well. For instance, information on users is often the responsibility of the HR department in larger organizations. As the need for directory-enabled applications grows (and policy-based networking is only one possible directory-enabled application), enterprises will have to face the inevitable task of deciding how all the necessary data can be maintained and shared. One important solution is the meta-directory. A meta-directory coordinates information about a single object or entity from a variety of sources in one place; it can therefore assemble a response to a query from many sources in real time. (For more details on meta-directories, see K. Kampman and C. Kampman, *All About Network Directories*, Wiley, 1999.) Network managers, therefore, should plan to be involved in the design and construction of a meta-directory to access the data their policy-based systems need.

Most enterprises are just starting to consolidate the information stored in many of their directories and few have deployed meta-directories. Since it may take a few years for enterprises to deploy enterprise-wide directories or meta-directories, many enterprises may choose to delay deploying policy-based networking systems until they get their directory house in order. Vendors are attempting to circumvent this problem by bundling the major directory products with their policy-based networking products, but this bundling doesn't solve the problems associated with getting the right user and application information that may be stored in other directories.

Schema Development

Although work on defining an information model for policy-based management began more than three years ago, policy-based networking is still in its relative infancy. It's taken time not only to agree on the logical description of network devices, policies, and related objects in the model, but also for the vendors to implement the information model within their own systems.

Because the DEN model seeks to define schemas, the directory serves as the point of interoperability. However, interoperability requires standard schemas and a standard information model. Standardization of the necessary schemas is continuing, but it is not complete. Currently, most vendors use proprietary DEN-compatible schemas.

The DEN information model is open-ended; that is, it allows vendors to define their own extensions to the schemas. This type of model is necessary in that each vendor's products have special options and features, and the schemas must reflect those special features so that policy management tools can properly configure those products. But if the vendors don't publish their own extensions, other vendors' policy-based network management systems will be unable to control all the features of other vendor's devices. Unless vendors publish their schema extensions, policy-based network management systems will evolve in much the same way as SNMP network management systems have: that is, a vendor's management system performs best with its own network equipment, offering limited management of other vendors' devices.

While it's likely that networking vendors will continue to use proprietary extensions to control the value-added features of their hardware, the DMTF's planned certification program for DEN compliance will help define the core features of every policy-based networking system. We expect the DMTF to start their certification program sometime in 2001, and network managers should press vendors for DEN compliance as certified by the DMTF when they're shopping for a policy-based networking product.

There's also the question of how managers can administer the schema for their policy systems. While the core schema that ships with a commercial system may suffice for many needs, network managers may elect to add extensions to customize the policy-based networking system to their organization. Directory services do support more direct access to schema information, as well as the ability to change schema (with the proper permissions) for applications. Typically, relational databases define a more rigid database structure that administrators can modify only with great care and effort. Directories, in contrast, are flexible by design, and applications can query directories, asking them to describe their structure.

Basic Requirements

As part of our ongoing effort to define the minimal requirements for a usable policy-based networking system, we'll now turn our attention to the requirements for the policy repository.

The basic requirements for the policy repository should include:

- LDAP support
- Distributed data store
- Support for multiuser management, including data versioning
- Authentication and access control

Whether the policy repository is a directory or a database, it should support what has become a standard protocol for accessing data, LDAP. It's not necessary that LDAP be the protocol used for accessing policies—that's the choice of the vendor, who may use a database that accesses via SQL or ODBC instead of a directory that natively supports LDAP. But other data that either is, or will be, essential to the deployment of policy-based networking systems, such as NOS-based user data, can be best accessed by means of LDAP.

Furthermore, on a large multisite network, a centralized data store may not provide the performance necessary to support access by large numbers of users on multiserver networks interconnected by slow WAN links; a distributed system, with local caches at various sites, may be a better solution. In addition, a single copy of the data store represents a single point of failure; if the directory server goes down, no one can access the network. Distributing the database across multiple servers, and then replicating the directory data between those servers, usually addresses these scalability and performance issues.

Multiuser management of policy-based systems places added demands on the policy repository. The repository should support versioning of data and rollback features so that changes can be traced back to administrators, or so that policies can be reset to previous versions in case of an error.

Last, but certainly not least, the policy repository must be secure. The policy repository should offer some means of authenticating users to ensure that only authorized personnel should be allowed to access the contents of the repository. Similarly, devices that require access to the policies, such as policy decision points, will also have to be authenticated by the repository.

Summary

Although we've often referred to policy-based network management as a directory-enabled application, vendors of policy-based systems have not yet exploited directories to their fullest. In fact, many of the current products do not use a directory for storing policies. This chapter presented some of the basic features of both directories and relational databases so you could see how they can be used as policy repositories.

Both storage technologies have strengths and weaknesses for storing policies. For instance, directories are well suited for use as distributed data stores. They also do a good job of supporting a hierarchy of objects with inheritance, which makes policy definition and organization easier. On the other hand, relational databases may be able to process complicated queries faster than databases and also provide better tools for ensuring data and transactional integrity.

The policy repository is an important focal point for data integrity, security, and scalability of the policy-based networking system. While the scalability issues may not be a concern in initial deployments of policy-based networking, due to the relatively small numbers of devices involved, we guarantee that scalability will become more of an issue as policy-based networking systems are used on larger networks. Network managers should therefore consider the design of the policy repository carefully, thinking about such issues as distributed data storage and replication strategies.

The next chapter continues in our series of four on the components of the policy-based networking framework. Chapter 7, " The Policy Decision Point," covers the procedures and protocols surrounding the policy decision points.

The Policy Decision Point

The policy decision point (PDP) is one of the new components that policy-based networking introduces to network management, one that aims to provide more intelligence to the management system. While network-wide policies are important for managing networks at a network-wide level, it's the PDP that must do much of the difficult work of translating policies into information that makes sense to the network devices that have to enforce the policies.

This chapter focuses not only on the policy decision point itself, but also on the way that a PDP interacts with a policy enforcement point. The procedure a PDP follows when translating a higher-level policy into a device-dependent policy is fairly straightforward and is usually implemented in vendor-specific ways. On the other hand, there's a lot of work and discussion (if not controversy) surrounding how PDPs should communicate with PEPs, and we'll devote quite a bit of this chapter to the discussion of these various protocols. The later part of this chapter covers some of the important issues of PDPs and policy distribution, such as scalability, security, and handling of non-policy-aware devices.

Basic Functions

The PDP serves two main functions in a policy-based networking system. First, it's an intermediate in translating higher-level abstractions of policies into configurations that are of use to policy enforcement points (PEPs). Second, the PDP can serve as the central point for distributing policies to PEPs, especially in three-tiered architectures.

In order to fulfill their role in translating and distributing policies to PEPs, PDPs have to be able to access the policies stored in a policy repository and know the capabilities of the devices the PDP controls. Both of these requirements can be met using a number of different protocols, which is why developers have adopted more than one approach to implementing policy-based networking. As an example, a PDP could use either LDAP or SQL to acquire policies from the repository, depending on whether the repository is a directory or a database, respectively. Similarly, the PDP could use SNMP, COPS, telnet/CLI, or CORBA (Common Object Request Broker Architecture) to transmit policies to PEPs. Each one of these protocols has advantages and disadvantages associated with it, and our discussion of these protocols will make up the bulk of this chapter.

For reliability's sake, multiple PDPs are required, which means that PDPs need a way to exchange policies and decisions. The PEPs also need a method for communicating with alternate PDPs in the event a PDP fails.

We mentioned in the previous chapter that the policy repository must ensure the integrity of transactions associated with policy creation and editing. In a similar fashion, the PDP must verify that the PEPs receive the proper policy information. In this case, verification means not only that the intended device received the policies but also that the device can actually enforce them. Verification thus requires knowledge of the device's capabilities.

At the same time, in order to reach an appropriate decision for configuring PEPs, the PDP should be aware of the operational state as well as the capabilities of the PEPs that it will configure. Other useful information includes the PEP's capacity and utilization. While *capability* is an ability to perform a desired function, *capacity* is a measure of how much of that capability the system has. *Utilization* refers to how much capacity for a particular capability has been used.

At the moment, very few devices on your network are policy-aware. This situation will most likely change over the next few years, as you upgrade device OSs or replace devices with newer models. But in the meantime, the lack of policy-aware devices means that some sort of policy translation module or policy proxy must work alongside the PDP. We're not talking about translating policies from one abstraction to another, as we described in Chapter 3, "What Are Policies?"—that's the PDP's job—but about translation from the lowest-level policy abstraction (i.e., device-dependent policies) in the PDP to configuration data (often called device-local or implementation-specific configuration data) that the network devices can use.

PDPs can communicate with PEPs in more than one way to distribute policies. In general, network devices aren't very intelligent, especially when it

TWO-TIER OR THREE-TIER?

You'll note that we frequently refer to the PDP coordinating multiple PEPs and aggregating information from them as well. Strictly speaking, that can occur only in a three-tiered policy-based networking architecture. Recall that in a two-tiered architecture, the PDP is colocated with the PEP that it controls, enforcing a one-to-one relationship between PDP and PEP. In the two-tiered architecture, PDPs don't really have the role of configuring or collecting data from multiple PEPs. Although there may be some occasions when a two-tiered architecture might be used, we feel that the three-tiered architecture offers the best flexibility and scalability, and it'll be the one we mention most often.

comes to dealing with changing network conditions. Device configurations are usually sent, or pushed, to each network device by a management console. Aside from requesting a particular configuration file when they boot, network devices don't actively request new configuration files when conditions change. But this situation is changing, particularly as network managers look to use protocols such as RADIUS or RSVP to reserve network resources (such as bandwidth using RSVP). There will be times when at least some network devices will request decisions on resource requests from a PDP, so the PDP must be able to handle these requests. In short, both push and pull mechanisms are important to policy distribution.

In Chapter 5, "Creating and Managing Policies," we detailed some of the policy conflicts that can occur and that should be resolved in the upper levels of a policy-based networking system. The PDP also has to resolve certain policy conflicts. We'll get into more details shortly, but these conflicts could be issues such as requesting the allocation of more bandwidth than a given port can handle or requiring more queues for buffering traffic than a device can support.

Considering the essential nature of networks to today's businesses, a network management system must be tamper-proof. In the previous chapter, we discussed what sort of data security the policy repository should support. The PDPs also need to be active participants in the security of the system, not only authenticating themselves to either a repository or a PEP, but also authenticating their sources of information (repositories and PEPs) and offering secure communication channels with the PEPs.

Extended Functions

In a three-tiered architecture, the PDP receives or retrieves policies and makes decisions on the configuration of the devices for which it's responsible.

Thus, the PDP serves as a distribution point. But the opposite role, acting as an aggregation point, is also something that the PDP can do. In this case, we're looking at a flow of information away from the PEPs and toward the policy console. The PDP may serve as an aggregator of device events or accounting information that should eventually make its way back to the network manager.

PDPs will also need to exchange information among themselves as a policy-based networking system grows. A single PDP may be sufficient for controlling dozens of, or even a hundred, devices, but larger networks, or those with a number of distributed sites, will require more than one PDP. In such cases, even though the central policy repository stores all policies, PDPs will still need to exchange policy information among themselves. For instance, if a PDP must change its local policies in response to a network failure, then other PDPs may also have to change their policies to maintain end-to-end consistency. Inter-PDP communication should be able to do this faster than if changes are first sent to the policy repository or policy console for action. But note that this type of inter-PDP communication is far from standardized.

Now let's move on to one of the thornier issues surrounding policy distribution, which protocol to use.

Methods for Distributing Device-Dependent Policies

As we've already noted, it's possible to use many of the protocols already used for network management, such as telnet/CLI, SNMP, HTTP, and CORBA, to distribute policy-based device configurations to PEPs; a new protocol, COPS, has also been proposed for exchanging information between PDPs and PEPs. (Note: In the case of two-tiered architectures, where the PDP and PEP are colocated on the same device, LDAP may serve to distribute policies directly to a network device, but we'll not include LDAP in our discussion here.)

The distribution of policies and policy-based device configurations depends on both push and pull methods of communication. When policies are created in a top-down fashion by a network manager and then distributed from the policy repository to the PDPs and finally to the PEPs, the system must include some type of notification method to inform PDPs that there are new or modified policies. The PDP can then request the pertinent policies from the policy repository. This is the process policy-based systems will most likely follow when network devices need to be provisioned or configured, for example, with QoS policies (such as those using DiffServ) or access control filters.

Under other circumstances, the network device may need to request a decision from the PDP. For example, a network device would need to query the PDP when it encounters a new situation that's not covered by its set of cached decisions (such as a new user logging in to a remote access server requiring RADIUS authentication), or when devices use RSVP to handle signaled QoS. A policy-based networking system should be capable of handling all of these situations.

The selection of protocols for exchanging policy-based data between PDPs and PEPs is still in a state of flux. Established methods for configuring devices, such as telnet/CLI (and SNMP, to a lesser extent), impose significant overhead if the state of the device needs to be maintained and changes must be made dynamically, which is the case for many QoS applications. Such protocols as LDAP, which are good at distributing information and therefore suited to accessing stored policy data, weren't designed to query clients and maintain session states, either. What's needed for effective policy-based network management is a protocol that can maintain state between PDPs and PEPs, dynamically update device configurations, and, perhaps most importantly, do so in a network-wide fashion; that's why such approaches as COPS and SNMPCONF are being developed. With these issues in mind, let's review the main features of some of these approaches.

Common Open Policy Service and Common Open Policy Service for Provisioning

The Resource Allocation Protocol (RAP) Working Group originally proposed COPS to the IETF as a protocol for controlling the allocation of network resources for signaled QoS using RSVP. This version of COPS has now been approved by the IETF as a proposed standard; RFC 2748 describes COPS and RFC 2749 describes the use of COPS with RSVP. This first version of COPS provides network devices with the opportunity to ask their policy server for an admit/reject decision for a particular RSVP session. But, with DiffServ, a router typically does not receive a signaling message telling it about the forthcoming packet stream; instead, it must be preloaded or provisioned with the policy decision ready for use when the packets arrive. The RAP Working Group is working on an extended version of COPS, often called COPS for Policy Provisioning (or COPS-PR), which extends COPS's capabilities to provisioning QoS or security policies. With COPS-PR, the network-wide policy/configuration data that a PDP downloads to a PEP is defined in Policy Information Bases (PIBs), which we describe shortly.

Common Open Policy Service

COPS is a client-server protocol that uses Transmission Control Protocol (TCP) as its transport protocol to reliably exchange messages between PEPs and a PDP. The PEP initiates sessions with a PDP, requesting a decision from the PDP in response to RSVP reservation (RESV) messages. Once a session has been established between and a PEP and a PDP, the PDP can also send unsolicited decisions to a PEP at any time to change a previously installed state. PEPs and PDPs also exchange keep-alive messages to detect a failure at either end.

A stateful protocol can be used to maintain a link between a PDP and a PEP to improve the efficiency and dynamic response of the policy-based networking system, especially when network conditions change. COPS maintains state in two ways: (1) the client and server share a request/decision state in which the PDP remembers requests from the PEP until they're explicitly deleted by the PEP, and (2) the PDP can associate state from various events (previous request/decision pairs) and use that information to respond to new queries differently than if it didn't have that information. Also, the PDP can push configuration information to the client as needed and can remove the information from the PEP when it's no longer applicable (for example, when a timer expires).

COPS is designed to be extensible. It uses self-identifying objects, which can be extended to support diverse client-specific information without requiring a rewrite of COPS. These self-identifying objects contain the data necessary for identifying request states, establishing the context for a request, identifying the type of request, referencing previously installed requests, relaying policy decisions, reporting errors, providing message integrity, and transferring client-specific/namespace information.

To distinguish between different kinds of clients, the type of client is identified in each message. Different types of clients may have different client-specific data and may require different kinds of policy decisions. At the moment, RSVP has been assigned a client_type of 1 in COPS, and it's been proposed that COPS-PR use a client_type of 2. But since client types represent a policy area (QoS versus security, for example), using COPS for provisioning may entail more than one client type. (That is, the system would use one client type for provisioning QoS and a different client type for provisioning VPNs.)

COPS takes advantage of a multilayer design to support new types of policy domains and extensions while maintaining backward compatibility. The COPS protocol is divided into three distinct layers, as described in Figure 7.1: the base protocol, as defined in RFC 2748; client-type usage directives, such as the one for RSVP, which is defined in RFC 2749; and the policy data model, such as the one for RSVP Policy Data, which is defined in RFC 2750.

The first layer of COPS defines the base protocol as the common denominator that must be supported by all COPS implementations.

In the second layer, each policy domain may be defined as a separate COPS client type. For example, RSVP is a separate policy domain with client type 1. As this book is being written, COPS-PR for provisioning is being defined as client type 2.

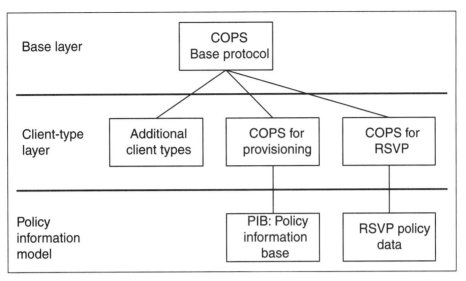

Figure 7.1   COPS layering.

The third and last layer in the COPS protocol stack defines the policy data model. Within a specific client type, COPS messages may include client-specific information. These objects are opaque to the COPS base protocol and can only be understood in the context of a specific client type and policy data model. This provides another level of extensibility where an existing COPS implementation may apply to a new policy domain or extend an already-supported domain by adding new information to the policy data model, or by using an entirely new policy data model.

COPS was originally designed to deal with signaled QoS using RSVP, where a PEP (such as a router) might be forced to require a decision from a PDP before dealing with a resource reservation request. Since a module other than the PEP is making the decision, the designers of COPS decided to call this process outsourcing. This sequence of commands in the outsourced decision process is shown in Figure 7.2.

COPS can also be used to configure PEPs in the following manner: The PEP makes a configuration request to the PDP for a particular interface, module, or functionality. The PDP then sends one or more decisions containing configuration data to the PEP, which the PEP installs and uses locally. A particular named configuration can be updated by simply sending additional decision messages for the same named configuration. When the PDP no longer wishes the PEP to use a piece of configuration information, it sends a decision message specifying the named configuration and a decision flags object with the remove configuration command. The PEP then removes the corresponding configuration and sends a report message to the PDP that specifies it has been deleted.

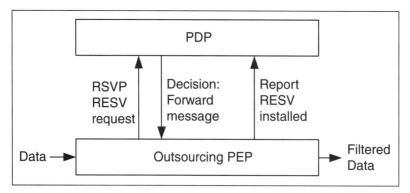

Figure 7.2 COPS command flow in outsourcing.

COPS avoids potential configuration conflicts from multiple PDPs by specifying that one—and only one—PDP controls a COPS client for a device at any one time. A device may include multiple clients, but these clients do not define overlapping functions. For example, one client might be defined for RSVP and a second might be defined for configuring access control. COPS grants a single PDP exclusive access to a client. This single access is not only exclusive of other PDPs, but also exclusive of SNMP and the CLI. Of course, SNMP and/or the CLI is able to disable the use of COPS (via device-local configuration) if and when local control of the device is required (for example, for emergency network debugging), but the closure of the COPS TCP connection informs the PDP that COPS is disabled. When COPS is enabled again, the TCP connection is reestablished and the PDP can restore the configuration to what the higher-level policies require.

COPS also includes options for security. The options cover both authentication of PDPs and PEPs and the integrity and secrecy of COPS messages. The COPS specs describe a COPS message integrity object that includes cryptographic keys and parameters similar to those found in IPSec. The message integrity object provides authentication and replay protection, but not encryption.

The integrity mechanism relies on a shared key known only to the PEP and PDP. The integrity object contains a digest (hash) of the message computed using the HMAC-MD5-96 cryptographic algorithm (HMAC is Hash-based Message Authentication Code). This hash is computed as a function of both the message and the shared key so that virtually any change to the message or to the key would form a new hash value that wouldn't match the originally computed hash value. The integrity object also includes a monotonically incremental sequence number, which allows the receiving entity to identify a replay (if it receives a seemingly new message with an old sequence number).

Mutual authentication takes place upon connection creation and it remains valid for as long as the connection is up and running. COPS can use either Transport Level Security (TLS) or IPSec, which performs authentication for the TCP connection, or the built-in integrity mechanism, which performs authentication for each client-type logical connection.

On top of the security offered by mutual authentication, the ongoing signaling must be protected from unauthorized third-party viewing, modification, or replay. The COPS built-in integrity feature protects all COPS messages from being modified by a third party, but does not encrypt those messages for secrecy. Optional transport security mechanisms such as IPSec can provide both integrity and secrecy for all communications on the TCP connection.

Common Open Policy Service for Provisioning

COPS-PR, or COPS for provisioning, consists of a series of proposed extensions to the original COPS protocol just described. The RAP Working Group proposed these extensions so that a COPS client-server system can be used to push policy-based configuration data to PEPs in situations other than those involving RSVP and PEP-generated requests. In the provisioning model, the PDP may proactively provision the PEP to react to external events (such as user input), PEP events, and any combination of these different types of events. Unlike COPS, COPS-PR makes no assumptions of a direct one-to-one correlation between PEP events and PDP decisions.

In order to handle the provisioning of policies to PEPs in response to external events rather than an RSVP-related request from the PEP, COPS-PR assumes that the PEP establishes a connection with its primary PDP upon booting. (A PEP will locate a secondary PDP if it fails to find its primary PDP.) When the connection is established, the PEP sends information about itself to the PDP in the form of a configuration request. This information includes device-specific information (for example, hardware type, software release, or configuration information). If the configuration of the device changes—a board is removed, a new board is added, or new software is installed, for example—in ways not covered by policies already known to the PEP, then the PEP sends this unsolicited new information to the PDP. On receiving this new information, the PDP sends to the PEP any additional provisioned policies now needed by the PEP (see Figure 7.3).

Provisioning may be performed in bulk (for example, a router's entire QoS configuration) or in portions (for example, updating a DiffServ marking filter). If conditions change so that the PDP determines that changes are required in the

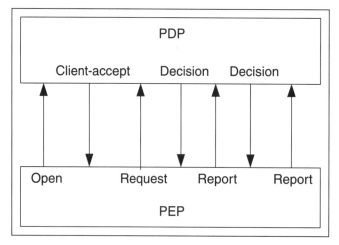

Figure 7.3 COPS command flow in provisioning.

currently provisioned policies, then the PDP sends the changes in policy to the PEP, and the PEP updates its local QoS mechanisms appropriately. (The provisioning model can also be used to configure PEPs for other services, such as VPNs on security gateways and access control lists on firewalls.)

Let's briefly review some of the differences in the two models. The outsourcing model is designed to provide a decision to a PEP in response to a request from the PEP, handling discrete operational events. On the other hand, the provisioning model sends decisions to PEPs without waiting for requests;

Table 7.1 Comparison of COPS and COPS-PR

ITEM	COPS	COPS-PR
Source of events	PEP	Mostly external to the PEP
PEP request describes ...	An operational event	A configuration scope rather than an event
Request/reply correlation	1:1 Event and its decision	1:N A scope and multiple configuration items
Context flags	Incoming, outgoing, and resource allocation flags	Configuration flags
Timing	PEP waits for results which must be delivered instantaneously	PEP does not wait: nonblocking operation. Loose timing which varies by the configured item

these decisions may be done in bulk or as incremental updates. The main points of both models are summarized in Table 7.1.

The Policy Information Base

In COPS-PR, PEPs can inform PDPs of their capabilities by means of a Policy Information Base (PIB). The proposals to define the COPS-PR protocol to handle provisioned QoS include the definition of a PIB that's similar to SNMP management information bases (MIBs) but focuses on policy decisions. By using PIBs in conjunction with COPS, a PEP can inform a PDP of its capabilities, thus providing the PDP with information that it needs to properly translate policies into device-specific configurations. New PIBs can be defined as needed to extend the usage of COPS-PR to new data items without changing the protocol. This is the same approach the IETF took with SNMP and MIBs. In fact, the design of COPS- PR has purposely been defined to leverage as many SNMP mechanisms as are appropriate. Some examples include the following:

- PIBs are defined by the Structure of Policy Provisioning Information (SPPI), a variant of SNMP's Structure of Management Information (SMI) used to define MIBs. The differences in the rules for defining a PIB are solely those needed for use with the COPS-PR protocol and network-wide policies/configuration.

- PIBs define a *policy rule class*, equivalent to a row definition in a MIB table, and a *policy rule instance*, equivalent to a particular row in a MIB table.

- PIBs use object IDs (OIDs) to name policy rule classes, which is the same naming mechanism used in MIBs.

The PIB can be described as a conceptual tree data structure where the branches of the tree represent types of rules or Policy Rule Classes (PRCs), while the leaves represent the contents of Policy Rule Instances (PRIs). There may be multiple instances of rules (PRIs) for any given rule type (PRC). For example, if one wanted to install multiple access control filters, the PRC might represent a generic access control filter type and each PRI might represent an individual access control filter to be applied. The tree might be represented as shown in Figure 7.4.

PIBs are a little simpler than MIBs because they do not need to include multimanager synchronization objects or objects for deleting one or more rows in a MIB table, nor do they need to specify procedures for how these additional objects are used. Since one and only one PDP can control a client (for a specific set of PIBs) at any one time, this exclusive access avoids SNMP's need to provide synchronization mechanisms to protect against multiple SNMP managers trying to access the same MIB objects at the same time. In addition,

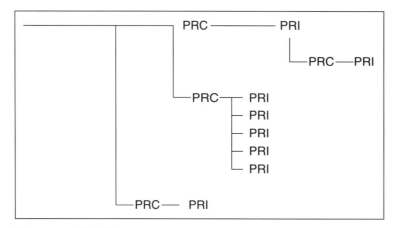

Figure 7.4   The PIB tree.

PIBs do not need other mechanisms to prevent overwriting data, which are included in some MIBs.

PIBs also differ from MIBs in the way they represent device interfaces. All interface-related policies in the PIB are defined, not per individual interface, but on a per-role basis. In the context of COPS and COPS-PR, roles are labels that abstract interface capabilities. For example, edge routers connecting corporate LANs to a WAN would contain an interface to the WAN (say, a T1 interface) that might be assigned a role called WAN-interface. All the T1 interfaces identified as WAN-interface would receive the same configuration information from the PDPs. Roles are useful for aggregating device interfaces to apply a common set of changes without having to name specific device interfaces.

Simple Network Management Protocol and SNMPCONF

SNMP is dominant in the areas of network status monitoring and statistics gathering. It has not been as widely used for configuration management as has telnet/CLI, however. Despite SNMP's relative lack of use as a configuration protocol, proponents of SNMP have suggested that SNMP could be extended to fill many of the roles required by policy-based networking systems, including policy distribution. SNMPv3 lacks some of the features needed to fulfill these roles, such as resource locking and the use of stateful sessions for device management, but the SNMPCONF Working Group is working on extending some of SNMPv3's features to support policy-based networking.

We'll review some of the basics of SNMP before moving on to discuss the details of the work that the SNMPCONF WG has done to adapt SNMP to policy-based networking.

Simple Network Management Protocol

SNMP defines a protocol for the exchange of management information. It also defines a format for representing that management information and a framework for organizing distributing systems into managing systems and managed agents. A number of specific database structures, called management information bases (MIBs), have been defined as part of the SNMP suite of standards. These MIBs specify managed objects for the common network management devices, such as bridges, routers, and LANs.

The SNMP network manager consists of four major components: the network management station (NMS), the NMS MIB and database, a set of network management applications, and the network management user interface. Two components of the SNMP reference model (see Figure 7.5) are of importance here—the network manager and the managed network entity. The NMS is the processing entity that monitors and controls the agents that it is responsible for. The NMS can read and write certain MIB objects in each agent to manage that network device. It can also store pertinent management information on each of the agents in its own database. The MIB of the NMS contains a master list of the MIBs from all of the agents that the NMS intends to manage.

The managed network entity consists of two key components: the agent and the agent MIB. The agent is the processing entity that receives requests from network management stations, processes them if they are valid, and sends the appropriate response. Agents can also be configured to send trap messages to report asynchronous, predefined events. Each message between an NMS and an agent contains a header and a protocol data unit (PDU); the PDU contains an SNMP command and any associated data.

An agent's MIB contains n objects, with each object having three primary attributes of name, syntax, and encoding. The object's name is a unique, preassigned object ID that places it within the SNMP OBJECT ID hierarchy. Three basic types of objects are defined for SNMP: a table, a row in that table (also called an entry), and a nonaggregate type commonly called a leaf. A table is comprised of 1 to n rows. Each row must have the identical number of aggregate objects within it. One or more of these aggregate objects are defined as an index for accessing that entry. Another concept we'll refer to occasionally is *instantiation*. In order for an NMS to access an agent's MIB objects, the NMS must know the object type as well as the object instance of the particular management object that it wishes to access. The object type can be compared to a definition while the object instance is a declaration. The object instance is also called the MIB variable.

The SNMP protocol defines four basic functions:

GET: Used by a manager to retrieve an item from an agent's MIB

SET: Used by a manager to set a value in an agent's MIB

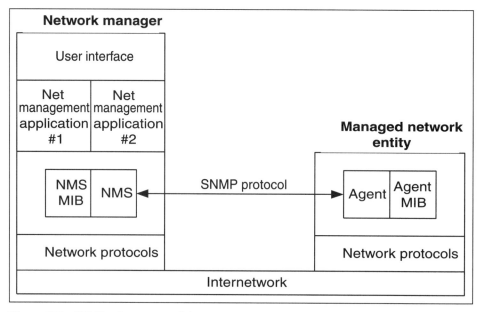

Figure 7.5   SNMP reference model.

GET-NEXT: Used by a manager to retrieve an item from an agent's MIB by
traversing the MIB tree

TRAP: Used by an agent to send an alert to a manager

When an agent receives a GET, GET-NEXT, or SET message, it will try to
retrieve, or modify, the object specified in the variable bindings and will send
a response back to the originator of the request. The set operation is atomic—
either all the variables get set or none of them do.

SNMP uses a transactional model, but it does not support the concept of a
long-term connection between a client and server. For this reason, SNMP
servers may not know whether or not devices have failed. Since messages
are sent over User Datagram Protocol (UDP), which is unreliable, the NMS
and the SNMP agent need an added way of ensuring that information is
delivered. Originally the trap message defined in SNMPv1 was used for
reports of error conditions or failures. To address the issue of reliable delivery, at least in part, the SNMPv2 documents defined the INFORM message.
SNMP INFORM messages are acknowledged by the manager so that the
managed device knows the message has been received. An important advantage of this approach is that multiple management systems can be kept in
sync with the managed devices in a network without polling and without
having to maintain a TCP connection to every managed device in the
network.

As another solution, the IETF has been working on a TCP-based SNMP implementation that would get around the lack of a connection/polling approach, and a connection could be established and maintained in order to allow messages to pass quickly between the client and server.

SNMPv3, which became a set of proposed Internet standards published as RFCs 2221 through 2275, defines security features, notably authentication and secrecy, which previous versions of SNMP lacked. Security-related processing occurs at the message level; the payload of an SNMP message is a protocol data unit (PDU). Security-related functions are organized into two separate subsystems: security and access control. The Security subsystem is concerned with privacy and authentication, and operates on SNMP messages. The Access Control subsystem is concerned with authorized access to management information, and operates on SNMP PDUs.

SNMPv3's security provisions are more complicated than those of COPS since SNMP must provide access control by multiple management entities to multiple managed objects on an object-by-object basis. This stems from the fact that SNMP has been designed from the beginning to support access by multiple NMSs.

Authentication within the User-based Security Model (USM) allows an entity to verify whom the message is from and whether the message has been altered. It further allows for timeliness, which protects against a message being intentionally delayed or replayed by a malicious party.

Two cryptographic functions are defined for USM: authentication and encryption. To support these functions, an SNMP engine requires two values: a privacy key and an authentication key. USM allows the use of two alternative authentication protocols: HMAC-MD5-96 and HMAC-SHA-96. USM uses the cipher block chaining (CBC) mode of the Data Encryption Standard (DES) for encryption with a 16-byte key.

Access control in the SNMP framework means controlling the management information that users can access. The View-based Access Control Model (VACM) accomplishes this by associating users to MIB views. VACM has two important characteristics:

VACM determines whether access to a managed object in a local MIB by a remote principal should be allowed.

VACM makes use of a MIB that defines the access control policy for this agent and makes it possible for remote configuration to be used.

The access rights for a group of management objects may be different depending on the security level of the messages containing the request. For example, an agent may allow read-only access for a request in an unauthenticated message but may require authentication for write access.

It is also possible to restrict the access of a particular group of users to a subset of managed objects at an agent. To achieve this, a MIB view, which defines a set of managed objects, controls access to a context. VACM makes use of the concepts of view subtrees and view families to define MIB views. (For more details, see David Zeltserman, *A Practical Guide to SNMPv3 and Network Management*, Prentice-Hall, 1999.)

SNMPCONF

When used for configuration management, SNMP deals primarily with device-local configurations. This specialized use makes it difficult to represent and distribute network-wide policies using SNMP alone. However, members of the SNMP community have defined a policy MIB and technology-specific MIB modules that they hope will fulfill many of the requirements of a policy-based networking system, at least for provisioning.

The SNMPCONF Working Group has been chartered to write MIB modules needed to facilitate configuration management, such as a MIB module which describes a network entity's capabilities and capacities that can be used by management entities making policy decisions at a network level or device-specific level (which we'll describe later in this section). It has also been chartered to create a Best Current Practices document which outlines the most effective methods for using the SNMP framework to accomplish configuration management.

The SNMP architecture provides for the definition of new MIB modules as needs arise. In the case of both policy-based and instance-based configuration, all that is needed is the definition of configuration objects. The important distinction to be made here is that some of the new objects will be aggregate configuration commands—that is, a policy—that can concisely convey to the managed element a series of configuration commands that should be executed. The new objects represent information at a higher layer of abstraction than has been common in previous MIB modules.

Given this architecture, adding support for policy-based configuration management within the SNMP architecture is accomplished by adding one MIB module, the Policy-Based Management MIB Module, or Policy Module for short. The Policy Module helps translate from one level of abstraction to another. It helps move from the mechanism-independent to the mechanism-dependent abstraction levels and helps move from the instance-independent to the instance-dependent level of abstraction. The Policy MIB Module Relation contains standard MIB tables that can tell the managed system what policy filters to apply, what roles apply to which instances, how long the policy should remain in effect, and if and how mechanism-dependent parameters (such as those for DiffServ) should be applied.

The first part of a policy in the Policy Table is a policy filter. The *policy filter* is an SNMP object which contains an expression that determines on which elements an action is to be performed. The policy action object contains what

A ROLE BY ANY OTHER NAME...

We discussed the term *role* earlier in this chapter, in the section on COPS, as well as in Chapter 3. However, during the development of the Policy Module, the SNMPCONF Working Group chose to use the term *role* for a different concept. In the SNMPCONF context, a role is an abstraction expressing political, financial, geographical, or architectural notions that cannot be derived directly from information stored on the device.

parameters are to be modified for instances in the system that match the policy filter expression.

The policy filter contains the roles that a specific instance must match before the policy action part is to be applied. The second part is a policy action that contains the operations the system is to perform on instances to which the policy applies. The policy table also contains pointer information for the scheduling of a policy, as well as information that can be of value when debugging and information about the status of each policy.

When the managed system must determine to which instances to apply the policy, it evaluates the roles and their associations with instances (such as a device's network interfaces). It accomplishes this function based on the filter object that is supplied with each policy.

The Policy MIB Module provides important information to the management system. This information includes the following:

- The current state of the policy.
- Global utilization information about the resources used by a particular policy.
- The mechanisms that the implementation supports. The Policy Module contains objects that identify the capabilities that the system supports.
- The specific instances that are associated with one or more of the roles identified earlier.

As Figure 7.6 illustrates, the Policy Module would be embedded in the network device and would act as a middle-level manager to assist in the configuration of specific policy-related MIB modules. Each technology-specific policy MIB would register with the Policy Module, informing the main module of its capabilities. The Policy Module, in turn, can then provide information to the management application of the device's capabilities.

In some cases, both mechanism- and implementation-specific attributes must be specified for an effective policy to be configured if the vendor has added extensions to a standard mechanism or has created a mechanism inside a particular domain. The higher-layer Policy Module can then point to these separate tables to allow management applications to operate on these different levels of abstraction as needed by the various users. This separation also avoids unnecessarily complex configuration of policy actions in the Policy Module. Debugging is potentially a bit easier since the policy action is an expression that an application would have to know how to parse in order to reasonably present the information whereas the mechanism and implementation-specific MIB modules contain the information in a form that most SNMP-based management applications are able to understand and display. This helps leverage the considerable investment in the current SNMP-based infrastructure.

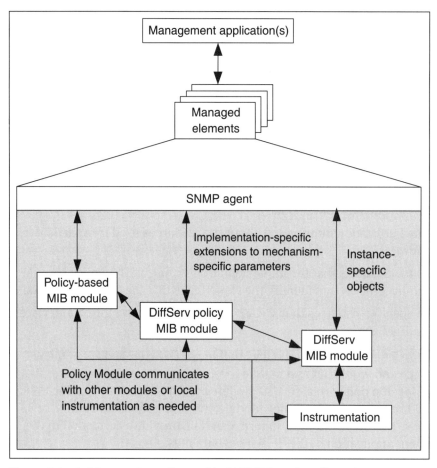

Figure 7.6 Architecture for policy-enabled SNMP-based configuration.

Other Methods

While much of the current discussion in IETF working groups has focused on using COPS, COPS-PR, or SNMPCONF for policy-based configuration of PEPs, there are other methods for configuring network devices, such as a Command Line Interpreter (CLI), CORBA, and HTTP.

Command Line Interpreter

The most widely deployed configuration tool for network devices is the command-line interface (CLI), which is likely to remain with us for some time. Nearly all current network managers use a CLI for a number of reasons. First, all network management tools are essentially element management tools and not "network management" tools as we've discussed the concept, so network managers have to touch each device independently. Furthermore, when it comes to performing simple tasks, graphical user interfaces are less efficient than text-based ones. Network managers frequently have to dial in to the network from a remote site to fix a problem, and graphical user interfaces often use too much bandwidth and are inefficient in that environment. Last, CLIs get the network manager closest to the system in the PEP and thus create a view that's easier to understand at an interface-specific level.

But using the CLI for policy implementation poses several problems. One serious problem is that a CLI does not provide a level of abstraction above the device, which means that network managers must perform a large number of configuration operations to configure a device. Also, the combination of large numbers of operations with the use of telnet to configure devices leads to significant overhead. Each telnet session is initiated separately and sends a login and line-by-line command strings.

Also, a network configuration application using CLI is not designed to track device status. Telnet/CLI has to sense indirectly that a device is down by means of SNMP traps or polling, usually through a different management station.

Finally, there are no standards for CLIs. Each vendor's implementation is different, although some vendors mimic Cisco's CLI to make their products easier to deploy in Cisco customer sites. A CLI is also less secure than other configuration methods since it depends on telnet (where a network manager's password might be intercepted by network snooping) and does not include machine authentication or encryption. One solution suggested by some vendors is to use CLI over Secure Shell (SSH), which provides public/private key authentication, and use IPSec to encrypt management traffic.

A policy-based networking system may have to support a CLI so that policy-based configurations can be distributed to non-policy-aware devices. This is where a policy proxy comes into play, for example. CLI is an important tool for configuring network devices, but its importance in that role will decrease as policy-based tools are developed and systems rely more on COPS, COPS-PR, and SNMPCONF.

Hypertext Transfer Protocol

In the last few years, another protocol, HTTP, has seen increased use as a network element management interface. HTTP, available on many devices and host systems, provides asynchronous capabilities between client and server. The Hypertext Transfer Protocol (HTTP) is the language that Web clients and Web servers use to communicate with each other. It is essentially the backbone of the Web. Behind every Web transaction is HTTP, in which the Web client requests a document and the server returns the requested data.

Many newer network devices include an embedded HTTP server, enabling anyone with a Web browser to manage the devices. The DMTF's work on WBEM (Web-Based Enterprise Management) is a major effort to define an information model (CIM, see Chapter 12, "Directory-Enabled Networks Initiative") that uses XML as a data description language and HTTP as a transport protocol for the control of desktop computers, servers, printers, and so on. While this effort does not yet have a direct impact on network management, it's worth watching because of the DMTF's work on integrating DEN with CIM; its work on the use of XML is a significant step forward in integrating management applications, and it may also be applied to network management applications in the near future.

For policy distribution, the PEP would act as the HTTP server, and a PDP with an HTTP client would connect to the PEP to send configuration data or retrieve device statistics. Furthermore, once a connection is established, either end can send a message to the other. HTTP supports the use of SSL to secure communications, allowing authentication and privacy during data transfer. While HTTP serves as the communication protocol for these sessions, another protocol would be required for configuration data so that structured management data can be exchanged between a PDP and a PEP. Some developers have started using XML for this role (see sidebar). But HTTP is still a point-based solution. It does not support the concept of network-wide configurations. Any network device configuration using HTTP in a policy-based networking system would be performed by a policy proxy and then only to support devices that do not include other methods of device configuration.

Common Object Request Broker Architecture

In telecommunications network management systems, there's a move toward using CORBA as a means of becoming less dependent on protocol-specific approaches using SNMP and CMIP (Common Management Information Protocol). CORBA was designed as a vendor-independent framework to simplify the development of distributed applications. It provides many of the services necessary for policy distribution, such as event notification services that support both push and pull distribution mechanisms. At least two vendors use CORBA to distribute policy-based configuration information in their policy-based networking products.

XML

Management systems need a mechanism to manipulate data generated by various applications and stored in different formats. The Extensible Markup Language (XML) meets this need. It is a meta-language that describes information and allows data to be formatted and exchanged between heterogeneous servers and clients over a network. XML is the more flexible big brother of the widely accepted Hypertext Markup Language (HTML) and is similar in concept to it. Both XML and HTML have their roots in Standardized Generalized Markup Language (SGML), which was designed to add structure and convey information about documents and data.

With markup languages, the main mechanism for supplying structural and semantic information is by decorating the document with elements comprising a start tag, optionally some content, and an end tag. A programmer specifies details about elements through Document Type Definitions (DTD), which define the information schema that provides a way to pass information between different vendors' products or send it directly to a Web browser. XML documents contain the actual information. XML tools validate the XML documents against the DTD.

XML is a markup language used to represent structured data in textual form. One XML goal is to keep most of the descriptive power of SGML, while removing as much of its complexity as possible. Whereas HTML is used to convey graphical information about a document, XML is designed to add structure and convey information about documents and data.

XML provides a way of identifying structured management information exchanges so applications can trade management data. Because XML parsers are available for many platforms, management information can be passed between management stations regardless of the underlying platform or operating environment.

Management information represented in the form of an XML document can be useful for assisting local processing on the client without incurring a round-trip to the server. For example, a PC server application can take XML-based management data from a remote device at defined intervals, parse it with a standard JavaScript, and present it via a browser to the manager.

CORBA is an open standard that allows objects to be stored and executed at remote locations, that is separate from the computer where the main program is running. CORBA sets the specifications for a client to request a server to perform an operation, and wait for that server to communicate the results back to the client. This communication happens via the CORBA bus.

CORBA is a complete distributed object platform (see Figure 7.7). It extends applications across networks, languages, component boundaries, and operating systems. A CORBA Object Request Broker (ORB) connects a client application with the objects it wishes to use. The client application does not need to know whether the object resides on the same computer or on a remote computer elsewhere on the network. The client application needs to know only two pieces of information: the object's name and how to use the object's interface. The ORB takes care of the details of locating the object, routing the request, and returning the result.

The services provided by CORBA include the following:

A naming service allows a CORBA client to locate a named CORBA object. It maps a human-readable name to a CORBA object reference.

An event service enables objects to dynamically register and unregister interest in specific events. Publishers and subscribers each connect to an event channel; publishers send messages (events) to the event channel, and subscribers receive these messages (events) asynchronously.

A transaction service allows transaction contexts between objects to be transparently propagated via Internet Inter-ORB Protocol (IIOP). It coordinates two-phase commits of transactions (flat or nested) among objects.

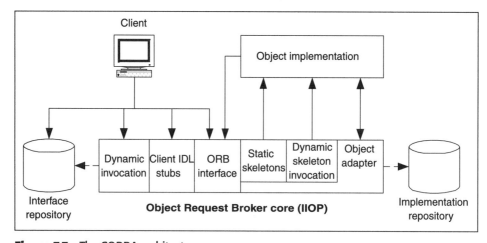

Figure 7.7 The CORBA architecture.

A security service provides features including encryption, authentication, and authorization to protect data and to control user access to objects and their services. It also manages the delegation of credentials between objects.

CORBA also defines the IIOP to govern how objects communicate over the network. Unlike HTTP, IIOP allows state data to be preserved across multiple invocations of objects and across multiple connections. CORBA embeds IP addresses in its Interoperable Object References (or IORs, which are basically object identifiers used throughout the system). Therefore, it won't work through firewalls or Network Address Translation (NAT) servers without specific CORBA gateway support. CORBA support in firewalls isn't very common, and it's nonexistent in most NAT routers. However, CORBA systems using IIOP can transport objects through firewalls.

Issues

As one of the newest components of policy-based networking, the PDP is surrounded by a number of unresolved and still-evolving issues. By and large, these issues do not impact the overall functionality of the PDP, but they do impact how the PDP performs its functions and how policy-based networking can integrate with other network management applications. The issues we'll focus on in this section include the following:

- Redundancy and reliability
- Scalability
- Distribution of policy-based configurations
- Handling of policy conflicts
- Migration of management systems from element management to policy-based network management

Redundancy and Reliability

It's inevitable that devices fail and PDPs are no exception to this rule. In order to ensure the maximum uptime of policy-based networking systems, PDPs need to maintain reliable communications with their PEPs and should provide for some level of redundancy.

As we mentioned earlier, both the PEP and remote PDP constantly verify their connection to each other via keep-alive messages when COPS is used. When a failure is detected, the PEP tries to reconnect to the remote PDP or, failing that, attempts to connect to a secondary (alternative) PDP. While disconnected, the PEP reverts to making local decisions—that is, using cached policies. Once a connection is reestablished, the PEP is expected to notify the PDP of any deleted state or new events that passed local admission control after the connection was lost.

In COPS, the PEP can connect to a secondary PDP in the event of the primary PDP's failure. In such situations, the secondary PDP can request information from the PEP describing its current policies and can update those policies based on what it learns from the PEP. For instance, the remote PDP may request that all of the PEP's internal state be resynchronized, that is, all previously installed requests are reissued. But the COPS protocol does not address how the two PDPs—the primary PDP and the secondary PDP—handle failover and resynchronization. In other words, COPS leaves it to other, unspecified mechanisms to ensure that both PDPs have the same policies. (If both PDPs don't have the same policies, a PEP could receive the wrong configuration data when attaching to the secondary PDP.)

SNMPCONF handles redundancy in much the same manner as SNMP does. SNMP achieves redundancy by the use of multiple management stations. As long as the management stations have the same access rights to managed objects on a device, no single management station owns the SNMP agents installed on a device. Since the majority of the communications between a management station and an SNMP agent (using GET and SET messages) is initiated by the management station, it's possible for one management station to take over in the event the original station fails.

The transport protocol for SNMP and SNMPCONF is UDP, which provides unreliable transport. As we pointed out earlier, the use of UDP means that any SNMP message may not reach its destination. SNMPv2's introduction of the Inform message addresses some of the concerns of unreliable Trap messages for sending error and fault messages, since Inform requires an acknowledgment from the destination. And well-designed SNMP applications take into account UDP's unreliability, checking device configurations after new data has been transmitted to a device's SNMP agent.

The issue of PDP redundancy is similar to that of policy repository redundancy, which we discussed in Chapter 6, "The Policy Repository." Since PDPs are crucial to the distribution of policy-based configurations to PEPs, a policy system should include backup PDPs. However, at this time, only a few vendors of policy-based networking systems currently provide this capability. Since the design of local PDP storage of policies is proprietary, each vendor has its own way of maintaining proper synchronization of the data that multiple PDPs store.

Scalability

Although the three-tiered architecture using PDPs as intermediate distribution points was developed as a way to make policy-based networking scalable to larger networks, the PDPs themselves can impact a system's scalability.

A PDP's performance is determined by the number of policies it must process and the number of PEPs it controls. If a number of policies must be compared for conflicts, for example, then it'd be best for the PDP not to query the policy repository for all pertinent policies because this could lead to significant delays in the decision-making process as the result of PDP queries being returned to the PDP. Many vendors have chosen to cache as many of the policies as possible at the PDP, treating the repository as more of a backup than as an active participant in policy distribution.

The number of PEPs that a single PDP can serve is still a matter of trial and error. In our conversations with vendors of policy-based management systems, vendors have suggested that a PDP can control on the order of a hundred or more PEPs. Vendors of two-tiered systems have suggested that a single repository can serve about 10 network devices. Thus, in order to expand a policy-based management system or improve its performance, a network manager has to either add more PDPs (in the case of the three-tiered system) or add more directories (in the case of the two-tiered system). In either approach, you'll have to pay close attention to how the PDPs or directories replicate data among themselves. There are a few standard methods for replicating data among directories or databases, but coordinating data among PDPs has not been standardized.

The issue of scalable policy distribution will also become more apparent as network managers look to utilize end-user hosts as policy enforcement points. Now systems have the task of distributing policies not to tens or hundreds of devices, but to thousands or tens of thousands of devices! A few vendors of policy-based networking systems have started to look at this problem. Some have suggested installing another layer of intermediate policy servers, forming two tiers of PDPs or policy servers. At least one other vendor has started implementing a system that uses IP multicasting to distribute policies to the appropriate agents located on end-user hosts and servers.

It's easy for vendors to suggest purchasing another PDP if the number currently installed in a PBN system isn't sufficient for controlling the network. But installing more than one PDP raises coordination issues. Policies need to be synchronized between the PDPs in much the same way as primary and backup PDPs must be synchronized. There's little, if any, work on policy synchronization in the standards bodies, which doesn't prevent vendors from developing their own proprietary methods for synchronizing multiple PDPs. But the lack of a standard does hinder interoperability between PDPs from different vendors.

Multiple PDPs may be required even in a policy domain whose network devices are all provided by the same vendor. There are two examples of this. First, a PDP may only manage a single aspect of policy (e.g., just network QoS, as opposed to security). In this case, some entity other than the PDPs must coordinate policies delivered by the multiple different PDPs to a single device. Second, there may be a PDP in each of several sites of an enterprise or a service provider. Each such PDP has local knowledge. It uses this local knowledge to validate policies as well as to manage its local elements. This local knowledge could be due to physical, geographical, or technical constraints (e.g., different types of devices). Therefore, since each PDP only controls a portion of the devices in the network (e.g., those network elements that it has knowledge of), multiple PDPs are required.

Distribution of Policy-Based Configurations

We've already spent much of this chapter discussing the pros and cons of the protocols a system can use to distribute policy-based configurations, so we won't go into any of the details here. At the moment, there is no clear leader in the race to select a single method for configuring devices in a policy-based networking system. In fact, it's likely that no single winner will emerge. Most commercial policy-based networking products currently support CLI as a primary method for configuring devices, recognizing that the majority of the devices installed on today's networks are not policy-aware.

Some vendors already support COPS for RSVP in their PDPs and many vendors have indicated that they will offer COPS support, including COPS-PR support, before long. But COPS support on a PDP means little if you don't have COPS-capable network devices. COPS clients for PEPs are relatively small applications, so it should be possible to upgrade many existing network devices to support COPS without replacing them, which will make the job of creating a policy-aware network somewhat easier than if you had to replace all of your equipment. Similarly, development of MIBs that work with the SNMPCONF's Policy MIB is rather straightforward and would only require the installation of a new set of policy-related MIBs on existing network devices.

The issue of policy distribution protocols is further complicated by your planned uses for policy-based networking. Much of the interest in policy-based networking is driven by the desire to implement QoS. COPS was designed with RSVP in mind. COPS-PR and SNMPCONF are designed for users with a broader range of situations requiring preprovisioning of policies, such as DiffServ, VPNs, or access filtering with firewalls. If you're planning to use any of these protocols and see the need for policy-based networking, then you'll want a system that supports the proper protocols.

Handling Policy Conflicts

As we've mentioned previously, the policy-based networking system is responsible for monitoring policies for possible conflicts. The system supposedly has a better knowledge of network devices and applicable policies than the network manager who's creating the policies does. Conflicts can occur at all levels of a policy-based networking system, but our focus here is the PDP. We've covered the other points for checking policy conflicts in previous chapters.

To recap the types of conflicts we might encounter, global conflicts are those based on the properties of the policy and not the specific devices (or their interfaces) to which the policy might apply. Whereas the policy console and policy management tool can check for global policy conflicts, checking for local policy conflicts that apply to all network devices that are controlled by its PDP or policy proxy is relegated to the PDP or the proxy.

One of the main decisions regarding conflicts that a PDP needs to make is that of satisfiability, that is, can a PEP provide the resources required to enforce a policy. For example, providing a specific class of service might depend on specific queuing behavior in all the network devices along the path through the network. But if that queuing behavior is not available on one of the interfaces in one of the target network devices, the policy cannot be satisfied. The PDP controlling that device then has to decide whether to fall back to a previous policy and inform the network manager that the policy could not be enforced, or it might use policy conditions to determine that a compromise can be reached to provide a somewhat similar class of service.

Migrating Management Systems

Policy-based networking embodies a paradigm of network management that differs significantly from that of past methods for managing networks. The network manager's view shifts from that of configuring and monitoring individual network elements to one that's network-wide, focusing on services.

This switch in viewpoint and operations will invariably give some network managers pause and require added training to ensure that policy-based networking is understood and used properly. Not only does this education have to include the definition of network services, but also how they're measured and how performance goals are met (via service level agreements [SLAs], for example). Mappings are also important, including mapping business policies to network services, and mapping network and application performance to SLAs.

At least in the first phases of deployment, policy-based networking has to be considered as an adjunct to, rather than a replacement for, traditional network management tools. Eventually, policy-based networking systems may subsume the traditional systems taking over the older functions as well as adding new ones. Both this transition, and the training that accompanies it, will take some time.

Basic Requirements

Since the PDP serves as an important intermediary in policy-based networking, it's crucial that this component perform certain functions, regardless of which protocol it uses. The basic requirements for the policy decision point (and any associated policy proxy) should include the following:

- Support for multiple configuration protocols
- PDP redundancy
- Review of policy translation procedures
- Alerts associated with policy conflicts
- Security

Since it doesn't appear as though a single protocol can currently take care of all the configuration needs of a network, the PDP has to be multifaceted when it comes to protocols. Essentially, that means the PDP has to be protocol-agnostic. When you're buying a policy-based networking system, you should ensure that the PDP includes a policy proxy and that the two modules work together to support device configuration via CLI, SNMP, as well as COPS if you are running RSVP.

A policy-based networking system is supposed to help support the business needs of a network, which means that it has to be reliable when mission-critical applications are run on the network. It's therefore crucial that a policy-based networking system includes backups for its PDPs or else there's little assurance that the system will be reliable.

Since the PDP and policy proxy automatically translate policies into device configurations, there's the unstated assumption that you can trust the PDP or policy proxy to make error-free translations. Whether it's merely to assure a curious network manager that the translations are correct or to help someone troubleshoot a device configuration, the system should provide the network manager with a way to review the translations stored on a PDP or policy proxy.

In a similar vein, the PDP should send alerts to the policy console when policy conflicts occur or when a translation cannot be performed. The latter situation might occur if new devices are installed on the network and the translation database hasn't been updated to include the capabilities of the new devices.

Last, but certainly not least, the PDP must enforce security for communications between itself and the PEPs it controls, as well as with the policy repository. (We already covered the repository's security issues in the previous chapters.) PDPs and PEPs must be able to authenticate themselves with each other using at least a shared key and a message digest, and messages transmitted between the two components should be encrypted.

Summary

Much of this chapter focused on the protocols that have been proposed for the distribution of policy-based device configurations from PDPs to PEPs. We've presented the pros and cons of COPS, COPS-PR, SNMP, and SNMPCONF, in particular, and those of CORBA and telnet/CLI to a lesser degree. COPS may be well suited for distributing decisions using the outsourced model favored by RSVP, but the jury's still out on which protocol is best for handling the provisioning model, which you might use for DiffServ, VPNs, or other security configurations. Both COPS-PR and SNMPCONF are likely techniques for provisioning policies.

The policy decision point is an important focal point for security and scalability of the policy-based networking system. While the scalability issues may not be a concern in initial deployments of policy-based networking, due to the relatively small numbers of devices involved, we guarantee that scalability will become more of an issue as policy-based networking systems are used on larger networks. Network managers should therefore consider how PDPs will be distributed through their network, what backup PDPs they will install, and how policies will be synchronized between all the PDPs.

The next chapter takes us to the lowest layer in our model of policy-based networking, the policy enforcement points. There we'll discuss the types of PEPs that developers and vendors are considering deploying in policy-based networking and what some of their major requirements are.

Policy Enforcement Points

Now that we've covered the details of what the upper layers of policy-based networking systems are supposed to do, we'll turn our attention to the underlying layer of equipment that needs to be managed, the policy enforcement points. This is where all of our work on creating and distributing policies bears fruit. The policy enforcement points (PEPs) control the traffic on our networks, helping the network support the business goals and policies we set at higher levels in the PBN system.

We've mentioned before that one of the main forces driving the use of policy-based networking currently is QoS. That means that two of the important types of PEPs are routers and switches. There are also other, newer devices such as traffic shapers and Web switches that can control traffic and can be used as PEPs. And, as we move to finer-grained classification systems for QoS (and other services), we have to include servers and desktop computers as policy enforcement points as well.

But there are other important services that can be controlled by policy-based networking, such as authentication, authorization, access control, and VPN tunnels, which involve firewalls, remote access servers, and VPN gateways. As we go through this chapter on PEPs, you'll see that there can be an overlap of functionality for different types of policies (QoS versus security, for example) in the same device. Also, you'll see the ultimate PEP may end up being the desktop as more network services are offered and controlled by policy-based networking.

Since there are so many kinds of PEPs, this chapter breaks down the PEPs into classes and presents the main requirements for each class. The latter part of this chapter covers some of the important issues of PEPs and their integration into policy-based networking, such as scalability, performance, and standardization.

Classes of Policy Enforcement Points

A PEP's main functions differ according to the service it's designed to support. For example, firewalls serve a different purpose from routers or VPN gateways. That's why we've decided to subdivide PEPs into different classes and discuss each of those classes separately. The classes of PEPs we've decided on are as follows:

- Routers and switches
- Web switches
- Traffic shapers
- Firewalls
- Remote access servers
- VPN gateways
- Address and name servers
- Servers and end-user hosts

It's not our intent to discuss the details of each class of equipment here—that would take a few books—but to present the details that are pertinent to using this equipment with policy-based networking.

Routers and Switches

The typical requirement for routers and switches within both the LAN and WAN is to provide end-to-end connectivity to all devices within the network. Many organizations may have additional requirements, such as controlling broadcast traffic, logically separating LANs (using layer 3 subnetting or layer 2 VLANs), as well as assigning various QoS levels to different users, groups, or applications. These various levels of service can include performance levels, bandwidth reservation, and/or access control.

These network devices may also have to support different services according to their location in the network. For example, routers in the backbone or core of the network are usually not designed for fine-grained classification of traffic flows, but handle aggregate flows containing traffic from different sources requiring the same level of service. On the other hand, edge routers at the LAN-

WAN boundary might be expected to perform a great deal of classification of individual flows (see Figure 8.1). In the backbone, the primary requirement is to process packets as fast as possible.

In the past few years, the division between routers and switches has gotten increasingly fuzzy. In the late 1990s, vendors began to introduce what were called layer 3 switches, routing switches, or switch-routers. These devices could perform layer 3 routing tasks at speeds equal to layer 2 switches since they used ASICs (application-specific integrated circuits) to perform forwarding decisions in hardware rather than in software like traditional routers. Layer 3 switches also offered an additional advantage: Like traditional routers, they could participate in routing decisions using protocols such as Routing Information Protocol (RIP), Open Shortest Path First (OSPF), and Border Gateway Protocol (BGP4). Many layer 3 switches also support advanced functionality such as RSVP signaling, IEEE 802.1P/Q, and IP DS field marking for prioritization, and policy control such as packet filtering and custom queuing.

Although the majority of packet forwarding is based on information contained in the link-layer and transport headers (layers 2 and 3 protocols), new

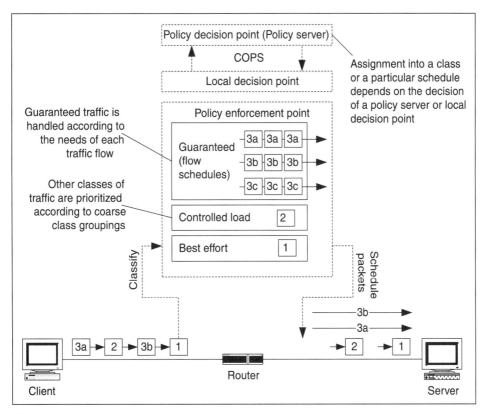

Figure 8.1   Router processing of packets.

switches have been designed to take advantage of information contained at layers above layer 3. These devices, often called layer 4 switches, can make traffic forwarding decisions based on URL, TCP port number, or even application type. Network managers can install these devices in front of server farms and use them to implement policies such as restricting access to a certain URL or giving a higher priority to traffic for a certain application.

We pointed out in the previous chapter that network devices can be configured using a variety of protocols, such as telnet/CLI, SNMP, HTTP, COPS, COPS-PR, and SNMPCONF. Almost all of today's routers and switches use SNMP for monitoring and reporting device status and use a CLI for configuration, but vendors have started to deliver devices that support COPS, COPS-PR, and SNMPCONF.

When it comes to handling traffic for deploying QoS, a number of different methods can be configured, depending on the router's capabilities. (We won't describe the techniques in detail here, but merely mention them; for more details see Geoff Huston, *Internet Performance Survival Guide: QoS Strategies for Multiservice Networks*, Wiley, 2000.) These techniques include the following:

Packet scheduling and prioritization. Simple FIFO (first-in, first-out) queuing, priority queuing, fair queuing, custom queuing, weighted fair queuing, per-flow queuing, and 802.1p Ethernet VLAN prioritization.

Congestion control. Random early detection (RED) and weighted RED.

Traffic shaping. Class-based queuing and TCP rate control.

The problem is that each vendor of networking equipment may have its own way of implementing these techniques. Difficulties arise when a policy-based networking system has to enforce device-independent policies. For example, if a policy decision point controls two different devices that each have different implementations of the same QoS technique (a queuing mechanism, for example), then these devices will interpret the policy differently *unless* there is a common device information model. IETF engineers are currently struggling with this issue for the QoS mechanisms that can be used with DiffServ.

Routers can also play a role in securing networks. Although firewalls can provide a greater deal of security by filtering traffic (see the later section on firewalls), routers can use access control lists (ACLs) to control an IP network. Vendors have only recently offered products that relieve the network manager of the tedium of configuring ACLs for each router, adding a GUI in some cases, and centralizing ACL generation for routers as well as firewalls. But it's only in the rare case that such centralized configuration products are tied to a policy-based networking system.

Layer 2 switches are often deployed using Virtual LANs (VLANs) to segment broadcast domains. The technology of VLANs allows multiple hosts to connect to the same switch and have their traffic isolated into groups that are established by the network operator. For example, suppose a single switch has all the hosts in the accounting department and all the hosts in the sales department connected to it. Using VLANs, the network operator can restrict traffic from the hosts on the sales LAN from being forwarded to the accounting LAN and vice versa. Network managers can configure VLAN membership by physical port number, by layer 3 protocol type, by MAC or IP address, or by other factors. Originally, each vendor implemented a proprietary technology for creating VLANs. However, the IEEE developed a VLAN standard (802.1p/Q) that has been widely accepted by network hardware manufacturers to promote interoperability.

Web Switches

A different type of switch that you may be likely to deploy, especially for Web sites supporting e-commerce, is a device that's known as a *Web switch*. This is a switch that's similar to the layer 4 switch we briefly described earlier, designed specifically for front-ending Internet or intranet server farms. Interest in Web switches has largely been driven by the increased use of the Internet for electronic commerce and as enterprises look for ways to improve the performance of their Web-based applications.

Web switches typically combine the functionality of a layer 3 switch with the following features:

- Rate shaping, traffic classification and prioritization
- Redirection of traffic to a local cache server
- Redirection of traffic based on URL request type (e.g., purchasing record requests versus JPEG file requests)
- Access filtering to restrict access to Web pages or servers
- Global redirection to route requests to Web servers closer to the end-user

Some products also combine the ability to encrypt and decrypt SSL sessions, further reducing the workload of the Web servers. Keep in mind that the use of these devices means that the data is no longer encrypted from end to end and the traffic is exposed before it gets to the server. Some of these products are also capable of load balancing other devices, such as firewalls.

Since these switches include support for bandwidth prioritization and access filters, such as for groups, URLs, and applications, a policy-based networking system could be used to configure these parameters, ensuring that they're coherent with similar parameters (and business goals) set for the rest of the network.

Traffic Shapers

Another relatively new network device has appeared for use at the LAN-WAN boundary to help manage WAN utilization: the traffic shaper. Traffic shapers are either companion devices to routers or they may be specially equipped routers. They are capable of delivering explicit-rate control for a large number of individual traffic flows based on parameters such as user, IP address, port, or protocol. These boxes gain tight control over the rate of each traffic class using a combination of techniques such as TCP rate control and class-based queuing, and enable network managers to establish multiple classes of traffic that can either be throttled back or marked for special handling in the carrier network.

A legacy router without traffic-shaping capabilities manages bandwidth using queuing access control, commonly via weighted fair queuing algorithms. Such a router cannot support explicit rate control over multiple traffic classes, and it generally offers looser control over service levels than the new traffic-shaping boxes.

Each vendor of traffic-shaping devices supplies a traffic management tool that controls the flows running through its boxes. The trend has been to scale these tools up so they can manage large networks with multiple subscribers, but so far only a few vendors have tied these devices into policy-based networking systems. Some vendors offer a policy-based management system for controlling these devices using proprietary protocols and designs.

Firewalls

Turning now to devices that address some of the security issues on networks, we'll start with a discussion of firewalls. Basically, a firewall is a network gateway that enforces security rules on the conversion of peer-to-peer communications. A firewall creates a boundary between two or more networks. Whether the firewall is software- or hardware-based, it uses what are called rules to determine if a data packet should pass through or be discarded.

The idea behind packet filters is simple: The firewall looks through the TCP/IP header of each packet sent through it and decides whether to transmit it or not (see Figure 8.2). Pertinent information scanned in the header includes source address, destination address, source port, and destination port. The major limitation of packet filters, however, is their inability to understand the activities of an application. As a result, some FTP or UDP query/response services are difficult to filter. To make the process easier, some firewalls incorporate so-called stateful packet filters. Stateful filters increase the intelligence of the filtering process by enabling the firewall to associate some new packets with packets that were previously sent through the firewall.

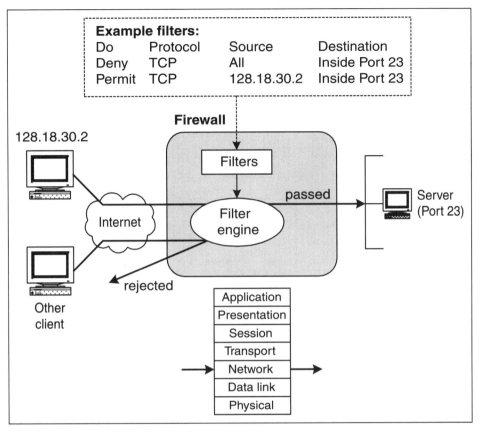

Example filters:

Do	Protocol	Source	Destination
Deny	TCP	All	Inside Port 23
Permit	TCP	128.18.30.2	Inside Port 23

Firewall

128.18.30.2

Filters

Internet

Filter engine

passed

Server (Port 23)

rejected

Other client

| Application |
| Presentation |
| Session |
| Transport |
| Network |
| Data link |
| Physical |

Figure 8.2 Packet-filtering firewall.

While packet filters monitor traffic on the network and transport layers of the protocol stack, application proxy firewalls function at the application level, which gives them control between client and server. In an application proxy environment, a client application first connects to a process on the firewall that listens for client connections (see Figure 8.3). After connecting to the proxy, the user is authenticated to the firewall. The proxy then connects to the desired remote host and relays the information being sent from the server to the client, and vice versa. At all times, the proxy application on the firewall remains on the link and can limit, at the application level, what that client or server is doing. All of this is transparent to the client.

Application proxies can also verify that the interaction between client and server actually conforms to the protocol in use, such as HTTP or FTP. Because they are more involved in the connection, proxy firewalls tend to have lower performance than packet filter firewalls.

However, during the past year or so, most firewall vendors have incorporated both packet filter and proxy technologies into their products. With a so-

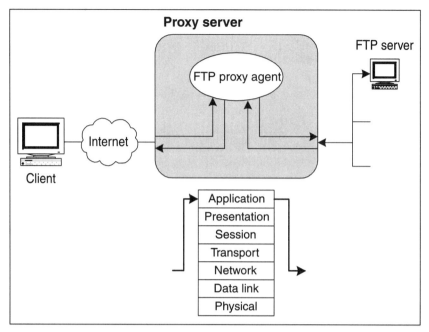

Figure 8.3 Application proxy firewall.

called hybrid firewall, the services best handled by packet filters (such as tel-net) can be packet-filtered, while those best handled by proxies (such as FTP) can be proxied.

One type of firewall engine cannot and will not be all things to all people. A packet-filtering firewall may be the fastest in passing data, but it is inherently the least secure of all methods. A proxy server firewall gives up the perfor-mance edge because of the increased overhead. Stateful inspection engines are both fast and secure, but lack some flexibility when adding custom ser-vices. Proxy-based firewalls examine and enforce security at the application layer, thus offering more stringent access controls. That's not to say that inspection-based firewalls are insecure; it's just that the two types of firewalls address different needs.

Reporting is crucial to firewall management because of the wide variety of attacks that can appear at a firewall. Good logging should present enough information to administrators for them to know when to quickly scan for important events. Until automated event correlation is developed, a network's best defense is the administrator who regularly monitors the logs.

A few years ago, most organizations had a single firewall. Today, firewalls are being used to support a host of activities, including the following:

- Intranet firewalls protect sensitive internal networks, such as human resources, from other internal users.

- Internet firewalls secure multiple Internet connections.
- Business partner firewalls securely connect with joint ventures, suppliers, and customers.

Today, it's not uncommon for a larger company to have a dozen, 50, or 100 firewalls protecting sensitive internal networks, multiple Internet connections, and business partner access. Managing multiple firewalls within a single organization has challenges of its own. Many products offer the ability to log in to separate firewalls from a single management station, but this forces administrators to manage each firewall on a one-by-one basis. Few products allow for a global view, which is where policy-based networking systems can be of use.

Control of firewalls using policy-based networking is still in its relatively early stages. Cisco is one of the few companies that includes control of both network services such as QoS and firewalls within a policy-based system. The system's design includes separate consoles for a network manager configuring QoS and a security manager configuring access via firewalls (and VPN gateways). Other vendors of firewall products have created policy-based management systems to help security administrators managing multiple distributed firewalls, but since many of these companies market only security products, they haven't integrated their systems with other policy-based networking systems. The definition and standardization of security policy has also not received as much attention as that for desktop and network device management, making integration of all these management approaches more difficult.

Remote Access Servers

Although VPNs are often used to provide remote access to corporate computing resources (see next section), dial-in access via modems and remote access servers has also been around for some time and still sees considerable use. Policy-based networking systems can be used to control remote access by controlling the authentication of dial-in users and setting authorization and access parameters via such protocols as RADIUS (Remote Authentication Dial-In User Service) and TACACS (Terminal Access Controller Access Control System).

A Network Access Server (NAS) is sometimes referred to as a Remote Access Server (RAS) as it typically allows remote access to a network. However, a more general picture is that of an edge server, where the NAS sits on the edge of an IP network of some type, and allows dynamic access to it. The core of what a NAS provides is dynamic network services. What distinguishes a NAS from a typical routing system is that these services are provided on a per-user basis, based on an authentication and the service is accounted for. This accounting may lead to policies and controls to limit appropriate usage to levels based on the availability of network bandwidth, or service agreements between the user and the provider.

Typical services include the following:

- Dial-up or direct access serial line access

- Network access (SLIP, PPP, IPX, NETBEUI)

- Asynchronous terminal services (telnet, Rlogin, LAT, and others), where the NAS implements the network protocol on behalf of the caller and presents a terminal interface

- Dial-out connections, in which the NAS initiates a connection over the public telephone network, typically based on the arrival of traffic to a specific network system

- Callback, where the NAS generates call to caller or initiates a network connection based on the arrival of a dial-in call

- Tunneling, in which the NAS transports the caller's network packets over a network to a remote server using an encapsulation protocol

NAS systems have come to depend on external server systems, such as RADIUS and TACACS, to implement authentication databases and accounting recording. The following is a look at how RADIUS can be used for the control of remote access sessions.

In the RADIUS client-server model, although the NAS functions as a server for providing network access (see Figure 8.4), it also functions as a client for RADIUS. The NAS is responsible for accepting user connection requests, getting user ID and password information, and passing the information securely to the RADIUS server. The RADIUS server returns authentication status, that is, approved or denied, as well as any configuration data required for the NAS to provide services to the end user.

RADIUS creates a single, centrally located database of users and available services, a feature particularly important for networks that contain large modem banks and more than one remote communications server. With RADIUS, the user information is stored in one location, the RADIUS server, which manages the authentication of the user and access to services from one location.

When a RADIUS implementation is tightly integrated with Windows NT, Novell NetWare, or UNIX, enterprise network administrators can use the passwords and groupings already created in the Windows NT domain, Novell's NDS, or UNIX Network Information Services (NIS) as the basis for authenticating remote users dialing in to any NAS. Some RADIUS servers also support LDAP for exchanging information with LDAP-compatible directories and other data stores. This tight integration with network operating systems and other sources of user data allows the network manager to use RADIUS to simplify administration while ensuring that security profiles for the users are current.

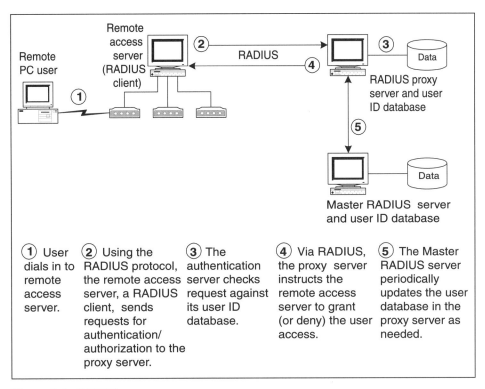

Remote PC user

Remote access server (RADIUS client)

RADIUS

Data

RADIUS proxy server and user ID database

Data

Master RADIUS server and user ID database

(1) User dials in to remote access server.

(2) Using the RADIUS protocol, the remote access server, a RADIUS client, sends requests for authentication/ authorization to the proxy server.

(3) The authentication server checks request against its user ID database.

(4) Via RADIUS, the proxy server instructs the remote access server to grant (or deny) the user access.

(5) The Master RADIUS server periodically updates the user database in the proxy server as needed.

Figure 8.4 RADIUS.

The authentication transaction serves an additional purpose beyond simply authenticating the user. Along with the authentication information that the RAS includes as part of a RADIUS request, the RAS also passes information about the type of connection the user is trying to establish. The RADIUS server can use this information to further qualify the user, possibly issuing a rejection based on this information.

Similarly, the RADIUS server includes additional information as part of the accept response it issues to the RAS. The RAS uses this information to control various aspects of the user's connection. This aspect of the authentication transaction is called attribute exchange.

Attribute exchange is controlled by the user's profile. Each profile lists attributes of two types: check-list attributes and return-list attributes.

Check-list attributes define a set of requirements for the connection. During the authentication transaction, the RAS must send attributes to the RADIUS server that match the checklist; if they don't, the RADIUS server will issue a reject even if the user can be authenticated. For example, by including appropriate attributes in the checklist, a variety of rules could be enforced. Only certain users might be permitted to use ISDN connections, or dial in to a particular RAS. Or, Caller ID could be used to validate a user against a list of legal originating phone numbers.

Return-list attributes are the attributes that the RADIUS server sends back to the RAS once authentication is successful. The return list defines additional parameters that the RAS should assign to the connection, typically as part of Point-to-Point Protocol (PPP) negotiations. For example, specific users could be assigned particular IP addresses or IPX network numbers, IP header compression could be turned on or off, or a time limit could be assigned to the connection.

RADIUS accounting is an additional feature of the RADIUS standard that permits a RADIUS server to track when users start and stop their dial-in connections and acquire statistics about each session. Using RADIUS accounting, the RADIUS server can maintain a history of all user dial-in sessions, indicating start time, stop time, and various statistics for the session as well as a list of current users showing which users are currently connected to which Remote Access Servers.

RADIUS supports the use of proxy servers, which store information for authentication purposes and can be used for accounting and authorization, but they do not allow the user data (passwords and so on) to be changed. A RADIUS proxy server depends on periodic updates of the user database from a master RADIUS server. When enterprises outsource remote access to an ISP, the ISP will often authenticate users using a RADIUS proxy server and the enterprise maintains a RADIUS server to keep control of user information for its employees and business partners.

Despite the popularity of RADIUS for control of remote access, the changing demands of authentication and authorization for remote users along with the increasing variety of mobile devices is leading to new efforts to refine network access servers and their authentication services. For example, the Network Access Server Requirements (NASREQ) Working Group of the IETF has been defining the requirements for network access servers, including support for authentication and authorization as well as other services. Some of the requirements for limiting operational access and restricting usage authorization include time-of-day restrictions, port locations, concurrent login limits, session expirations and idle timeouts, packet filters, and QoS parameters.

Since RADIUS (and any of its likely successors) has proven valuable as an integrator of authentication services from network operating systems and other sources of authentication data, it should fit into the scheme of policy-based networking. In some ways, RADIUS servers already enforce policies for remote access, but they're not integrated into policy-based networking products. The LDAP support that some RADIUS products include also makes exchange of user data with other repositories easier, but policy-based control of RADIUS servers hasn't yet appeared.

Virtual Private Network Gateways

Although there are many ways to create virtual private networks (VPNs), three protocols—Point-to-Point Tunneling Protocol (PPTP), Layer 2 Tunneling Protocol (L2TP), and IP Security (IPSec)—can be used to create VPN tunnels across the Internet by encapsulating IP traffic within other packets. In this situation, the VPN protocols protect the encapsulated packets either by authenticating the packet's contents, encrypting the contents, or both (see Figure 8.5). Tunnels can be created in two ways: either between two sites using a VPN gateway at each site, or between a VPN gateway and a mobile user employing VPN client software. (See David Kosiur, *Building and Managing Virtual Private Networks*, Wiley, 1998, and David McDysan, *VPN Applications Guide: Real Solutions for Enterprise Networks*, Wiley, 2000, for more details.)

Using such protocols as PPTP or L2TP, tunnel setup is aimed mainly at remote-access tunnels between a mobile user and a gateway. Authentication is often based on either PPP's authentication mechanism, using a RADIUS server supporting Password Authentication Protocol (PAP) and Challenge Handshake Authentication Protocol (CHAP), for example, or by means of security tokens. In the case of IPSec, however, a more involved procedure was designed for authenticating computers (either an individual's computer or a gateway) to provide better security for any transactions using the protocol.

Using IPSec with the Internet Key Exchange (IKE), a system can set up security associations (SAs) which include information on the algorithms for authenticating and encrypting messages, the lifetime of the keys employed, the key lengths, and so on. Each pair of communicating computers will use a specific set of SAs to set up a VPN tunnel. For our purposes, we can think of the VPN gateway as a policy enforcement point.

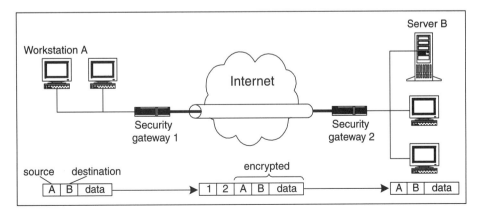

Figure 8.5   VPN schematic.

Network managers might choose to create policies governing the specification of an SA's contents according to the endpoints of the tunnel. For instance, an SA could be created to use triple DES (3DES) to encrypt data transferred between offices in the United States, but a different SA specifying only DES encryption would be used to create a tunnel involving an office in a country where export restrictions apply. Other information that can be controlled via a policy-based system includes IP address assignments, authentication method, and client software updates. Some vendors are also looking to combine the specification of QoS parameters with VPN tunnel setup.

At the moment, the vendors of VPN products offering policy-based control of tunnel parameters use proprietary systems and have not standardized on an information model or a policy language for VPN-related policies. These systems typically use SNMP to communicate with VPN gateways to distribute policies, although some devices include LDAP to access authentication and authorization data directly from a directory.

One group within the IETF—the IP Security Policy (IPSP) Working Group—has been working to develop a language for describing packet filters and SA policies for use with VPNs, along with a management scheme for IPSec credentials.

Address and Name Servers

Two other network services that can be managed via policy-based networking are IP address services and domain name services. Although this can be accomplished for static address and domain name servers, the move toward dynamic address assignment using Dynamic Host Configuration Protocol (DHCP) and related links to Domain Name Service (DNS) using Dynamic DNS (DDNS) makes the use of policy-based networking even more beneficial.

The Dynamic Host Configuration Protocol (DHCP) is designed to provide a centralized approach to the configuration and maintenance of an IP address space, allowing the network administrator to configure various clients on the network from a single location. DHCP permits IP address leases to be dynamically assigned to workstations, eliminating the need for static IP address allocation by network and systems management staff. Leases determine the length of time for which an IP address is valid for use by a device.

DHCP is a client-server protocol. DHCP servers store ranges, or pools, of available IP addresses. The servers assign addresses to client devices on TCP/IP networks in response to requests from the DHCP client software installed on those devices. All of the common operating systems include DHCP client software as part of their TCP/IP software, which simplifies the task of using DHCP for assigning addresses and related configuration information, such as subnet mask, primary gateway, and primary DNS server.

DHCP servers can distribute addresses based on one of three different allocation policies: manual, automatic, and dynamic. In dynamic assignment, the DHCP server assigns an IP address from its pool of available addresses along with a lease period during which the address is legitimate. At the end of the lease, the address is returned to the pool of addresses for reassignment, unless the client requests a renewal.

Like DHCP, DNS is a client-server protocol. The main function of the name server is to answer standard queries from clients. The DNS client is software in a network host that initiates a DNS query or lookup, usually on behalf of a network application, then interprets the responses from a name server and returns the appropriate information to the application that requested it. DNS clients are a standard part of TCP/IP software in every major operating system.

In the past, DNS was designed to work with static IP addresses. The introduction of DHCP made address assignment a more dynamic process, one that DNS wasn't designed to track. The batch orientation of DNS zone transfers cannot keep up to date with dynamic addressing. The extensions for notification and incremental zone transfers that we described earlier only reduce the time during which different DNS servers will have an inconsistent view of the DNS name space.

To provide better coordination between DNS and DHCP, the IETF defined Dynamic DNS in RFC 2136. Dynamic DNS allows DHCP servers to automatically pass IP address assignment information to DNS servers, reducing the amount of manual data entry and improving the update speed for DNS (see Figure 8.6). This link between DHCP and DNS servers allows DNS servers to track network nodes that have addresses assigned by DHCP, whether the assignments are made statically or dynamically.

DHCP and DNS servers actually fit into policy-based networking systems in two different ways. First, they can be sources of data for policy rules and policy translations, mapping user and server names to IP addresses that PEPs can then use during policy enforcement. Second, the DHCP and DNS servers can be controlled by policy-based networking to ensure that user machines receive addresses from the proper pool of IP addresses and that subdomains and machines are named following the organization's naming rules. When DHCP and DNS servers serve this second role, they can be considered policy enforcement points and configured via a policy-based networking system.

Servers and End-User Hosts

While the focus of many early systems for policy-based networking has been the control of edge devices such as edge routers, firewalls, and VPN gateways, future systems may well have to account for servers and end-user hosts as

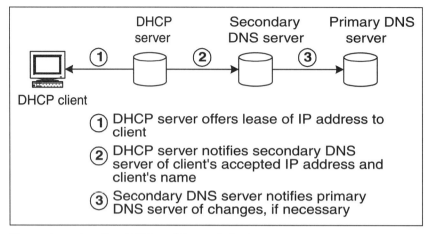

Figure 8.6   Coupling DHCP and Dynamic DNS.

policy enforcement points as well. In fact, a few vendors have started to look at these computers as PEPs, both to provide finer-grained classification of traffic and to deal with traffic classification problems that can arise when traffic from the host is encrypted.

Some problems with network congestion can be resolved by enforcing policies at the desktop, requiring the host computer to be well behaved with regards to the network traffic it generates. The easiest way to assure that a desktop is well behaved is to provide a gatekeeper in the desktop at the entry point into the network. This gatekeeper controls the traffic into and from the network according to rules or policies set by the network manager.

In a desktop context, a gatekeeping function can be used to meter and firewall the desktop-generated traffic into the network. This gatekeeping capability shapes the traffic, causing specific packets of data to enter the network at different rates or denies network entry based on the packet type, packet attributes, packet content, or the application generating the traffic.

Traffic shaping might be set by a network manager to control what a desktop application does, at what rate, and when it is permitted to do it. A second important desktop-based element is the ability to signal its performance requirements to the network infrastructure. In other words, if the desktop-based traffic requires any specific network service such as higher priority, the specific network packets must be recognizable by the network infrastructure.

In a network context, the desktop traffic needs to be able to identify specific network packets and the applications that generate or receive them in order to request the appropriate network transit class of service. Collectively, the traffic shaping and signaling from the desktop can be set by policies.

POLICY-BASED NETWORKING VERSUS ENTERPRISE MANAGEMENT SYSTEMS

Using the host for policy-based networking, as we describe it in this book, is not the same as controlling hosts via enterprise management systems, which may also use policies. In the latter case, the management systems aim to control the configuration of each host's operating system and the applications that can run on the host. Both systems make the use of policies, but to control different entities. As policy-based networking moves toward using the host to enforce policies, there will inevitably be some overlap between the two management systems, which will have to be ironed out. As we'll see in Chapter 12, "Directory-Enabled Networks Initiative," there's already a strong tie between the two approaches, since the DMTF's Common Information Model started out as a model for enterprise control of hosts and has now been extended to include network devices and services.

In general, vendors have adopted one approach to host-based enforcement points; that is, they install agent software on the host to receive policies and enforce those policies on any traffic the host generates before it's transmitted on the network. Where the vendors differ is where the agent software is located in the operating system and how the agents receive their policies.

One approach is to install an enforcement software module as a shim that sits between the Winsock 2 interface and the protocol drivers in the network stack (see Figure 8.7). Additional software serves as the interface between the enforcement modules and the policy distribution system, usually using SNMP MIBs. The policy agent implements policy controls based on objects stored in a MIB or using information sent by a policy-based networking system. The policy agent enforces bandwidth restrictions, assigns priority, generates alarms based on certain thresholds, and provides access control.

Another approach has been to install the policy enforcement engine above the Winsock layer and provide an API for other applications to use. Some vendors have also installed packet classification engines and priority queues on network interface adapters (NICs), either in silicon or software.

One problem that's often mentioned in connection with host-based agents is the possibility of users tampering with the agents, to get their traffic classified with a higher priority, for instance. None of these first-generation policy agents are tamper-proof, to our knowledge; most vendors currently are more interested in getting the technology into the field and plan to address security problems later if they arise.

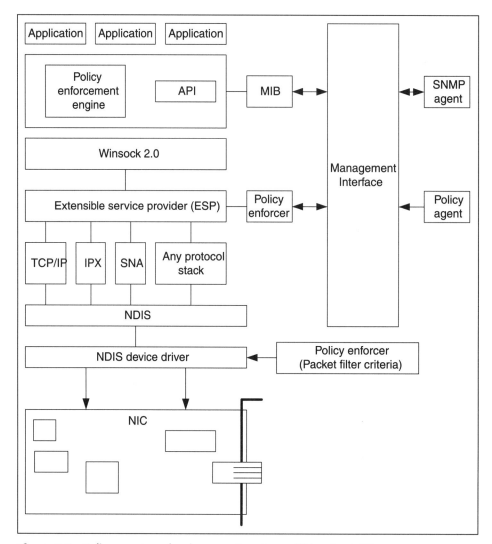

Figure 8.7   Policy agents and enforcement engines within a host OS.

Issues

It's not easy to select issues relating to PEPs as a whole when there can be so many different kinds of PEPs. We've already mentioned some of the device-specific issues in our prior descriptions of the different classes of PEPs, so we'll only mention a few major issues here. The issues we'll focus on in this section include the following:

- Encryption and traffic classification
- Third-party control of PEPs
- Performance
- Integration

Encryption and Traffic Classification

Most PEPs depend on information—such as source and destination IP addresses—contained within the packets they're processing in order to enforce policies. (The exceptions are host computers serving as PEPs, which can classify packets as they're formed before they're put on the network.) Policies may also depend on other information, such as application and session information, which requires investigation of more of the packet's contents. But VPNs that employ encryption can hinder packet classification and policy enforcement, since encryption of a packet's contents can prevent a PEP from examining the packet fields that it needs to enforce a policy.

If a host computer encrypts the packet before it's transmitted on the network, then only policy enforcement based on source and destination IP addresses would be possible since a PEP cannot see the rest of the packet's contents, which would allow enforcement based on higher-level protocols or application formation. If enforcement based on other packet attributes is necessary, then the best solution is to have the host computer classify and mark the packet (using the unencrypted DS field in the IP header, for example) at the same time as it encrypts the packet. One other solution that's been proposed is to have the host use RSVP to signal to an edge device what treatment the following flow from the host should receive.

On the other hand, if an edge device such as a router (acting as a VPN gateway) is responsible for encrypting the packet, then the edge router can also mark the packet for a particular QoS treatment (using the DS field, for example) at the same time as it encrypts the packet for transmission on a VPN tunnel. This is essentially the same procedure as that performed by the host; it simply assumes that traffic on the internal LAN is secure against attack and does not need to be encrypted.

Third-Party Control of PEPs

Considering the proprietary implementations of queuing, traffic shaping, and other QoS-related techniques that vendors install on their networking hardware, it may prove difficult for one vendor's policy-based networking system to configure devices from another vendor. This may be true whether a CLI, SNMP MIBs, or COPS PIBs are used to distribute policy-based configurations.

Many vendors of policy-based networking systems currently use telnet/CLI or SNMP to configure devices from other networking vendors, but it's unlikely that these systems can optimize some of the devices' parameters as well as the original manufacturers can. If fine-tuning of the devices is necessary, a network manager may have little choice but to use the same vendor for the networking equipment and a policy-based networking system. However, at this point in time, there's too little field experience with QoS to tell if a great deal of fine tuning of the devices is necessary to meet most customers' needs.

The IETF has been working on standard PIBs for services such as DiffServ, which improves the prospect of having an acceptable least common denominator for device configuration. However, vendors will still be able to add their own extensions to the PIBs, which could lead to a situation similar to that found with SNMP, where vendor extensions lock in customers to their management systems. Time will tell.

Performance

Network managers familiar with access control lists know that these filters exact a toll on router performance. Furthermore, in some cases, proprietary performance-enhancing features on some routers will not work when access lists are used. Although a policy-based networking system eases the task of network management by shielding the network manager from all the details of each device's configuration, the policy-based system also makes it possible for the network manager to create policies that distribute too many rules to the PEPs. Just when we're trying to improve a network's performance by deploying QoS, we may be reducing the performance of the devices expected to enforce QoS.

While there's very little public data that show how policies affect a router's performance, vendors generally agree that a large number of filters will reduce a router's performance. This is especially true as the filters become more complicated—as for layer 4 switches—where more than the usual 5 tuples (source and destination addresses, source and destination ports, protocol) have to be examined before a forwarding decision is made. Just as many layer 3 functions have been coded into ASICs to increase the performance of layer 3 switches, vendors are now turning their attention to coding classification engines in ASICs to provide faster classification (at layers above layer 3) to keep up with today's faster network speeds, such as Gigabit Ethernet.

Integration

As you've made your way through this chapter, it should have become obvious that many equipment vendors have chosen to implement their own brand of policy-based networking to control their products. Even the simple word *pol-*

icy can have vastly different meanings. (In all fairness, some of these vendors introduced the use of policy into device management before policy-based networking as we now know it was formulated.)

The proliferation of proprietary policy-based management systems from different vendors makes it difficult, if not impossible, to combine the management of this wide variety of devices into a coherent system. Yet integrated management of a wide variety of devices is one of the promises of policy-based networking, as we mentioned way back in the first chapter.

It seems likely that this fragmentation of effort will eventually diminish and that policy-based networking vendors will offer systems that can control many, if not all, of the devices we described in this chapter. Some vendors' policy-based networking systems already control multiple classes of devices, such as routers and firewalls and VPN gateways.

As the DMTF's integration of DEN with the Common Information Model matures and the various IETF working groups standardize more components of policy-based networking, it will be easier for vendors to get their systems to work together. Of course, vendors will always be looking for value-added features that can distinguish their products from their competitors' and this could lead to proprietary extensions of MIBs and PIBs. In many ways, the market is still a little early in the standards development stage, so vendors have had little choice but to use their own approaches to policy-based networking, acting pragmatically to get a product to market.

Selecting PEPs for Policy-Based Networking

We've covered a wide range of network devices in this chapter, including some that are only in the very early stages of integration with policy-based networking. The two primary uses that most customers plan for policy-based networking are QoS and security, so routers, switches, firewalls, and VPN gateways are high on the list for policy support. They're also the most common devices on networks today, which means you'll have to consider how a policy-based networking product supports your current devices, and what upgrades or replacements may be necessary.

If you're planning to deploy some of the devices we've described in this chapter and want to control them using a policy-based system, we suggest checking a few features of the vendor's products:

- If it's an individual device, such as a router or firewall, does it require a CLI to configure or does it support other clients, such as SNMP or COPS, for configuration?

- If the device is controlled by a policy-based system from the vendor, compare the system's architecture to the ones we describe in Chapter 4,

"Architectures for Policy-Based Networking," to see if it's capable of distributed management of multiple devices.

- Ask the vendor if its policy-based system can, or will later, interoperate with other policy-based networking systems, perhaps by using the same policy repository or exchanging policy data via LDAP or XML. Or can the vendor's products be controlled by some other vendor's policy-based networking system?

Summary

Many different classes of devices—routers, switches, firewalls, VPN gateways, Web switches, traffic shapers, remote access servers, and even end-user hosts—can serve as policy enforcement devices. Currently, the main focus is on routers, firewalls, VPN gateways, and traffic shapers. As policy-based networking takes hold over the next few years, its concepts and products should be applied to some of the other network devices we've mentioned to further leverage your management system.

This is the last chapter in our series describing the components of the policy-based networking architecture. In the next chapter, we cover a related and important feature, that of monitoring network behavior.

CHAPTER 9

Monitoring Network Behavior and Policies

So far, we've talked about the provisioning and enforcement of policies. But there's one more aspect of network management that we need to consider: that of verification of the policies' actions. In other words, how is the network performing with the policies that you created and that the system distributed to the enforcement points?

Network managers need feedback to determine how their networks are running. But they don't want that feedback to take the form of lines of upset users outside their office doors or angry phone calls from customers telling them their connection is slow and applications are timing out. Network managers need to be more proactive about monitoring the health of their networks, whether it's for use with traditional methods of network management or with policy-based networking.

In the past, network managers have had a direct causal relationship with their network devices. They'd configure a device and monitor the performance of that device. If they wanted to know more about the performance of their entire network, they'd collect data from a number of devices and consolidate that information at a network management console to get some idea of how the network as a whole was performing. But that approach doesn't tell the network manager the effect of a device's configuration on the entire network, and it doesn't enable the network manager to learn how a particular service, say, forwarding of high-priority traffic with minimum delay (a definition of Gold service, perhaps), is performing.

Policy-based networking isolates network managers from this direct relationship between a manager's configuration of devices and measurement of the network's response. Much of the network manager's intelligence or experience in configuring devices is transferred to, or taken over, by the policy management tool and policy decision points. Network managers are therefore one step further removed from intimate knowledge of what the devices they're responsible for are doing. (This is the price we have to pay to enable machine-based configuration and dynamic response to changing network conditions. It will no doubt bother some network managers who want to be on top of things all the time. But it's also necessary if enterprises are going to deploy new network services with a limited pool of experienced network managers.) But network managers need to know the effect of their policies on the network, so they need feedback of how their network is performing once a set of policies is distributed. This is true for both services as well as individual devices.

Just as policy-based networking provides a global view of the network and focuses on network services rather than individual network devices, policy-based networking requires a similar service-oriented view of network performance. Unfortunately, as we'll see in this chapter, most network monitoring systems are oriented toward individual network elements rather than services, complicating the integration of monitoring systems with policy-based networking systems.

Policy-based networking also brings with it other items that need to be monitored, the policies themselves. When troubleshooting a network, network managers may need to ensure that the correct policies have been distributed to the proper PEPs and that translation from highly abstract business policies to device-dependent configurations is performed correctly (see Chapter 3, "What Are Policies?").

In this chapter, we review the basics of network monitoring, pointing out how monitoring is being extended to include measurements of services. Then we discuss service-level agreements and their importance for verifying services before we talk about how network monitoring can be integrated with policy-based networking. Last, we point out some of the important locations in the policy-based networking architecture for monitoring policies and policy translations. Keep in mind that, although much of our focus will be on the approaches to monitoring QoS, there are other policy domains, such as security and VPNs, which also require monitoring. Different domains have different monitoring needs.

Providing Feedback to Policy-Based Networking Systems

Policy-based networking systems require feedback at a number of levels since they span the gamut of high-level business-oriented policies to individual device configurations (see Figure 9.1). But getting appropriate feedback remains a problem—one that's not unique to policy-based networking—since traditional infrastructure management has been split along technological lines. For example, some tools monitor the performance of individual network devices while others monitor the traffic flowing through the network; some tools look at application software performance while others look at transaction response. This fragmentation makes it difficult for information technology (IT) management to report on, let alone monitor, the performance of a particular business service or process.

When tying feedback to policy-based networking, there are various levels of feedback that can prove useful. First, there's element-related feedback, which tells the system (and the administrator) whether a device is not operating properly—this could be a network device as well as a server. Second, there's service-level performance, which relates more closely to the business-level rules originally input into the PBN system.

One of the challenges IT managers face today is how to integrate these various monitoring tools to obtain an appropriate view of network, service, and

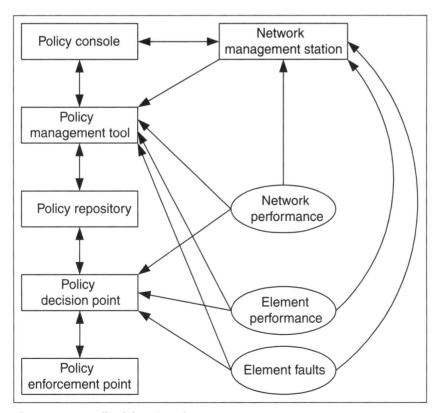

Figure 9.1 Feedback locations for PBN systems.

application performance. Vendors still produce a veritable grab bag of nonintegrated, platform-based tools that provide only pieces of the necessary solution. Policy-based networking doesn't make this task any easier, but it does offer one logical location for integrating the results, since, ultimately, we're interested in meeting business requirements and that's where policy-based networking starts—relating network resources to business requirements.

The frameworks that have been developed for network management are usually based on a framework developed by the ISO (International Standards Organization), which recognizes five different types of management: fault management, performance management, account management, configuration management, and security management. Of these five management areas, we concentrate on the monitoring aspects of only two: fault management and performance management. We'll discuss security management and its relation to policy-based networking in Chapter 15, "Policies for Network Security."

Monitoring Network Behavior

There are basically four types of monitoring that would be of interest to us: element monitoring, active networking monitoring, service monitoring, and application-level monitoring. Of the four, element monitoring has been practiced for the longest period of time. There's been a trend to offer more tools for application-level monitoring over the past few years, especially driven by the interest in Web-based applications and electronic commerce. Application-level monitoring is also important for end-to-end measurement of performance, since the user's experience is what counts, and that's often tied to how his or her application performs. Unfortunately, as we'll see later in this chapter, there hasn't been a great deal of progress in service monitoring, partly because a service requires the integration of many different devices and factors at a variety of levels.

Element Monitoring

As the name implies, element monitoring focuses on measuring the performance of individual network devices or individual interfaces within a network device. Element monitoring is usually done passively, that is, an agent installed in the monitored device detects a problem or condition of note when a device or application does something.

Polling allows the network management station to collect statistics on interfaces and devices from the passive monitoring agents, but it doesn't allow the system to proactively prevent network problems. For that, we have to turn to active monitors, which we discuss in the section following this one.

Element monitoring is usually done by means of SNMP. As we pointed out in Chapter 7, "The Policy Decision Point," SNMP has been a standard for network management for quite a few years, and the standard is now in its third version. SNMP defines a protocol for the exchange of management information called the Structure of Management Information, or SMI. It also defines a format for representing that management information and a framework for organizing distributing systems into managing systems and managed agents. A number of specific database structures, called management information bases (MIBs), have been defined as part of the SNMP suite of standards. These MIBs specify managed objects for the common network management devices, such as bridges, routers, and LANs. Two components of the SNMP reference model (see Figure 9.2) are important to our discussion here: the network manager and the managed network entity.

The SNMP network manager consists of four major components: the network management station (NMS), the NMS MIB and database, a set of network management applications, and the network management user interface. The NMS is the processing entity that monitors and controls the agents that it is responsible for. The NMS can read and write certain MIB objects in each agent to manage that network device. It can also store pertinent management information on

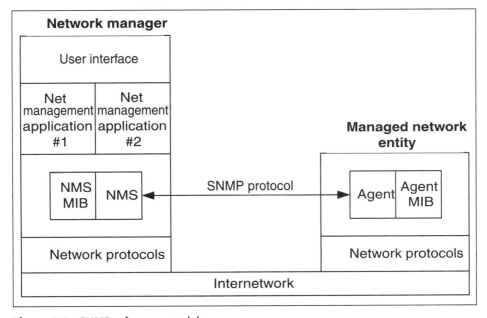

Figure 9.2 SNMP reference model.

each of the agents in its own database. The MIB of the NMS contains a master list of the MIBs from all of the agents that the NMS intends to manage.

The managed network entity consists of two key components: the agent and the agent MIB. The agent is the processing entity that receives requests from network management stations, processes them if they are valid, and sends the appropriate response. Agents can also be configured to send trap messages to report asynchronous, predefined events.

The various management information bases described using the SMI of the SNMP architecture enable a network management station to gather element-based status information at arbitrary frequencies. The underlying approach of the element polling systems is that the polling component, the network management station, is configured with an internal model of the network; status information, gathered through polling individual agents installed on elements, is integrated into the network model.

Standards such as remote monitoring (RMON) and RMON2 (see Figure 9.3) provide a basis for effective traffic analysis and troubleshooting of switched networks. The RMON standard, currently defined in RFC 1757, was designed to provide proactive monitoring and diagnostics for distributed LAN-based networks. Monitoring devices, called agents or probes, enable an effective means of instrumenting critical network segments for user-defined alarms and a wealth of vital statistics.

The RMON standard was crafted to be deployed as a distributed computing architecture, in which the agents and probes communicate with a central management station (a client) via Simple Network Management Protocol (SNMP). The basic RMON standard only specifies monitoring and diagnostics for network traffic at the MAC (data-link) layer. As an extension of the RMON standard, the RMON2 standard (RFC 2021) defines specifications for monitoring network traffic above the MAC layer.

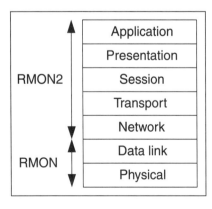

Figure 9.3 RMON versus RMON2 coverage of protocol layers.

A drawback of the original RMON-based probes is that because they view the traffic on the local LAN segment, they are not able to identify network hosts and sources beyond the connection to the managed device. To do so, a probe/agent must be capable of identifying traffic at the network layer that will provide statistics for all hosts accessing that segment, no matter where they are located or how the network is connected. With RMON2-based agent/probes, all RMON groups map into all of the major network-layer protocols. In addition, RMON2 defines the specification for monitoring application-layer traffic, which enables administrators to monitor network applications by outlining how logical filters can be constructed for remote agents.

RMON2 alarms, statistics, history, and host/conversation groups can be used for troubleshooting and maintaining network availability based upon application-layer traffic—the most critical traffic in the network. Furthermore, with RMON2, any MIB object can be locally tracked and recorded in a historical log.

In a switched network stand-alone monitors called sniffers must be placed near the client or server in order to generate useful information. But populating a switched network infrastructure with the necessary probes can be an expensive prospect. Using RMON2 information that's available on many network devices allows management systems to parse a large amount of application data without additional hardware. Although RMON and RMON2 reports can add significantly to network traffic, RMON and RMON2 probes generate reports only on demand, so care should be used in heavily congested networks.

The network element polling approach can indicate whether each network element is operating within the configured operational parameters, and can alert the network operator when there are local anomalies to this condition. But such a view is best described as network-centric, rather than service-centric. Polling devices can therefore help a policy-based networking system to determine the state of the devices it's controlling, but the approach isn't well suited to determining whether a particular service is performing as expected. For that, we need to employ other methods.

Active Network Monitoring

In addition to polling devices to gather device and network statistics, a network management system can also take advantage of active monitors. These active monitors either can be special devices in the network whose sole job is to periodically test the network and report results, or they can be software agents residing on servers and end-user hosts.

Active network monitoring requires the injection of packets (often imitating a normal user query) into the data stream; collection of the packets at a later time; and correlation of the packets for information regarding delays, drop, and fragmentation conditions for the paths traversed by the packet. The most common probe tools in the network today are ping and traceroute.

The most common probe tools are the Internet Control Message Protocol (ICMP) Echo Request and corresponding ICMP Echo Reply packets, which comprise the functionality of the ping utility. In its basic form, ping takes a target IP address as an argument, directs an ICMP Echo Request packet to that address, and waits for a matching ICMP Echo Reply response.

A ping response indicates that a working path to and from the device exists. The two paths may be the same, but in general, they are not.

A typical use of ping is to regularly test the paths to a number of sites to establish a baseline of path metrics. This enables a comparison of a specific ping result to these base metrics to give an indication of current path load within the network. There are some problems with ping, however. For instance, a router's response to a ping may be given a low scheduling priority because the routing protocol operation is a more critical function. It's therefore possible that extended delays and loss may be related to the load of the target router processor rather than to the condition of the network path. Also, ping packets usually do not occur in bursts, but many typical TCP flows may, meaning that the ping results may not reflect actual application performance along the same path.

The second common ICMP-based network management tool, traceroute, is based on the ICMP Time Exceeded message. Here, a sequence of UDP packets is generated to the target host, each with an increased time to live (TTL) value in the IP header. This generates a sequence of ICMP Time Exceeded messages sourced from the router where the TTL expired. These source addresses are those of the routers, in turn, on the path, from the source to the destination. The complete output of a traceroute execution exposes not only the elements of the path to the destination, but also the delay and loss characteristics of each partial path element.

In a DiffServ environment, ping and traceroute pose some engineering issues. The network's QoS admission filters may choose a different classification for ICMP packets from that chosen for TCP and UDP packets; as a result, the probe packet may be scheduled differently or may even take a completely different path through the network.

Here are other techniques for measuring one-way delay and loss which are better-suited than ping and traceroute for measuring the service parameters of unidirectional flows, such as you might encounter using RSVP and IntServ. A one-way approach relies on a pair of sender and receiver probes using synchronized clocks. The Internet Provider Performance Metrics (IPPM) Working Group of the IETF has been developing these measures for one-way flows, as well as refinements of measurements for two-way flows.

Actively monitoring traffic by using network devices can incur a delay—for some high-capacity routers, the debug mode needed to enable this kind of granularity introduces unacceptable processor overhead. On the other hand, active monitoring allows you to look at application behavior from the perspective of a virtual service, rather than of a server.

Service Monitoring

One of the fundamental concepts of policy-based networking is that the system allows the network manager to deal with the network at the level of business objectives rather than at the level of individual devices. This is in line with the philosophy of providing services on the network. To be effective in providing and managing network services, the network manager therefore also has to have an idea of how each service is performing and whether the requirements of each user of the service are being met. Monitoring services requires more than just looking at each network element between the source and destination of a flow, for instance.

One challenge for network managers is that a sequence of snapshots of element status values cannot readily be reconstructed into a comprehensive view of the operational status of the network as an entire system. An implicit assumption is that if the network is operating within the configured parameters, all service-level commitments are being met. Unfortunately, this assumption may not be well founded.

Currently, the main focus of policy-based networking vendors and customers alike is QoS, so we discuss many of the details surrounding QoS monitoring in this section. There are a number of parameters we can use to characterize the health of a service. Some of the characteristics that would be defined for QoS include delay, jitter, reliability, burst capacity, and traffic volume. (We say more about these characteristics in Chapter 13, "An Introduction to Quality of Service," but see the sidebar for a brief review.) Even if we confine ourselves to measure these characteristics from one edge of a public network to another (say site to site over a service provider's network) and don't concern ourselves with the end-to-end performance between a user's desktop and a server, for instance, the characteristics we've mentioned are not solely a function of individual devices and their performance.

A management system can poll each active network element to retrieve the number of packets dropped and the number of packets successfully forwarded. From these two data items, the relative proportion of packets dropped can be calculated on an element-by-element basis, and a series of element measures can provide a per-pass dropped proportion by multiplying the individual packet forwarding measurements.

But delay is somewhat more challenging to measure on an element-by-element basis using element polling. In general, delay is not easily measured using network element polling.

Measurement techniques using polling and modeling can track the performance of the network, on an element-by-element basis, but they cannot track per-path service levels across the network. Probe techniques, particularly one-way loss and delay, can perform such a complementary role of per-path service monitoring.

TYPICAL QoS PARAMETERS

The fundamental characteristics of QoS are delay, jitter, reliability, burst capacity, and traffic volume. *Delay*, also called latency, is the minimum time that elapses between requesting and receiving data and can be affected by many different factors, including bandwidth, an internetwork's infrastructure, routing techniques, and transfer protocols. *Jitter* is the variation in the delay. Some networks offer the ability to exceed an agreed-upon capacity of a link for a certain amount of time. The *burst capacity* of a network is the maximum throughput that the network will accept for relatively brief, unsustained periods.

To improve the monitoring of services, both the monitored elements and the management stations need a better understanding of the services provided and the role each element plays in providing a service. One approach is to expand the functionality of the polling system by expanding the management model to include components of the service architectures. Efforts are underway at the IETF to standardize the MIBs relating to the DiffServ model and the operation of IntServ and RSVP. For the DiffServ model, it is first necessary to define an abstract model of the DiffServ admission router's operation, by looking at the major functional blocks of the router. (See Chapter 4 of Geoff Huston, *Internet Performance Survival Guide*, Wiley, 2000, for more information.) The first of these blocks is the definition of the supported behavior aggregates provided by the network. Within the network path, the initial active path element is the traffic classification model, which can be modeled as a set of filters and associated set of output streams. The output stream is passed to the traffic-conditioning elements that are the traffic meters and the associated action elements. (See Figure 9.4.)

From this generic model it is possible to define instrumentation for SNMP polling, where each of these five components—the behavior aggregate, the classifier, the meter, profile actions, and a queuing discipline—correspond to a MIB table. Using this structure it is possible to parameterize both the specific configuration of the DiffServ network element and its dynamic state.

A comparable MIB is defined for the Integrated Services (IntServ) architecture and an additional MIB for the operation of guaranteed services. (For more details on RSVP, see David Durham and Raj Yavatkar, *Inside the Internet's Resource reSerVation Protocol*, Wiley, 1999.) The Integrated Services MIB defines the per element reservation table used to determine the current reservation state, an indication of whether the router can except further flow reservations, and the reservation characteristics of each current flow. No performance polling parameters or accounting parameters have been included in

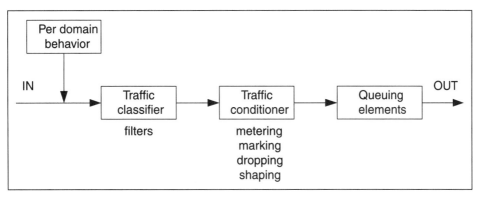

Figure 9.4 Router model.

the MIB thus far. The guaranteed services MIB adds to this definition with a per-interface definition of a backlog. This is a means of expressing packet quantization delay, a packet delay term that is the packet propagation delay over the interface, and a slack term. However, these are per-element status definitions and do not include performance or accounting data items.

The Integrated Services MIB is being further defined as an RSVP MIB for the operation of IntServ network elements. The MIB enables a management system to poll the IntServ network element to retrieve the status of every active IntServ reserved flow and the operational characteristics of each flow, as seen by the network element.

Currently, the development of policy information bases (PIBs) for Differentiated Services and Integrated Services have mirrored the work we just described for the MIBs, as far as service monitoring is concerned.

Application-Level Monitoring

While it's necessary to monitor network devices and services to inform network managers and policy-based networking systems of the network's health and performance, the ultimate judge of network performance in many cases is the end user. This is especially true when business requirements are taken into account. The end user is interested in how applications work on the network, not the underlying services and devices that the network must support to enable the applications to work. Thus, the network manager also has to depend on some kind of application-level monitoring to observe, or anticipate, the performance of the end user's applications.

The best and most direct way to ensure that application service levels are meeting required targets is to actually measure and report on the quality of service delivered to the application user, in terms of end-to-end availability and response time.

In order to effectively determine application performance and availability it is necessary to monitor the active transaction of an application as well as the application's environment. The best place to perform this transaction monitoring is a subject of debate among vendors competing to develop an effective solution for application performance management. In today's distributed client-server environments, there are several locations along the end-to-end network path between the user and the server from which to monitor and characterize application performance; these are the server, the network, and the client.

Active monitors can be a part of server applications. They can also function as agents that reside on the server and monitor specific server processes, watching for load and health metrics in addition to maintaining counters and running averages for applications. In many cases, server-side monitoring gives network managers a better view of the virtual service the network is offering, although it lacks the granularity and remote-control capabilities of a client agent.

Active testing of key applications and services by constant, periodic generation of synthetic transactions by agents designed to simulate real users is the most practical and flexible solution to this problem. Rather than build up a picture of service levels layer by layer or by only looking within the core infrastructure, this approach generates the same kinds of transactions end users generate to measure what an end user really is experiencing. The active agent approach involves the controlled generation of simulated end-user transactions to key applications and services.

This synthetic transaction approach offers a valuable benefit: the ability to create a repeatable and controlled environment for both baselining and trending purposes. But the approach does have a few pitfalls—for instance, it doesn't say anything about misconfigured desktops if they're a cause of a problem.

Service-Level Agreements and Policy Goals

Thus far, we've concentrated on the methods that a manager can use to monitor a network and all of its components ranging from individual network devices to applications. We'll soon discuss how this information can be used in policy-based networking systems. But before we do that, we need to mention one more aspect of network monitoring, that of service-level agreements (SLAs). SLAs are an attempt to provide a common understanding of terms about availability and performance between a network service provider and a customer. An SLA can be set internally, between the IT department and other departments (the customers) requiring the IT services, or externally, between an enterprise and its Internet service provider (ISP).

The SLAs that document service-level guarantees have one main purpose: They help keep conflicts between you and your service provider to a minimum by setting reasonable expectations of service. SLAs benefit you, the client, by providing effective grading criteria and protection from poor service. They benefit the service provider by providing a way of ensuring that expectations are set correctly and will be judged fairly. Remember, some SLAs include some kind of monetary reimbursement for lost or poor service, but that's a last resort; you'd really rather have good service than compensation for poor service.

Service level agreements, or SLAs, are meant to ensure that your expectations regarding network performance, maintenance, and problem resolution are met by your ISP. Three basic items are covered in an SLA: availability, effective throughput, and delay. Some SLAs include a limit of the demand level, that is, no more than x transactions per hour are allowed. One of the purposes of SLAs is the documentation of customer expectations and what an ISP is willing to provide in common terms. At the moment, this is done by means of a signed contract.

Network availability is a simple measure of the uptime of the network links available to you, complicated only by the fact that it's measured over all your sites. If you measured network availability over a month's time, the formula would look like this:

$$\frac{(24 \text{ hours} \times \text{days in month} \times \text{number of sites}) - \text{network outage time}}{(24 \text{ hours} \times \text{days in month} \times \text{number of sites})}$$

Even for so simple a measure as network availability, check to see what's included in the service provider's definition. Availability guarantees should include all components of the provider's network, the local loop to the network, and any Customer Premises Equipment (CPE) provided by the service provider (such as a Channel Service Unit/Digital Service Unit (CSU/DSU) and router). Excluded items may include a customer-provided CSU/DSU, router, or other access device; the local loop when provided by the customer; network downtime caused by the carrier's scheduled maintenance; customer-induced outages; dial-in links; and acts of God.

Note that there's an important distinction between network-based availability and site-based availability. For a network consisting of 10 sites, an average network availability of 99.5 percent would allow 36 total hours of downtime in a 30-day month. If the SLA is written around site-based availability instead of being network-based, then any one site can be down for only 3.6 hours in the month. The distinction can be very important when computing downtime.

Two standards groups are working on the definition of standard terms for SLAs, especially for use with policy-based networking. The DMTF's SLA Working Group and the Service Provider Directory-enabled Network Application (SP-DNA) Working Group of the Directory Interoperability Forum (DIF) focus on defining SLA-related policy objects that can be used as part of the Common Information Model and stored in directories. These service-level objects (SLOs), which include such items as bandwidth, delay, and jitter, will make it easier to construct an SLA by using standardized terms. Plus, when SLOs are standardized, different parties can agree on what's being monitored as part of an SLA. This will be important not only for enterprise customers dealing with an ISP, but also for arrangements between ISPs.

A few key implementation issues have a direct impact on the usefulness of SLAs to the network manager. The first issue is where the measurements are taken: end-to-end or just within the ISP's network cloud (see Figure 9.5). The local loop can have a profound impact on network performance, but it is ignored in a switch-to-switch implementation. Performance measurements and troubleshooting must be performed end to end.

It should be obvious that the location of the monitoring devices will affect the results of your monitoring. For instance, if you're interested in monitoring the performance of your service provider's network, then you'll most likely locate monitors at the LAN-WAN boundary and check network traffic between your different corporate sites. But then you're not likely to discover performance problems within your own LANs. If you want to monitor performance on your own internal networks, you'll have to place monitors at different points on your LANs, say, between LAN segments and your routing core, or in front of server farms, for instance. If QoS or another service is provided only from the LAN-WAN boundary, then measurements from end to end are less applicable.

The location of these monitors is also dependent on what you're trying to compare the measurements with. In other words, are you most interested in determining the service guarantees of your service provider or in guaranteeing

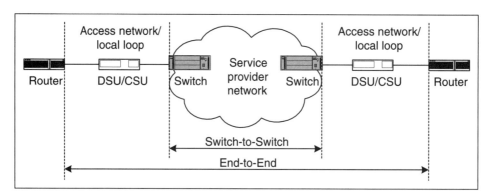

Figure 9.5 Measurement points.

the end-to-end performance of your network supporting a customer's application? If it's the latter, then you need to think about end-to-end monitoring.

The second issue is utilizing a measurement system that is independent of
the network you are measuring. Use an objective system that is not biased
toward either switch or router architectures. Also, keep in mind that how this
information is presented is almost as important as the information itself.

Agreeing on definitions of measured parameters and how they're measured
is an important task, but one that's not easy to accomplish, particularly
because there's no standardization of these metrics among ISPs. Although it'll
be some time before standardized metrics for IP network performance and
availability are agreed upon, check out the work of the IETF's working group
on Internet Provider Performance Metrics (IPPM) to see the latest efforts.

Integrating Monitoring with
Policy-Based Networking

We pointed out earlier in this chapter that SNMP is probably the most common way to collect statistics about the state and performance of network
devices. If you recall our discussion of policy decision points (PDPs—see
Chapter 7), we mentioned that PDPs not only serve the role of distributing
policy-based configurations to devices, but they can also serve as aggregation
points for information from the PEPs they control. Although some developers
would like to use COPS for both of these roles, it's also possible for SNMP to
be used for both roles on a PDP. In fact, SNMP may well have a leg up on
COPS for these dual roles since the protocol's already been used widely for
network monitoring. But let's also look at how COPS can be used to obtain
device status information from PEPs.

One difference between COPS and SNMP, which we mentioned in Chapter 7,
is that SNMP management stations poll the SNMP agents for information, while
the COPS client can send information to the COPS server at any time, as long as
the session between the client and server is still in place. Thus, there should be
no delay in learning of a change in a device or network condition using COPS,
whereas there might be a delay using SNMP, depending on the time between the
polls. On the other hand, the COPS responses may add to the network and NMS
load without adding information beyond what polling provides.

Although the policy information base (PIB) defined for COPS-PR uses a
modeling language and information structure related to that used by SNMP
MIBs, very few PIBs have been defined. Furthermore, SNMP has been around
for quite a while and developers have written MIBs for a number of devices
and uses. The focus of PIBs so far has been on the control of DiffServ and
IntServ, and PIBs have not yet been extended to monitoring the devices they

control. For instance, the currently proposed specifications for the DiffServ QoS PIB depend on the DiffServ MIB for monitoring devices.

PIBs also differ from MIBs in the way they represent device interfaces. All interface-related policies in the PIB are defined, not per individual interface, but on a per-role basis. (See Chapter 7 for more on roles.) In contrast, an SNMP MIB is aimed at interface-specific configuration and monitoring. While it's possible to use a PIB to apply the same policies to two similar (but not identical) interfaces having the same role, the MIB must allow each interface to have different status, different statistics, and different low-level configuration.

One of the reasons for integrating network performance data with policy-based networking is to make the management system more dynamic, enabling it to respond to device failures and changing network conditions. It may sound trite, but PDPs can trigger adoption to network conditions, but only if the conditions are known. But we have to get theoretical here, since no vendor has yet released a PDP that can change a PEP's configuration based on changes in network conditions.

Let's look first at a scenario in which SNMP is used to acquire the status of network devices. In this case, the SNMP monitor would have to inform the PDP of any changes in status. If SNMP is also used for configuring PEPs, then the SNMP monitor might well be part of the PDP and the appropriate PEPs would be configured from the same PDP (or messages would be transmitted to other PDPs if PEPs controlled by other PDPs also had to be reconfigured). If the PDP used COPS or another protocol to configure the PEPs, then there would have to be some sort of exchange between the SNMP monitor and the COPS-enabled PDP. In either case, the SNMP monitor should also inform the network manager of the change (either directly or by posting an alert to the policy management console).

On the other hand, if the system depended solely on COPS for monitoring and configuring network devices, the interplay between PDPs and PEPs is simpler. In this scenario, the PDP would maintain open sessions with the PEPs that it controls and alerts can be generated by either the client (PEP) or the server (PDP) at any time. Thus, a PEP can immediately send device statistics or alerts to the PDP and the PDP will respond as part of the same session. It's still possible that there may be some delays, however, if the PDP should require added information from other sources—such as the policy repository or policy management tool—before it can reach a new decision on how to proceed.

Considering the current inability of PDPs to proactively respond to changing network conditions, today's PBN systems depend on network managers' responses to network conditions. They must initiate the distribution of new policies (or revert to an old set of policies). Many PBN vendors have included proactive PDPs that can dynamically respond to changing network conditions in their projections for policy-based networking, but these projections place such advances at least one to two years in the future.

Many vendors of policy-based networking products have partnered with leading network monitor vendors to link their policy-based networking systems with network measurement systems and monitoring devices. Since some of the policy-based networking products already include open APIs for accessing data within the system, the vendors are using these APIs to exchange monitoring data with their policy products.

Monitoring Policies

So far, we've only talked about monitoring network performance and services. But if you recall the introduction to this chapter, we mentioned that it's also necessary to monitor the policies themselves as they work their way through the system. First, network managers may need assurances that the policies they created resulted in the proper device configurations. This may be particularly important when they're troubleshooting a network problem. Also, since policy-based networking introduces new components into network management—like the policy decision point and the policy management tool—there should be some way of monitoring the functions and performance of these devices.

Let's revisit the general architectural framework for policy-based networking that we originally introduced in Chapter 2, "Introduction to Policy-Based Networking." We've redrawn it in Figure 9.6 to indicate many of the locations where we could monitor policies. Of these possible monitoring points, we'll discuss what we consider to be the four most important ones:

- Between the policy management tool and the policy repository
- Between the policy repository and policy decision points
- At each policy decision point
- Between the PDP and each PEP

In Chapter 6, "The Policy Repository," we brought up some of the issues surrounding the policy repository, especially with regards to maintaining data integrity. As an adjunct to the basic structure of the repository that supports data integrity, a network manager might also want to obtain some basic statistics about the transfer of policies between the policy management tool and the repository. These statistics should include the following: Did all policies get to the repository? Which policy consoles use this repository? Which users (i.e., network managers) use this repository? And which users created which policies?

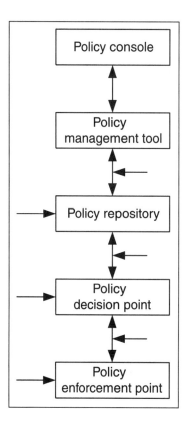

Figure 9.6 Possible locations for monitoring policies.

Now let's turn to the communications between the policy repository and PDPs. In this case, we'd like to know which policies a PDP exchanged with the repository. (We use the word *exchange* here because some repositories may be able to push policies to a PDP while other repositories, such as those using LDAP, will send policies to a PDP in response to a query from the PDP—the "pull" method—see Chapter 7 for more details.) We'd also like to know which PDPs interacted with a particular repository. Looking at the PDP's communications with the repository, we'd like to know which repositories the PDP retrieved policies from, and the policies it retrieved (or received in response to a query).

Since the PDP is a major component in the decision-making processes of a policy-based networking system, we particularly want to make sure that it's functioning properly. That means we'd like to know what policy conflicts were detected and what were the results of the policy translations that the PDP performed. In the case of the first task, it'd be best if the PDP forwarded alerts of policy conflicts (and the action taken) to the policy management tool and policy console to keep the network manager aware of changes. Consistent policy depends on consistent policy translations, which means it's necessary to monitor the translations.

Last, let's turn to the links between a PDP and the PEPs that it manages. On the PDP end of things, we'd like to know how many PEPs the PDP has interacted with and what policies-based configurations the PDP sent to each PEP. Also, it's useful to know what roles the PEP has advertised to the PDP. On the PEP side of things, it'd be nice to know how many, and which, PDPs the PEP has interacted with, and what configurations (or policies) the PEP has received from each PDP. It would also be useful to know which protocols were used to transmit the roles and policies. This latter information could prove useful to a network manager since it can tell him or her if a PDP-distributed policy has been overridden (for troubleshooting purposes, for example) by a policy sent directly from an SNMP management console.

Additional monitoring of policies is required if desktops are used as policy enforcement points. Since the systems currently proposed for setting and enforcing policies in a user's computer are not secure against tampering, a network manager should check the desktop's system to ensure that unauthorized persons have not altered the policies. Otherwise, the users may choose to override the system's policies and give their traffic higher priorities, defeating one of the purposes of the system-wide policies.

Policy monitoring is at a very early stage of development. You won't find many vendors that include any policy logs in their current products, despite their obvious value to the network manager. One or two products do allow network managers to drill down into policies to discover the resulting configuration files, but they do not actually log policy translations.

Summary

We've just completed an admittedly brief survey of a rather wide-ranging topic, that of network monitoring. In today's services-oriented network infrastructure, there's more to network monitoring than simple element monitoring. Network managers and policy-based networking systems require input from service and application-level monitors in addition to the information garnered from element monitors. Unfortunately, few if any network management systems can provide all of this data.

Integration of network monitoring information with policy-based networking is still in a fledgling state. Currently, policy-based networking systems are not capable of dynamically reacting to network faults or changes in network performance, although that is the future goal for most of these systems. At present, it's still the network manager who must react to changes in the network by creating and initiating the distribution of new policies.

We also pointed out that policy-based networking systems require yet another kind of monitoring—monitoring of the policies, their translations, and distribution within the system. This, too, is a relatively new aspect of policy-based networking, one that customers will have to push their vendors for.

To summarize the past eight chapters, we present a detailed example of how a policy-based networking system works, illustrating policy translations and distributions, in the next chapter.

An Example of Policy Processing

We originally started the book by showing you the concepts behind, and framework of, policy-based networking. Then we took apart the framework to investigate the functions of and issues surrounding each of the components of a policy-based networking system. To close out our discussion of the components and their functions, we reverse that trend of dissecting the system (at least a little bit) to show how everything works together, from the policy console to the PEP, to use policy to do something useful in managing a network.

The Scenario

Let's take a look at a scenario that most likely occurs in every large business. A company's Accounting Department has to process sales orders, product inventory, shipping information, and payroll information on a daily basis and then generates monthly and quarterly reports that indicate how the company is doing. You'd expect network traffic to increase toward the end of each reporting period when the department has to accumulate the sales and inventory data. Since this involves getting information from salespeople on the road as well as shipping centers and warehouses that may be scattered around the state—if not the country or the world—and not just the servers in the Accounting Department, the increased network traffic is not isolated to one small portion of the network.

In the past, one way of dealing with this necessary increase in network traffic would be for the network managers to ask other users of the network to limit usage of the network during the times when Accounting needed priority, say, the last few days of the month or the quarter. But this doesn't always work, since most users don't have a good idea of what impact their computing activities have on the network. For instance, they may understand that transferring large files via FTP can slow down others' use of the network, but it's more difficult for them to gauge the effect of browsing the Web or sending e-mail.

So let's turn to the use of policy-based networking as a solution for proactively managing the network to guarantee that the Accounting Department has the network resources it needs when it needs them. We'll start out by defining a set of high-level business policies that describe the behavior of the network and then describe how these policies are translated from one level of abstraction to another by the different components of a policy-based networking system until we finally get to device configurations for the PEPs on the network.

Just to recap the general architecture for policy-based networking before we talk about policy translations and distribution, recall that the general model for policy-based networking consists of a policy console, the policy management tool, the policy repository, policy decision points, and policy enforcement points.

A network manager would use the policy console to author and edit policies and monitor the status of the network. The policy management tool works in conjunction with the policy console to translate the rules that managers create in the editor into entries that match a predefined schema for storage within the policy repository. The policy repository stores the rules and policies required by the system. The next component in the architecture, the policy decision point (PDP), is responsible for accessing the policy data stored in the repository and making decisions based on those policies. PDPs base their decisions on requests from network devices or applications, policies stored in the central repository, and changes in network conditions. PDPs may have to include a translator module called a policy proxy to convert policy decisions into commands understandable to older devices that are not policy-aware. The remaining components of the architecture—the policy enforcement points, or PEPs—are the network devices that actually implement the decisions that the policy decision points have passed to them.

Figure 10.1 illustrates the main steps of distributing and translating policies from policy console down to the PEPs.

We should also review the components of a policy. In basic terms, policies consist of conditions and corresponding actions. The basic building block of a policy is a *policy rule* (or simply, rule), which is a simple declarative statement associating a policy object with a value. For example, a policy rule can define a destination, such as destIPaddr = 192.168.72.12, or it can define an action, such

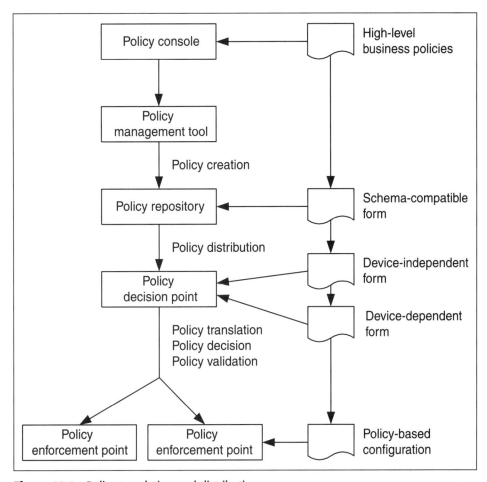

Figure 10.1   Policy translation and distribution.

as Priority = Gold. Policy rules define either conditions or actions. Each policy includes one or more conditions and one or more actions, as shown in Figure 10.2. The conditions define when the policy rule is applicable.

Now let's turn to our example.

Some Basic Assumptions

Before we actually start describing the policies, we need to mention some assumptions that we've made about the network, the business, and so on.

We'll assume that the Accounting Department must issue reports for each month. The reports are due on the first of the month, and it takes them 10 days to gather the information and prepare the report, so traffic gets heavier

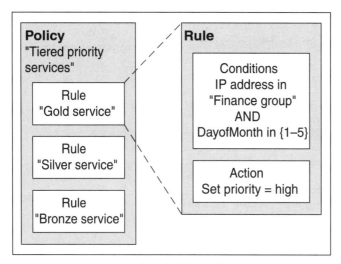

Figure 10.2   Conceptual model of a policy.

during the last 10 days of the month. Quarterly reports are due on the 15th of the month immediately following the end of the quarter, and work on this begins as soon as the previous monthly report is finished. The company in this example has a fiscal year that matches the calendar year, so quarters end at the end of March, June, September, and December. That means that work on quarterly reports occurs in April, July, October, and January.

Second, we assume that the Accounting Department is on its own subnet. This will simplify the translation of the term *Accounting Department* into IP addresses.

Business-Level Policies

Even before the network manager can create any policies that are specific to Accounting Department traffic, he or she has to create some policies for general network operations. (We'll label these policies so we can more easily track them as they get stored and translated by the system.) These might be some typical policies:

General_1: Provide high QoS to multicast traffic to the corporate management subnet during business hours and all day Sunday.

General_2: Provide high QoS to nightly backup operations on the HQ_Server from 2 A.M. to 4 A.M. local time on weeknights and Saturdays.

General_3: Provide lowest priority QoS for Quake traffic.

Now the network manager can create policies for other specific situations, such as the one we've described for the Accounting Department. In our scenario, those policies could be as follows:

Acct_1: Provide high QoS for traffic to or from the Accounting subnet during the last 10 days of the month, or first 15 days after the end of a fiscal quarter.

Acct_2: Provide medium QoS for intracompany Web usage during business hours from the Accounting subnet.

Acct_3: Provide medium QoS between the two accounting servers that share database, directory, and other information.

Typically, a network manager would use the graphical user interface of the policy console to create these policies. Figure 10.3 illustrates how a typical policy might look on a policy console.

The actual policies entered at the policy console might look something like this (based on terms similar to those used in Figure 10.2):

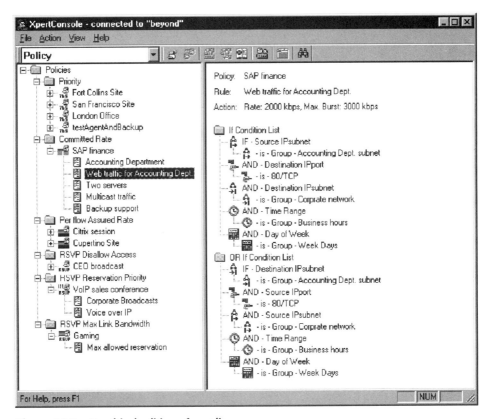

Figure 10.3   Graphical editing of a policy.

General_1:
IF   SourceIPsubnet is CorpManagementSubnet
        AND   DayofWeek is WeekDays
OR   SourceIPsubnet is CorpManagementSubnet
        AND   DayofWeek is Sunday
THEN   Priority = High

General_2:
IF   Destination is HQ_Server
        AND   TimeofDay is 2 A.M. to 4 A.M.
        AND   DayofWeek is WeekDays
OR   Destination is HQ_Server
        AND   TimeofDay is 2 A.M. to 4 A.M.
        AND   DayofWeek is Saturday
THEN   Priority = High

General_3:
IF   Application is Quake
THEN   Priority = Lowest

Acct_1:
IF   SourceIPsubnet is AccountingSubnet
        AND   DayofMonth is last10days
OR   DestinationIPsubnet is AccountingSubnet
        AND   DayofMonth is last10days
OR   SourceIPsubnet is AccountingSubnet
        AND   DayofMonth is EndofQuarterPlus15
OR   DestinationIPsubnet is AccountingSubnet
        AND   DayofMonth is EndofQuarterPlus15
THEN   Priority = High

Acct_2:
IF   SourceIPsubnet is AccountingSubnet
        AND   DestinationIPsubnet is CorporateSubnet
        AND   TimeofDay is businessHours
        AND   DayofWeek is WeekDays
        AND   IPport is 80
OR   DestinationIPsubnet is AccountingSubnet
        AND   SourceIPsubnet is CorporateSubnet
        AND   TimeofDay is businessHours
        AND   DayofWeek is WeekDays
        AND   IPport is 80
THEN   Priority = Medium

Acct_3:
IF Source is AccountingServer1
   AND Destination is AccountingServer2
OR Source is AccountingServer2
   AND Destination is AccountingServer1
THEN Priority = Medium

We've assumed here that the network manager previously defined the labels AccountingServer1, AccountingServer2, AccountingSubnet, CorporateSubnet, CorpManagementSubnet, HQ_Server, businessHours, last10days, EndofQuarterPlus15, the IP port number for Quake (26000) and the parameters defining the different priorities (such as bandwidth, queuing mechanism, and so on).

Policy Schema Representation

Once the network manager defines the appropriate policies at the policy console, the policy management tool translates them into a form that's compatible with the schema defined for the policy repository (see Figure 10.4). Although we haven't said much about the details of the Common Information Model (CIM) and the DEN extensions so far, we'll use the policy objects and schema that are very similar to those recommended by the DMTF's CIM and DEN model. (More details on CIM and DEN are in Chapter 12, "Directory-Enabled Networks Initiative.") One advantage to this approach is the ability to reuse objects such as policy conditions. For instance, HQ_Server and AccountingSubnet only have to be defined once in the system.

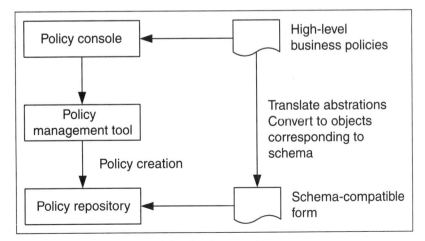

Figure 10.4 Processing policies for the repository.

Converting the original policies entered at the console to forms compatible with the repository's schema requires translating some of the abstractions within the policies. For instance, the abstraction AccountingSubnet would be translated to 192.168.12.0/21. Similarly, HQ_Server is translated to its IP address of 192.168.2.15 and weekdays is translated to MTWRF. (Note that we use some standard labels (defined within CIM) to represent times, such as timeOfDay and dayOfWeek. DayOfWeek is represented by the string SMTWRFS, where blanks (_) are used to indicate inapplicable days.)

The priorities set for different classes of network traffic are arbitrary, using a representation that's convenient for the network manager and that can be defined within the policy-based system. In our example, the priority levels are Lowest, Low, Medium, High, and so on, but they could also be called, Bronze, Silver, and Gold, for instance. What the network manager needs to define for the system at some point is what each priority class represents. For instance, Lowest priority might just be the typical best-effort forwarding of IP networks, while Medium might mean a minimum bandwidth of 256 Kbps with a minimum latency of 115 milliseconds and a packet drop rate of no more than 5 percent.

What is stored in the repository could still be labels (or names) for the condition values rather than fixed information such as IP addresses and subnet values. When the information is sent to the PDP, though, the information must be resolved. The following policies are what the PDP would receive.

```
General_1:
                if (((srcIPsubnet == 224.0.0.0/17 ) &&
                    (timeOfDay == 0800-1700) && (dayOfWeek == _MTWRF_))
                    ||
                    ((srcIPsubnet == 224.0.0.0/17) &&
                    (dayOfWeek == S_____)))
                then
                      priority = 6
                endif


General_2:
                if (((srcIPaddress == 192.168.2.15) ||
                    (destIPaddress == 192.168.2.15))
                  &&
                   (timeOfDay == 0200-0400)
                  &&
                   (dayOfWeek == _MTWRFS))
                then
                      priority = 6
                endif


General_3:
                 if (IPport == 26000)
                then
```

```
                    priority = 0
             endif

Acct_1:

             if (((IPsubnet 192.168.12.0/21) &&
                  (dayOfMonth in last10days))
                 ||
                  ((IPsubnet 192.168.12.0/21) &&
                  (monthIn [April, July, October, January]) &&
                  (dayOfMonth in [1-15])))
             then
                  priority = 6
             endif

Acct_2:

             if (((srcIPsubnet == 192.168.12.0/21) &&
                  (destIPport == 80) &&
                  (destIPsubnet == 192.168.0.0/16) &&
                  (timeOfDay == 0800-1700) && (dayOfWeek == _MTWRF_))
                 ||
                  ((destIPsubnet == 192.168.12.0/21) &&
                  (srcIPport == 80) &&
                  (srcIPsubnet == 192.168.0.0/16) &&
                  (timeOfDay == 0800-1700) && (dayOfWeek == _MTWRF_)))
             then
                  priority = 4
             endif

Acct_3:

             if (((srcIPaddress == 192.168.12.17) &&
                  (destIPaddress == 192.168.24.8))
                 ||
                  ((srcIPaddress == 192.168.24.8) &&
                  (destIPaddress == 192.168.12.17)))
             then
                  priority = 4
             endif
```

The policies should be grouped together to form a policy group, such as all policies related to the Accounting subnet. Once they're grouped, the policy management tool can examine the policies to determine whether there are conflicts between policies.

The policies also need to be associated with PEPs, such as the router attached to the Accounting subnet. Once this association is created, each policy may be tested for any conflicts with other policies. A policy can now be deployed to one or more policy decision points. The policy management tool would send a notification to the PDPs that there is a new policy for them. This notification message might include references to the PEPs affected as well as information about where to find the policy in the repository.

Conversion to Policy-Based Configurations

The PDPs would now retrieve the policies from the repository and notify the policy management tool of receipt. Each PDP might also verify the validity of each new policy at this point.

The PDPs would perform the appropriate actions for each PEP to instantiate the policy on each PEP associated with the policy and for which that PDP is responsible (see Figure 10.5). The PDP would then provide status information to the policy management tool regarding the success of the deployment operation.

In order to allow an existing device, which has no concept of the policy schema, to use policy, a PDP would use a policy proxy to provide the appropriate mapping from policy data to device configuration actions. This may involve operations that do not directly map to device capabilities, for example, handling time and date-related conditions, which are not supported by many PEPs today.

The PDP would validate the policy data, then filter the policy data based on the time information. For instance, policy Acct_2 would be translated and sent to the PEP (along with other rules in effect) only Monday through Friday at 8 A.M. At 5 P.M. Monday through Friday, the PDP would understand that a time period within a rule has expired, which would cause the PDP to reevaluate what information should be configured on the PEP. In this example, the PDP would cause the configuration related to policy Acct_2 to be removed from

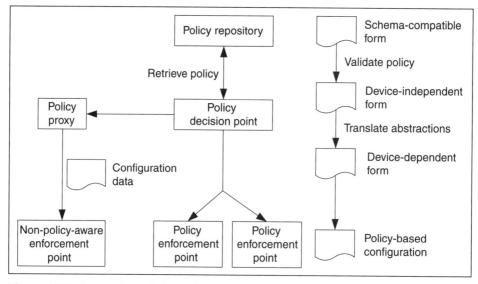

Figure 10.5 Processing policies at the PDP.

the PEP. At 8 A.M. on Monday through Friday the PDP would again reevaluate the policy data and would add the configuration information relative to policy Acct_2 to the configuration of the PEPs associated with the policy. The non-time portions of the condition list would be converted into an access control list (ACL) on the router with the source subnet, destination subnet, and destination IP port number when the time condition is true.

To continue the example, configuration relating to policy Acct_3 would always be on the PEP since it does not have a time component. The two condition lists would be converted into ACLs for the router, each ACL specifying a source and destination pair.

The policy labeled General_1 again is subject to time conditions. When one of the time conditions evaluates true, an ACL will be configured on the router to match traffic with a source subnet matching a multicast address.

The policy labeled General_2 also contains a time condition and when the time conditions evaluate true, the PEP will be configured with two ACLs, one matching the address for the backup server as the source address and the other matching the destination address to allow traffic going to and coming from the backup server to have better QoS.

The policy labeled General_3 contains no time conditions, so would be converted into an ACL matching port 26000 (the registered port for Quake, a multiuser game) as the source or destination port on a packet, and provide it with the lowest priority. If a device has a feature that provides less than best-effort priority, this value may be mapped to such a capability on that device.

Since the policy labeled Acct_1 has date-based conditions, it would be converted to an ACL matching the specified subnet as the source or destination subnet just prior to the period of enforcement (either the last 10 days of the month or the first 15 days of the month after the end of the quarter). The ACL would not be configured for the PEP (for this rule) during other time periods.

Prior to deploying the policy-based configuration to the device that's the PEP, the PDP would determine the current configuration. If there were a configuration containing a feature that conflicts with the operation of this PEP, the PDP would provide feedback to the policy management tool about the condition and would not deploy the policy. If not, the PDP would issue commands (e.g., SNMP set commands, telnet/CLI, etc., as appropriate for the device) to delete the current configuration or free resources which will no longer be used. At this point, the PDP will actually send the configuration commands to the device so that the PEP can act in accordance with the policy.

Once the policy-based configuration has been sent to the PEPs, the PDP would determine the success of the deployment and provide feedback to the policy management tool. In order to determine the success for this example, the PDP would query the device and examine the information relating to the configuration of the PEPs to determine whether the configuration now matches what the PDP expects based on the policy data. If no errors were encountered during the deployment and the configuration is correct, the PDP reports success.

What about the traffic priorities? Rather than get into a lengthy discussion of QoS mechanisms to explain how the priorities a network manager has created can be converted to PEP configurations, we'll defer the details to Chapter 13, "An Introduction to Quality of Service," and Geoff Huston's book, *Internet Performance Survival Guide* (Wiley, 2000). For simplicity's sake, we'll just point out that the DiffServ model developed by the IETF for QoS depends on three main functions: classification, conditioning, and scheduling. Classification encompasses filters and classifiers. Conditioning depends on meters such as token bucket policies, levels (defining in-profile and out-of-profile traffic), and actions such as drop, mark, or forward to a traffic conditioner. Scheduling consists of queue sets and threshold sets. A threshold set is composed of a drop method, such as a tail or random drops, and minimum and maximum threshold levels. A queue set consists of a threshold set, a priority group, the service description (weighted RED, for instance), and the bandwidth (usually expressed as a percentage of the bandwidth supported by the interface).

In order to convert the network manager's priorities (0 to 7 in our example), a PDP would have set the parameters for all of the items we just listed for any PEP in the network path that supports DiffServ. For COPS-capable devices, for instance, a PDP could do so by using the Differentiated Services Quality of Service PIB being developed by the IETF.

Provisioned versus Outsourced Policies

What we've discussed so far is a top-down example of provisioning policies using a push model, that is, policies are moved from the network manager at the top level down to the PDPs and PEPs. As we pointed out in Chapter 4, "Architectures for Policy-Based Networking," there will also be occasions when a PEP will request a policy-based configuration from its controlling PDP in order to process a network event. This could happen if a router receives an RSVP request for resources or a sales agent dialing into the corporate system has his or her session controlled by RADIUS and a policy-based system.

Summary

You've just seen a concrete example of how policies are generated and distributed within a policy-based networking system, all the way from the network manager to the policy enforcement points. Although the example was relatively simple, you can see that configuring a policy-based networking system requires setting some basic policies that govern the network's behavior followed by creating other policies that cover the exceptions.

Now the next two chapters will cover the last topics of this section, the standards that are being developed for policy-based networking, and the role they play in the framework we've devised. Then we'll move on to a new section on applications of policy-based networking.

11

The Role of Standards in Policy-Based Networking

Standards play a part in every aspect of our lives. Standards particularly play an important role in technology when customers, developers, and vendors are concerned with getting different pieces of technology to work together. We've already mentioned many of the standards that are under development for policy-based networking in past chapters. But so far we've presented the necessary standards and the issues they seek to solve in a somewhat haphazard fashion, discussing the standards in the sections covering the affected components. This chapter aims to bring together some of that same information, but also adds to it by discussing the importance of the standards and the processes they govern in developing and extending the power of policy-based networking.

The Value of Standards

To understand the aim of this chapter, we need to turn back to our first chapter, where we pointed out that policy-based networking systems are supposed to make management tasks easier for network managers. Recall that policy-based networking is a shift in the way that networks are managed and network resources are allocated. Instead of emphasizing devices and interfaces, a policy-based networking system focuses on users and applications. It does this by hiding the user to device mapping from the network manager and relying on a set of network entities to provide dynamic associations between users of the network and traffic they generate.

In essence, policy-based networking allows network managers to express business goals as a set of rules, or policies, which are then enforced throughout the network. Policy-based networking systems allow such rules to be defined centrally but enforced in a distributed fashion. This architecture makes it possible to apply rules either enterprise-wide or within domains, such as specific user groups or geographic areas.

In addition, policy-based networking systems can automate many tasks that network managers have had to perform manually in the past, such as configuring switches and routers to prioritize traffic from specific applications. As a result of this automation, policy-based networking systems enable organizations to use services such as QoS that would otherwise be too configuration-intensive to deploy.

Some network managers can realize the benefits of policy-based networking by using a system from a given vendor that is designed to work specifically with that vendor's network equipment. But the real world isn't so neat—many more networks today are composed of products from more than one vendor. Furthermore, you may eventually want to tie your own policy-based networking system with that of your service provider and there's no guarantee that the two of you will be using the same product. Standards will allow management of more types of devices on your network, for a wider variety of services, and will allow more organizations to use policy-based networking by promoting improved interoperability. Interoperability can provide more benefits of policy-based networking to a wider market than proprietary approaches can.

But what parts or processes of policy-based networking can, and should, be standardized to promote interoperability? First, there's data reuse, whether it be device configurations or the policies themselves. By using the same configuration across multiple devices, the administrator can achieve consistent behavior in the managed environment and reduce, or better yet eliminate, duplication of effort.

Automation of management tasks is one feature that distinguishes policy-based networking from most implementations of management tools with existing technologies (e.g., SNMP). One aspect of automation is the desire of managers to be able to reuse management data where that reuse makes sense, and for the tools to support such reuse. In other words, wherever possible, the tools support management information reuse, and do not require the manager to duplicate information already in the management system.

But common information does not necessarily require a common format (i.e., schema). In other words, it is possible to have common information for QoS management, and common information for security uses, but have completely different formats for the different uses of data. But this would cause a duplication of information that could be common (e.g., user information used for access control), and so would be a bad thing because it would lead to greater differences between disciplines than necessary.

The key to providing a solution for these requirements is the data used to manage the environment; what that data represents, how it gets from the manager to what the data affects, and the functionality that supports reuse and automation. And that depends on how the data is stored in a repository, which brings us to the issue of schema definitions, our second item of interoperability. In fact, the definition of schemas for computing and network devices is such a big topic that we'll devote the entire next chapter to the main effort for standardizing management objects and schema, which is shepherded by the DMTF.

In addition to standard schemas for policies and management data, policy-based networking systems depend on standards for data access as well as policy distribution in order to interoperate (see Figure 11.1). As examples of how standards can promote interoperability among components of policy-based networking systems and thereby increase their power, we'll focus on four major areas that standards impact:

- Sharing policies among organizations
- Sharing policies among policy domains
- Sharing information among PDPs
- Supporting multivendor networks

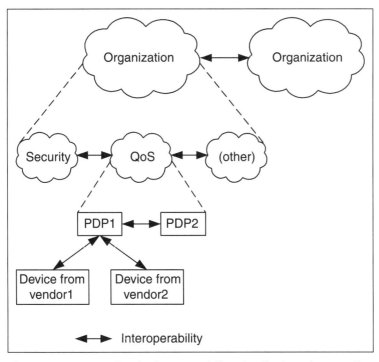

Figure 11.1 Improving the interoperability of policy-based networking components.

Sharing Policies among Organizations

Although much of our attention thus far has been focused on policy-based networking within a single organization, it's highly likely that service providers—either ISPs or Application Service Providers (ASPs)—will deploy policy-based networking to manage new services, such as QoS, for their customers. In the simplest case, the service provider could allow its customers to use a predefined set of policy templates to define the special needs of their services.

But interoperability issues arise when the enterprise customer already has a policy-based networking system and wishes to exchange policies written on its system with the service provider's system. Having the capability to exchange policies at a high level of abstraction will become increasingly important in the future as enterprises seek assurances of QoS from their ISPs using service-level agreements (SLAs). (The same issues arise when one service provider wants to exchange policies with another service provider, to provide end-to-end QoS, for instance.)

In order for these systems to be interoperable, the systems should be built upon the same information model (here's where the CIM/DEN work of the DMTF becomes especially valuable) and have a common language, a policy description language, for describing the policies that need to be shared. Another factor that will affect interoperability is how access controls are applied to repository objects, such as policy rules. Let's look at each of these issues in more detail.

Schemas

Schemas can be defined for different data stores, such as databases and directories (after all, a directory is just a special-purpose database). We'll focus on the use of schemas within directories, although some of the same issues are applicable to databases.

A directory's schema defines the set of objects that can be created in that directory and the set of attributes that can be used to describe those objects. Regardless of the physical characteristics of the directory (if it's hierarchical, relational, or flat files, for instance), the schema defines the contents of the directory in such a way that a directory-enabled application can search, add, or modify the contents of the directory. This schema, then, often defines both the directory name space (the actual information in the directory) and the objects the directory can accommodate (users, printers, and so on).

The Lightweight Directory Access Protocol (LDAP), now in its third version, is a commonly accepted standard for accessing data in directories. But, while LDAPv3 assumes that a given directory conforms to an X.500-like hierarchical naming model, the protocol does not specify the schema for the directory's content. In general, given the range of information a directory can contain, the likelihood of fully standardized schemas is quite low. Fortunately, we have a good basis for a standard schema for policies and policy-based networking in the work started by the DEN Ad Hoc Working Group and now continued by the DMTF in its Common Information Model (CIM).

But, as we'll see in the following chapter, the DMTF's work on incorporating policies into CIM is not finished. Although the DMTF has published the first version of CIM that includes policy classes, there's room for further refinement and definition of other classes concerning network devices and services.

The DEN information model is open-ended; that is, it allows vendors to define their own extensions to the schemas. This type of model is necessary because each vendor's products have special options and features, and the schemas must reflect those special features so that policy management tools can properly configure those products. But if the vendors don't publish their own extensions, other vendors' policy-based network management systems will be unable to control all the features of other vendor's devices. Unless vendors publish their schema extensions, policy-based network management systems will evolve in much the same way as SNMP network management systems have: That is, a vendor's management system performs best with its own network equipment, offering limited management of other vendors' devices.

While it's likely that networking vendors will continue to use proprietary extensions to control the value-added features of their hardware, the DMTF's planned certification program for DEN compliance will help define the core features of every policy-based networking system. Compliance with schema is relatively straightforward. A schema provider, such as a vendor of a policy-based networking system, is compliant with the schema when it has published the complete schema definition, including all class definitions and attributes. Likewise, the schema provider must comply with the rules for defining schema extensions; any new class must be defined as a subclass of an existing class defined in the base schema.

If two policy-based networking systems comply with the DMTF's CIM and do not include any extensions, then they should be able to share schemas and data with few, if any, problems. However, should two systems incorporate vendor extensions, they would have to discover each other's schema and map data between the schemas according to the differences noted in the discovery process. Directory vendors generally have their own methods for schema discovery and mapping, although the LDAPv3 protocol includes some standardization of schema discovery methods.

Some combination of XML (the Extensible Markup Language) and LDAPv3 could be used to support on-the-fly publishing and discovery of directory schemas, thereby enabling applications to determine how to best interpret, process or display information found in a directory server developed by another vendor. There's been some work along these lines, resulting in DirXML, originally proposed by Novell, and the Directory Services Markup Language (DSML).

DirXML is a directory-enabled application that sits on top of Novell's eDirectory. It's a peer technology to such things as Novell Directory Services (NDS) Corporate Edition. One function of eDirectory is to provide notification when a change to the stored data occurs. DirXML provides a means for monitoring and revealing the data and changes through an XML interface. It exposes the directory data to other applications through XML.

DSML is an XML document type for schema and data interchange. DSML provides a format for directory interoperability across various Internet protocols, including the HTTP and Simple Mail Transfer Protocol (SMTP), not just LDAP. In this way, DSML helps directory vendors to expose their schemas and entries to Internet-oriented applications through multiple protocols, using XML as the common denominator.

XML generally—and DSML specifically—is well positioned to become a core interface in most commercial meta-directory and general-purpose directory environments. As vendors integrate XML with their meta-directory products and services, directory data integration and interchange should become easier. But it may be another year or two before enterprise customers can realize these benefits, since the industry is still in the early phases of XML adoption.

Policy Description

Although there's been a lot of work, particularly by the DMTF and IETF, to promote interoperable schemas and policy definitions at the repository level, we still have some way to go to achieve interoperability at the highest levels of policy-based networking systems, such as that of the policy console, management tool, and repository. One reason is the lack of a standard language for describing policies. Such a standard is necessary if we're going to exchange policies between policy-based networking systems, such as between and an enterprise and its service provider.

There's currently little visible activity on defining a standard policy definition language (PDL), at least within working groups defining policy standards. One reason for the delay may be the desire to wait until classes describing the items comprising a SLA are standardized within CIM and the DEN extensions. Another reason for slow progress on a PDL has been the number of other issues that the standards committees and vendors have faced as they try to roll out policy-based networking systems; many vendors, for instance, are 6 to 12 months behind their own projections for the availability of some features in policy-based networking. So, they've had to focus on the more immediate problems for single-domain policy-based products before dealing with such cross-system issues as a PDL.

One likely candidate for a multipurpose policy description language is XML. The DMTF has already created XML mappings for Web-Based Enterprise Management (WBEM), which is aimed at desktop and system management and uses CIM. With DEN extensions becoming an integral part of CIM, the DMTF will extend its XML mappings of CIM to include DEN.

Access Control

When policies are shared between organizations or even across domains, it's necessary to control access not just to the repository itself, but also to individual policies and their components (i.e., rules). For example, a network manager may be allowed to use predefined rules to create new policies for the organization's traffic, but the network manager might not be allowed to modify those rules. Similarly, a network manager might have access to some policies (the ones pertinent to a particular department), but not to others written for other organizational groups, even if they're stored in the same repository. This approach requires access control at the object level in the repository, something that not all data stores are designed to support.

For directory-based repositories, LDAP currently supports mechanisms for the authentication of clients and for ensuring the privacy of data transported across a network. LDAP authentication can be performed by means of either HTTP Digest Authentication or Secure Sockets Layer (SSL). Also, since policy rules are reusable objects within the repository, access to the repository will have to be granted on an object-by-object basis. The IETF standards for LDAP-enabled directories now support object-based access, but vendors of LDAPv3 directories have not uniformly implemented this feature.

On the other hand, the IETF is creating an access control specification for LDAP directories that can apply to both the contents of directories and the resources to which the directory points. These access rights can be applied to objects in the directory (such as rules and policies), to the attributes of objects in the directory, or to objects that the directory references (other network resources). And the Open Group is attempting to create a standard authorization API. On the other hand, however, these standards are still embryonic, and it's unclear how far they will go. The simple fact that applications will always need to create custom access controls that have complete symmetry with their features and functions continues to make creating standards in this area difficult at best.

Sharing Policies among Policy Domains

Within an organization, it's likely that different managers will handle different areas of responsibility—a network manager handles QoS and an IT manager handles security, for instance. They might use different consoles, or even different vendors' products for setting policies. The data they use should be shared and reusable.

Again, sharing the same information model is important but so is sharing the same mapping of the information model to the data model. (In other words, using a data store with the same mappings.) Some vendors already offer different consoles for different areas of responsibility, but no vendors yet claim that their products are interoperable with those from other vendors at the data store level.

If managers of different policy domains are to work together and share data, schemas for the different domains—such as networking and security—must be defined. Much of this book has focused on the networking side of things, and work on schemas for network devices and services is progressing well. But work on other domains is much further behind. For example, the DMTF work on security in CIM has so far focused on the authentication and authorization of users and not on firewall policies or VPN tunnel parameters. A few working groups within the IETF—the Dynamic Host Configuration (DHC) and IP Security Policy (IPSP)—are working on schemas for their respective areas (address management and VPNs) for use with CIM.

Sharing Information among PDPs

The two situations we just discussed—sharing information among organizations and sharing policies among domains—are probably the most significant interoperability needs as policy-based networking evolves over the next few years. But it's quite possible that some organizations will find themselves integrating policy-based networking systems from different vendors, perhaps due to a corporate merger or acquisition of another company. In such cases, it might be necessary to keep the existing PDPs in place but ensure that they can communicate with each other to guarantee consistency in network policies and responses to network events.

PDPs may need to communicate with each other for two reasons. First, a PDP may have to implement a new policy or change a decision because one of the PEPs that it controls has changed state in some way that affects its capabilities—perhaps it's gone down or become congested. Since the new policy or decision could affect the provisioning of an end-to-end service, other PDPs involved in controlling the devices providing that service need to be informed of the change. (Likewise, the network manager and the policy management tool need to be informed of the change, but we'll let that go for the moment.)

Second, PDPs may also have to assume new roles. We mentioned that, in the COPS protocol, each PEP has a primary and secondary PDPs. Similarly, any good policy-based networking system should have backup PDPs to ensure the system's robust and reliable. There's no telling when a backup or secondary PDP has to take over the function of the main (or primary) PDP, and other PDPs will need to be informed of these changes in function. If they aren't aware of the changes, some PDPs may fail to update the backup PDP with the latest information and the system will get out of sync.

Unfortunately, very little has been done to address these situations. Vendors aren't very interested in resolving the first situation that we described. After all, they'd just as soon sell you more of their equipment to replace a competitor's system. But customers often can't afford to do that.

Any current solution to intra-PDP communication is therefore vendor-specific. Some vendors have elected to use the policy management tool as the mediator of all communications among PDPs, forcing all communications through the management tool. This may suffice for a small number of PDPs, but making the management tool a single point of failure in this communication path could be troublesome, especially as the number of PDPs on a network increases.

Supporting Multivendor Networks

At the lowest level in their architecture, policy-based networking systems need to work with network devices from more than one vendor. It's rare to find a network of any appreciable size that's built out of products from only one vendor. One way that policy-based networking systems deal with multivendor networks is to use standard protocols, such as SNMP, CLI, and COPS, to distribute policies. However, even when standard protocols are used, each vendor of a policy-based system must create its own set of rules for translating policies into configuration commands for network devices from other vendors.

There's been some work, such as that by the DiffServ Working Group of the IETF, to standardize the definitions of services and how they're supported by different queuing and traffic-shaping algorithms within a network device. As they're being developed, the terms are being incorporated in the DiffServ MIBs and PIBs that are being developed concurrently.

To support the dynamic nature of networks, it's important that a policy-based networking system includes both push and pull mechanisms for distributing policies. SNMP and CLI are good for device-specific configurations and can therefore be used as the final step in distributing policy-based configuration to PEPs. However, neither of these methods includes a way for PEPs to notify a PDP that they need new configuration data, such as in response to network events arising from RSVP or RADIUS.

COPS supports client-pull methods for distributing policies while COPS-PR is designed to push policies to PEPs. However, COPS and COPS-PR currently support QoS-related policies only, and neither protocol has yet to be extended to accommodate other types of policies, such as security-related policies.

For its part, CORBA's strengths lie in the ready availability of APIs for creating distributed applications and its event service, which can be used to push and pull policy data as required. On the downside, CORBA is not well suited for interdomain policy management because of the limited support for CORBA in firewalls and on NAT servers.

Many networking vendors have started to introduce COPS-compatible devices or upgrades for existing products. COPS is likely to become an important standard for distributing policy data between PDPs and PEPs, but probably not the only one. But the use of COPS and PIBs does not obviate the need for SNMP, which is still required for monitoring and setting local configuration. At the same time, defining policy MIBs for use with SNMP-based management stations also makes it possible for existing SNMP systems to provision services.

Considering the proprietary implementations of queuing, traffic shaping, and other QoS-related techniques that vendors install on their networking hardware, it may prove difficult for one vendor's policy-based networking system to configure every last detail of a device from another vendor. This may be true whatever method is used to distribute policy-based configurations. If fine-tuning of the devices is necessary, a network manager may have little choice but to use the same vendor for the networking equipment and policy-based networking system.

Summary

Many of the first-generation products for policy-based networking do not adhere to some of the newer standards being developed for policy-based networking, such as the DMTF's Common Information Model and the extensions originally developed by the DEN Ad Hoc Working Group. Despite their lack of support for these developing standards, the products are still of use to customers.

This chapter attempts to show how the power of policy-based networking is increased by the use of standards. Standards can prove particularly useful when sharing policies among organizations, such as between an enterprise and its service provider; sharing policies among policy domains, such as between network and security managers; coordinating PDPs from different vendors; and supporting multivendor networks.

Some of the important protocols that impact these uses are LDAP, SNMP, CORBA, COPS, and XML, as well as the Common Information Model with its

DEN extensions. In many cases, the protocols need further refinement to meet all the needs of policy-based networking, such as access controls, policy descriptions, and service descriptions.

The next chapter continues this discussion of standards for policy-based networking, focusing on the primary information model proposed for policies, the DMTF's Common Information Model and the DEN extensions.

Directory-Enabled Networks Initiative

One of the more important developments in policy-based networking has been the work of the DEN Ad Hoc Working Group and the Distributed Management Task Force (DMTF). These two groups have focused their efforts on the development of an information model that's suitable for use in policy-based networking, among other areas. As such, they've been strong proponents of what's come to be called directory-enabled networking.

While we've pointed out that vendors have been just as likely to select a database as a directory for policy storage in their products, directories offer the opportunity to integrate a wider variety of data. This opportunity goes beyond policy-based networking as we've described it. Sharing a wider variety of data in a common data store such as a directory affords developers the opportunity to create applications that use information about users and networks without creating that information from scratch or duplicating the info.

But keep in mind that this concept of information integration via a directory is not fully developed or widely implemented. We're still somewhat early on the adoption curve for enterprise-wide integrated directories. As we'll see in this chapter, all the data definitions for network-related objects haven't been worked out. Plus, many enterprises still face the task of integrating their data; some have started on the road to data and directory integration, but many have not. It's not unusual to hear stories of companies maintaining upward of a hundred different directories! But the interest in directories has grown considerably in the past few years and more directory integration projects are started (and successfully completed) each year. This rising use of enterprise-wide directories will definitely impact the use of directories in policy-based networking.

It's worth pointing out before we begin that there's a distinction between DEN and directory-enabled networking. The acronym *DEN* is meant to represent the industry initiative that produced the DEN specification defining an information model and LDAP mapping. On the other hand, *directory-enabled networking* is a broader term, encompassing a design philosophy where applications use information stored in directories to take advantage of the network. Our focus in this chapter is on DEN and its relationship to policy-based networking.

DEN, Common Information Model, and Policy-Based Networking

As we pointed out in Chapter 3, "What Are Policies?," there are various levels of abstraction when policies are represented in a policy-based networking system, starting at the administrator-defined level, moving through device-independent abstractions and device-dependent abstractions until we get to configuration data.

At the highest level in our framework for policy-based networking, that of the policy repository, the policy representations are defined by schemas. A schema defines the set of objects that can be created in a data store and the set of attributes that can be used to describe those objects. Anyone can define a schema, but schemas are better suited for representing standard objects that are simple and exist within static boundaries, not the complex network elements and services which exist in a constantly changing environment. In order to model the interaction between network elements, services, and clients of the network, which is fundamental to the development of policy-based networking, it's beneficial to create an information model. Within our context of policy-based networking, an information model describes three things: the composition of policy rules, the characteristics of devices that are being controlled by policies, and the relationships and interactions among the objects being managed.

Not only does the development of an information model help describe managed objects and their relationships with each other, but it also provides a common format for describing objects that makes it easier to share data across domains (between QoS and security management applications, for example). Multiple systems that employ different repositories can also be derived from the same information model by mapping their data to the model. This way, both repositories can be optimized for their specific needs while retaining the ability to exchange information with each other. As we'll see in this chapter, DEN and CIM are all about defining an information model that's appropriate for describing not only users and desktop computers, but also networks, network elements, and network services.

But once we enter the world of network components including routers and switches, we need other representations of policies, ones that the devices will understand—the device-dependent policies (see Figure 12.1). This brings us back into the realm of MIBs and PIBs, which contain their own object definitions relating to a device's capabilities, operational state, and configuration. In order to create objects for MIBs and PIBs that will be used to control a network device, the policy decision point (PDP) in our architecture has to retrieve the pertinent information from the policy repository. The classes defined within the information model and stored in a repository according to the schema derived from the information model determine what information the PDP needs to retrieve by describing the attributes of the classes and the relationships between the classes. For instance, a server could consist of attributes such as server name, serial number, network address, and operating system. We'll have more to say about classes later in this chapter.

CIM and DEN provide an extensible model that ranges in granularity from the very fine (a chip on a card in a slot of a chassis of a network element) to a

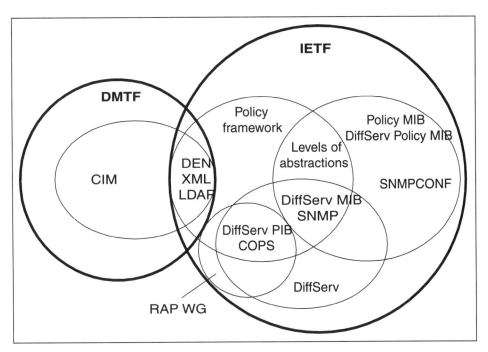

Figure 12.1 Fitting standards together.

very high level (such as an autonomous system using the BGP4 routing protocol, for example). Administrators can make use of the entire range of granularity when defining policies, and the PDPs can then extract the appropriate information from a policy repository at their required level of granularity in order to translate higher-level policies into device-dependent policies for distribution to the policy enforcement points.

Now, with this framework in mind, we'll discuss the evolution of the DEN specification and show how some of DEN's components can be used in policy-based networking.

What Is the Directory-Enabled Networks Initiative?

While policy-based networking has been on the minds of many networking engineers for at least the last few years, it wasn't until some of the leading vendors looked to apply the capabilities of directories to managing networks that interest in policy-based networking became noticeable. In May 1997, Microsoft and Cisco announced their Directory-Enabled Networks (DEN) Initiative, aimed at integrating networks and directory services for the purposes of providing advanced management of network elements and services. To encourage industry input into the development of the specification, Microsoft and Cisco held an open design preview in November 1997. Representatives from a broad spectrum of networking and directory service vendors as well as corporate and academic customers attended. This initial design preview followed an announcement of the Directory-Enabled Networks Initiative that September.

Many of the vendors who attended the design preview formed the DEN Ad Hoc Working Group (AHWG) for the express purpose of drafting a DEN specification. To ensure that the specification included customer input, the AHWG also formed a Customer Advisory Board, which included representatives from Fortune 500 companies such as Texaco, Charles Schwab, Sprint, and the University of Washington. The goal of the DEN AHWG was the specification of a directory services information model and schemas to facilitate the interoperability of distributed applications, management tools, and network elements.

The DEN developers wanted to integrate directory services and networks in order to build networks that could respond more intelligently to changing network conditions and application requirements. By integrating directories and the network, the DEN Ad Hoc Working Group felt that applications would be able to leverage the network infrastructure on behalf of users to deliver better performance, security, reliability, and quality of service.

Through such integration, the directory takes on a new role. Today, directories act as a repository for information about users and computing resources, such as servers and printers. The DEN Initiative aimed at extending directories to include information about network devices, services, and applications. More significantly, the DEN work attempted to include in the directory information about the relationships among all the elements in the directory.

In this expanded view of directory services, users along with computing and network resources (such as devices, operating systems, management tools, and applications) use the directory service to publish information about themselves and to discover other resources and obtain information about them. Once information about users, network elements, and services is available in a single location, it is possible to define and manage the network based on policies. As the repository for information about people, devices, services, and so forth, and their relationships, the directory essentially controls which users can log on to the network, what capabilities they possess, what their preferences are, and what types of operations they can perform.

A related initiative was the DMTF's development of the Common Information Model, which was originally focused on system management. The early versions of CIM already defined such classes as managed elements (such as servers, desktop computers) and applications, but, short of a network interface card (NIC) installed in a computer, CIM lacked any classes defining network devices or services. Nor did CIM include the concept of policy.

Recognizing that there was no information model for network management, especially one that afforded a global view of networks and their services, the DEN Ad Hoc WG used some of the concepts of X.500 directory structures and some of the classes defined in CIM to take a stab at defining an information model that could be used for policy-based networking. The working group also elected to define a mapping of the information model to LDAP as part of its efforts to promote directory-enabled networking.

After about a year's work, the DEN Ad Hoc Working Group finally reached the stage at which it felt it had a workable information model. At the same time, it made sense to merge the DEN information model with CIM since the two models shared similar roots and, once combined, would help the sharing of information among more types of applications.

In fall of 1998, the DEN Ad Hoc Working Group's Customer Advisory Board submitted its final draft of the DEN specification to the DMTF. Although much of the original DEN specification was already based on the concepts of the DMTF's CIM, the DMTF now committed its resources to incorporate the DEN specification into the CIM specifications.

So DEN has come full circle. It started using some of the concepts and classes of CIM, extended those concepts and classes to networks and policies, and now has become an integral part of CIM, extending it into new fields and applications.

Although the DEN specification has become part of CIM, we'll focus our attention on the network-related parts of CIM, only discussing CIM to show that the DEN specification has been incorporated into, and expanded by, CIM. To accomplish this, we'll start out by describing the classes originally defined by the final specification from the DEN Ad Hoc Working Group and then show how those classes have been integrated into later versions of CIM and what other network-related classes have become part of CIM since then.

Components of DEN

The initial draft of the DEN spec laid out an information model, a usage model, and a schema for integrating networks with directory services, as well as an initial mapping of the schema to LDAP.

We'll focus on the information model and schema, since modifications that followed the release of the original DEN spec have led to new LDAP mappings by the DMTF.

The information model describes the relationships among the directory objects that represent users, applications, network elements, and network services. In essence, the information model governs how objects interact with each other. The DEN information model has three parts: 10 base object class hierarchies that form the basic framework; an extensible schema based on inheritance and the aggregation of component objects or classes into a larger entity; and simple mechanisms for establishing relationships among objects.

One benefit of the information model is that it enables diverse applications to share a common namespace and schema along with common rules that govern how those objects interact. As a result, applications that have completely different purposes can exchange information and knowledge about common objects. For example, an application from one vendor could populate a DEN-enabled directory with information describing the salient characteristics of the network. An application from a second vendor could use this information to provision services across the network, while a third vendor's application could be used to manage network devices.

The usage model, on the other hand, defines how existing network services and protocols work with the elements in the information model to accomplish specific goals, such as coordinating IP address allocation across multiple Dynamic Host Configuration Protocol (DHCP) servers, and establishing and propagating remote access login policy.

The Directory's Role

The authors of DEN noted that the directory has a special role to play in directory-enabled networking. While the directory will act as the root for a range of information, it won't necessarily be the single repository for this information. In particular, there is a large amount of nonstatic, or volatile, information that must be maintained, including information about the state of network links, the flows active through a router, and the data rate for each flow.

This information is likely to reside in memory caches, file systems, and various databases throughout the network. When appropriate, information about these other information stores (in essence, *meta* information) will reside in the directory.

The directory also may store user data, such as authentication and access rights, user profiles, IP infrastructure data (such as startup files for routers), and address and name server data. Policy-based management systems can leverage the inheritance of the underlying directory, giving managers the ability to aggregate policies based on a whole company, specific organizations within a company, and specific users.

In the DEN specification, the schema can be implemented on any directory that has an extensible schema, so that new classes and attributes can be added. The schema also supports inheritance so that new class definitions could be created from, and inherit the characteristics of, existing definitions. Last, the schema supports LDAP v3.

The Schema

The DEN schema defines the object classes and their related attributes that can be represented in a directory service. The schema defined in the DEN spec incorporates concepts from, and is complementary to, both X.500 and the Common Information Model (CIM) defined by the Distributed Management Task Force (DMTF).

A directory's schema defines the set of objects that can be created in that directory and the set of attributes that can be used to describe those objects. The DEN spec defines 10 base class hierarchies: person, network device, application, network protocol, network media, network service, profile, policy, location, and linked container (see Figure 12.2). Of these 10 base classes, network device, network protocol, network media, network service, profile, policy, and linked container were new classes introduced by the DEN specification.

These base classes are organized under a class called Top, which is an X.500 base class that forms the starting point for all the other classes. The first eight classes are important for characterizing the elements of a networked system. The location class was provided so network managers, for example, can physically locate a device, such as a particular port on a switch in a particular wiring closet. The designers defined the linked container class so there would be a standard way to implement a forward-linked list of containers, which is useful for establishing an explicit search order for locating a profile.

The person and application classes were drawn from X.500, while the device class borrowed from both X.500 and CIM. For example, the DEN authors aug-

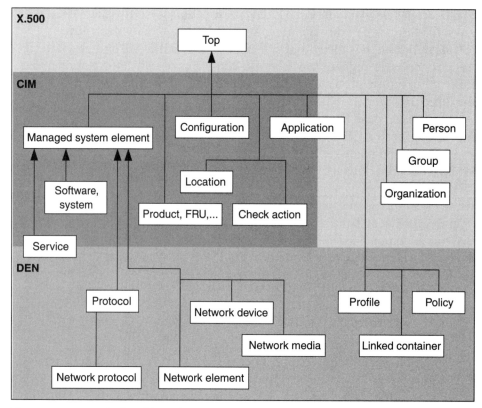

Figure 12.2 DEN's class hierarchy.

mented the X.500 definitions of the person and device classes so they can be used to describe and control the interaction among users, applications, network elements, and services. The protocol and media classes were also taken from CIM, although they'd been refined in the DEN spec to reflect a network, rather than a pure systems, orientation.

The person class is an X.500 class that defines objects that represent people. The DEN spec defined additional attributes to enable network services to be personalized on a per-user basis.

The application class was derived from the X.500 application process class, which defines an object that performs information processing for a particular application. The DEN application class allows applications to be represented as generic resources.

Because there are many approaches to defining profiles, the DEN schema defined abstract base classes rather than detailed structural classes so that it could accommodate other approaches, and used LDAP to access the information contained in the profile class.

Specific Classes

As we noted previously, the *network device class* draws from both X.500 and CIM. X.500 defines the generic concept of a device, but does not define the logical functionality of a device. CIM has a very rich definition of a logical device, but did not specifically define the concept or functionality of a network device. DEN extends and enhances the CIM definition (while maintaining compatibility with X.500) of a logical element to include network elements. The logical aspects of a network element are realized in the NetworkElement class. The DEN spec defines more than a dozen objects within the device class.

For example, a physical element is a class for representing any physical component of a system. One criterion for identifying a physical element is that a person must be able to physically attach a label to the object.

A physical component is a superclass for chips and physical media. The chip subclass represents all chip components, such as CPUs and ASICs, and is used to model the chips in network elements, such as special router ASICs. Physical media is drawn from CIM and represents diskettes, removable hard drives, and other system media.

A physical package is a container object—that is, one that's specifically designed to consist of other objects— and is used to define the characteristics of components that can physically contain other physical elements. It's a superclass representing hardware modules, such as router interface processors, and is the most general class used to represent a piece of network hardware. For example, cabinet is a subclass of physical package that represents a piece of hardware that can potentially stand alone in the network. Other devices include network card, network ports, slot, wired and wireless connections, and connectors.

CLASSES AND SUPERCLASSES

A *class* is a collection of instances (often called objects), all of which support a common type, that is, a set of properties and methods. Classes can be thought of as nothing more than a mechanism for classifying objects encountered in the real world. A class defines a set of properties and other features that are part of the defining criteria for that class. For example, the class Person may have the property Name. Therefore, if something is classified as an instance of the class Person, then it must have a name.

A subclass is derived from a superclass. The subclass inherits all features of its superclass, but can add new features or redefine existing ones. A class is said to be a subclass of another class if all instances of the first class are also instances of the second class.

As its name implies, the *protocol class* is used to represent different protocols. The network protocol subclass is used to group together common characteristics of different networking protocols, including identifying networking protocols by networking layer.

For example, the layer one subclass abstracts the common characteristics of layer one, or physical layer, networking protocols, which are concerned with mechanical, electrical, and other characteristics of how bits get onto the physical wire. The layer two subclass abstracts the common characteristics of layer two, or data-link layer, networking protocols, such as Ethernet and token ring, which frame data and provide error and flow control functions. The layer two subclass is further subdivided into dedicated media and shared media protocols. Similarly, the layer three subclass abstracts the common characteristics of layer three, or network layer, networking protocols, such as IP and TCP. This subclass further subdivides into connectionless and connection-oriented protocols.

The DEN specification took the *media class* defined by the CIM schema, which is used to represent physical media such as tapes and removable hard drives, and reworked it into a new network media class for representing network communication. Two subclasses were proposed under network media, LAN media and WAN media.

The *service class* represents a generic function that is available on the network. It provides a template of attributes and behaviors that describe a network function or a set of functions that can be invoked. Using this class, application developers will be able to match services to users, groups, and other objects. Among the service subclasses outlined in the initial DEN specification are connection, QoS, AAA (authentication, authorization, and auditing), security (including IPSec and certificate services), and multimedia services.

The *profile class* offers a way to organize profiles into different categories. Profiles define the characteristics and needs of an object. The DEN spec identified half a dozen subclasses under the profile class, including user, group, organization, organization unit, service, and device profile. In addition, a remote access profile has been defined as a subclass under user profile. This subclass expresses user profile information for remote access applications based on RADIUS and is one of the most fully defined aspects of the initial DEN spec.

The *policy class* encapsulates information that governs the use of network resources in a particular context and the way in which different network resources interact with each other. A policy is a template of attributes and behaviors that describe a function or a set of functions that can be invoked that control how various entities interact with each other. General policies can be used to control how groups of entities use a service or a set of services, while specific policies, which inherit from more general ones, control the use of a service by a particular entity. Under policy, a handful of subclasses have been defined, including security, networking (with subclasses for routing and

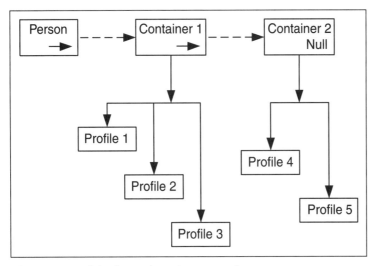

Figure 12.3 Linked container class example.

switching policies), configuration, usage (with subclasses for compression and encryption policies), and provisioning policy.

Another class that the DEN specification added to the schema is the *linked container class*. The linked container class can best be understood via a diagram (see Figure 12.3).

In this example, the person object contains the distinguished name of *container 1*, which holds profile objects that apply to a user. (See Chapter 6, "The Policy Repository," for an explanation of distinguished names.) Container 1 holds the distinguished name of *container 2*. Since container 2 does not hold the distinguished name of another container, this is the end of the chain. Using linked containers, for example, and starting at a person object, a network service could follow the distinguished name link to the first container and search for applicable policy information in that container. If no applicable policies are found, the service follows the distinguished name link to the next container and so on, with the search order controlled by the forward links.

Common Information Model

The DMTF's Common Information Model is organized into nine components or models, as shown in Figure 12.4: core, physical, database, applications, system, user, logical network, policy, and device. In addition, vendors can create extensions to CIM.

The core model is the part of CIM (see Figure 12.5) that establishes the major design patterns for representational issues that are not specific to a particular management domain or resource type. The common models—systems,

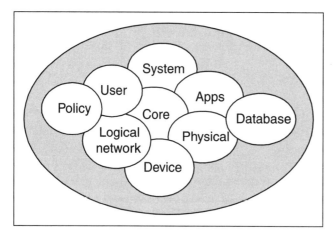

Figure 12.4 Components of CIM.

device, applications, or physical—leverage the constructs defined in the core model to represent issues in specific management domains or resource types.

The physical common model (see Figure 12.6) describes objects that can be tagged with a label, occupy space, and are subject to the laws of physics. These objects include chassis and docking stations, chips, physical media, connectors, and cables. Relationships between these objects, mostly dealing with containment and location, are defined as associations in the model. The main goal of

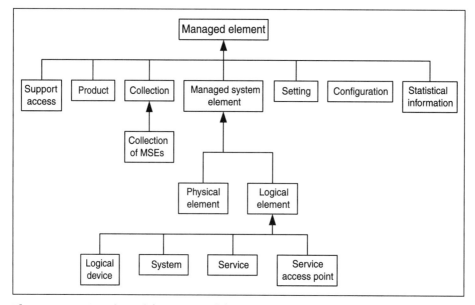

Figure 12.5 Overview of the core model.

the physical model is to describe the general packaging, enclosure, component, and cabling information for inventory and asset management.

Although the Common Information Model originally was repository-agnostic, directory services are now the preferred repository, partly due to the influence of the DEN specification. The DMTF now specifies LDAP as the access protocol for CIM and had released LDAP mappings for various submodels of CIM.

For more details on CIM, see Winston Bumpus et al., *Common Information Model: Implementing the Object Model for Enterprise Management* (Wiley, 2000). Also check out the DMTF's Web site at www.dmtf.org for up-to-date specifications of CIM and DEN schema and LDAP mappings.

Relationships between Objects

Directories are not designed to maintain relationships between objects they contain, yet policy-based networking requires relating objects and services to one another. The linked container class provides a means to establish such relationships between objects in the directory. In particular, linked containers can be used to represent the various relationships that policies and profiles can have relative to each other. For example, policy objects can apply to various combinations of service consumers and services.

The Common Information Model uses association classes to express relationships between instances of classes in the model. The design of associa-

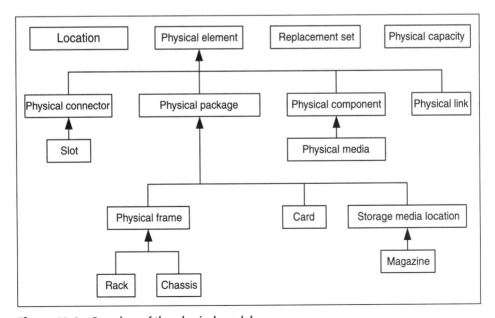

Figure 12.6 Overview of the physical model.

tions resembles the OMG CORBA relationship service. That is, an association allows two previously unrelated classes to be associated without modifying either of them. This is done by creating a new association class, which has references to each of the classes to be associated.

An *association* is a group of links that have a common structure and set of semantics. However, associations are not just simple pointers. A pointer is an attribute of an object. The key difference is that a pointer belongs to an object and is used to reference another object. However, an association does not belong to either object—an association is a separate class that depends upon both objects. In addition, an association is inherently bidirectional. An aggregation is a special type of association. It represents a relationship where some objects are a part of another object.

Associations and aggregations describe relationships between two classes and the characteristics of those relationships. For example, an OSPF service runs inside a router (which is a physical element); an association would be defined to describe that relationship.

The Distributed Management Task Force and DEN

While the DEN specification was a solid foundation for representing network devices and services within an information model, the DMTF further enhanced DEN as it incorporated DEN's classes and relationships into CIM.

To understand how DEN was incorporated into CIM, we should look at DEN's three submodels: the physical submodel, the logical submodel, and the policy submodel. The physical submodel describes the physical structure and connectivity of network devices. For example, a router might consist of a particular processor card, a certain amount of RAM, and two or more interface cards. On the other hand, the logical submodel describes the logical connectivity and topology of a network, its services, protocols, and administrative domains. The logical submodels handle such items as subnets, for example. Last, the policy submodel describes how entities are controlled and provisioned. By creating these submodels, DEN allows a developer to independently model the structure of a device as well as its behavior.

The physical model aspects of DEN, which include definitions of networking hardware, were incorporated into CIM 2.1. The DMTF incorporated the logical model of DEN, which includes definitions and interrelations of protocols and network services, into CIM version 2.2. The first LDAP mappings of schemas were released by the DMTF in May 2000 and covered CIM's core and physical classes. Since policy was a new concept to CIM when the DMTF accepted the DEN specification, it took longer for the

DMTF to integrate policy into CIM, finally releasing the policy submodel in CIM version 2.4.

Now let's look at two of the more important (to us) components of CIM, the network model and the policy model.

The Network Model

The network model focuses on basic networking concepts, describing the network-centric elements that make up LANs, MANs, and WANs. The network model also describes associations that enable clients—users, applications, and host computers—to be bound to services that are available on the network. It also describes relationships between different types of network elements and services. The purpose of the network model is to model the logical characteristics and capabilities of the managed objects that form a network. (The physical aspects of network objects are described and modeled using the physical model of CIM.)

Classes that are part of the network model occur in various places of the CIM hierarchy, as shown in Figure 12.7. For example, the AdminDomain class is a subclass of the System class, while the ProtocolEndpoint class is a subclass of the ServiceAccessPoint class. Since the LogicalNetwork class describes a collection of many logical elements, including protocols and services, it's defined as a collection of ManagedSystemElements.

The NetworkService class is the root of the network services submodel. Network services represent generic functions that are available from the network that configure and/or modify the traffic being sent. Its subclasses are the ForwardingService and RouteCalculationService classes.

Other submodels that have been developed as part of the network model include BGP (Border Gateway Protocol), SwitchService (which includes VLANs), QoS services, and IPSec. Let's look a bit more closely at two of the submodels, QoS services and IPSec.

The QoSService class conceptualizes a QoS service as a set of coordinated subservices, serving as a common base class for defining subservices needed to build higher-level QoS. To that end, QoSService subclasses are as follows:

PrecedenceService, which defines how traffic is forwarded based on the value of the ToS byte of a packet

DiffServService, which defines how traffic is forwarded based on the value of the DiffServ Codepoint

8021Pservice, which defines how traffic is forwarded based on the value of the Priority field in the 802.1p header.

The IPSec class aims to model the configuration of IPSec negotiations using the Internet Key Exchange (IKE) protocol. Its development within the DMTF

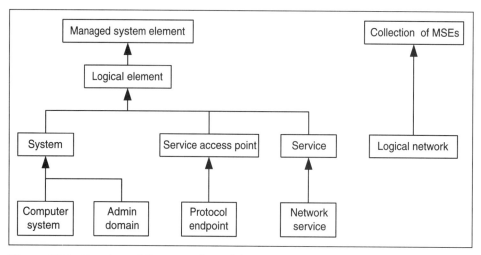

Figure 12.7 Overview of the network model.

was coordinated with the work of the IETF's IPSec Policy Working Group and uses classes within CIM's user-security model and network model.

Policy Model

It should come as no surprise that the policy model within CIM resembles the way we've defined policies in this book. (See Chapter 3, for instance.) Again, the policy class is a subclass of the ManagedElement class (see Figure 12.8). An instance of policy consists of PolicyRule instances, which themselves are composed of one or more instances of PolicyCondition and PolicyAction. The policy model also includes a class for collecting policies, called the Policy-Group class.

The policy model also includes a way to define where the policies are stored, for administrative purposes. This is done via the PolicyRepository class, which is part of the AdminDomain subclass of the System class.

DEN Usage in the Industry

When the DEN Ad Hoc Working Group submitted its draft of DEN to the DMTF, 175 vendors endorsed the draft. All of those vendors have committed resources to the development of DEN and support for policy-based management systems. So what part does DEN currently play in the development of policy-based networking?

Various networking vendors, such as 3Com, Alcatel, Cisco, Lucent, Marconi, and Nortel, as well as many smaller companies, have already shipped parts of

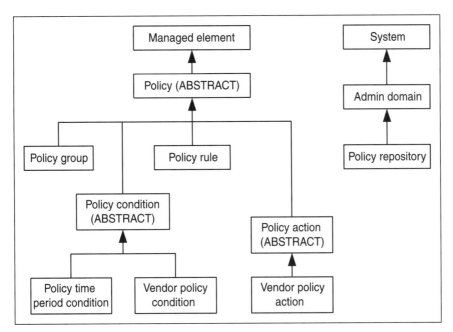

Figure 12.8 Overview of core policy model.

their policy-based networking systems. Many shipping and announced policy-based networking products have been touted as being DEN-compliant. For many, this means that the vendors are using an object model for defining devices, services, and policies that follows the same structure as that found within the DEN/CIM model. It does not necessarily mean that a product uses the full information model as specified for CIM, or that it uses the DMTF's LDAP mappings for CIM and the DEN extensions.

Keep in mind that the DEN information model is open-ended; that is, it allows vendors to define their own extensions to the schemas. This type of model is necessary in that each vendor's networking products have special options and features, and the schemas must reflect those special features so that policy management tools can properly configure those products. But if the vendors don't publish their own extensions, other vendors' policy-based network management systems will be unable to control all the features of other vendors' devices. Unless vendors publish their schema extensions, policy-based network management systems will evolve in much the same way as SNMP network management systems have: That is, a vendor's management system performs best with its own network equipment, offering limited management of other vendors' devices.

While it's likely that networking vendors will continue to use proprietary extensions to control the value-added features of their hardware, the DMTF's certification program for DEN compliance helps define the core features of every policy-based networking system. Compliance includes the following:

- Compliance with the DEN-related portions of the CIM core schemas
- Compliance with the DEN-related portions of the CIM physical model
- Compliance with the DEN-related portions of the CIM network model
- Compliance with other models relevant to the application domain
- Compliance with the CIM-to-LDAP mapping guidelines (if LDAP is used in the product)
- Compliance with the CIM rules for defining schema extensions
- Publication of the information model and schema definitions

Summary

If you're interested in making more of your networked applications work together and reducing duplication of the data that they need to work, then you should investigate consolidating your data within enterprise-wide directories and using CIM for network and systems management. If policy-based networking is an integral part of your company's information strategy, then consider how a vendor's policy-based networking product is designed to take advantage of the CIM/DEN specifications, and whether the product meets the requirements of the DMTF's compliance tests.

Now we'll move to the third part of this book, where we discuss some of the actual applications for policy-based networking.

PART

Three

Applications of Policy-Based Networking

There are two main areas of applying policy-based networking, quality of service (QoS) and security. QoS policies include decisions concerning traffic classification and forwarding, including the myriad decisions about queuing algorithms, drop precedence, and bandwidth allocation. Security policies can include such things as access control, VPN tunnel setup, as well as control of public key infrastructure (PKI). Since policy-based networking can shield network managers from the details of each device's configuration for these policies, making the day-to-day maintenance of networks a bit easier, enterprises and service providers alike are anxious to apply policy-based networking to their networks.

CHAPTER 13

An Introduction to
Quality of Service

Many network managers for enterprises and service providers are looking to utilize QoS to deal with the increasing bandwidth demands due to new users and applications. While QoS features are useful, organizations still have to figure out how to apply these capabilities in their networks. In particular, network managers have to determine which QoS features should be turned on in each network node, so that the resulting flow of traffic meets users' needs. Furthermore, the demand for QoS treatment on business networks will only increase as new applications, such as voice over IP and streaming multimedia, are deployed.

Policy-based networking systems are needed because QoS capabilities, while desirable, are often too difficult to implement. Some of the issues include the complex and difficult learning curves for switches and routers; the workload associated with configuring QoS parameters and a large enterprise network; and the lack of the system-wide view.

But before we can describe how you can apply policy-based networking for the control of QoS on a network, we need to provide some background on QoS. That's the focus of this chapter. Then, in the following chapter, we'll discuss the ways policy-based networking has been designed to control QoS.

The Need for Quality of Service

Over the past several years, it has become clear that the nature of traffic on local and campus networks is changing. Whereas text-based data was often the only type of traffic on enterprise networks a few years ago, multimedia-oriented traffic is on the rise. Similarly, the volume of traffic on enterprise networks has steadily increased. As a result, mission-critical applications are vying with non-mission-critical applications for network resources.

Likewise, timing-sensitive applications, such as videoconferencing and video training, are at the mercy of bulky file transfers. Without some sort of QoS capabilities, the network must provide best-effort service to all comers.

What does QoS mean to users? In the broadest sense, QoS is the network performance as perceived by users. It can be measured by the amount of time it takes for screens of information to be displayed on a user's monitor, for example. The user's perception of the quality of sound or video in multimedia applications (that is, whether it's smooth or choppy) is also a measure. Ultimately, QoS is just that—the quality of the service that the user receives from the network.

However, user perception isn't the only issue in evaluating the quality of service a network provides. If a network is highly congested, clerks in the order entry department may be limited by how many orders they can process in an hour. Similarly, SAP R/3 operations may be bogged down by FTP or Napster traffic. If the quality of the network service is poor, then business processes can suffer, which can have a concrete impact on an organization's productivity and its bottom line. Basic QoS capabilities provide network managers with a level of control over their network traffic that can help ensure that mission-critical applications don't suffer as overall network traffic increases. Likewise, certain types of multimedia traffic must be protected from data traffic and vice versa.

In today's networks, traffic is handled on a first come, first served basis. When congestion occurs and memory buffers on devices such as switches and routers are filled, packets are dropped. Typically, the last packets in are the ones that are jettisoned, regardless of what application they belong to. Furthermore, traditional network traffic is relatively bursty and tends to arrive in unpredictable chunks. For example, when a user downloads a file from a file server or opens a Web page, a large block of data gets transferred. Such transfers can interfere with the transmission of other types of data, such as SNA traffic, on the network.

To address these problems, QoS technologies change the basic functioning of networks by allowing them to provide different levels of service for different types of traffic. For example, you can use QoS techniques to ensure that SAP R/3 traffic is always transmitted and never dropped while Napster traffic gets the lowest level of service.

Some organizations may be able to solve network performance problems by adding bandwidth to the network. Certainly, more bandwidth will make data move faster. However, it won't make congestion go away or prevent router and switch buffers from overflowing and dropping packets indiscriminately. If you consider the speed mismatch between gigabit-speed backbones, 100-Mbps Ethernet links in building risers, and 10-Mbps Ethernet to desktops, you're bound to have congestion points.

Nor will bandwidth alone address the problem of mission-critical and timing-sensitive applications getting bogged down in file transfers or Web-page downloads. The unpredictability of network traffic is a major cause of congestion, since the bottleneck may move around depending on what network users are doing on any given day, at any given time of day. If you want better control over which traffic gets through and which doesn't, you need some sort of QoS scheme. Likewise, if you've been running a separate network for mission-critical applications (such as an SNA network) and want to consolidate this with non-mission-critical traffic, you need some type of CoS/QoS to ensure each type of traffic gets handled appropriately.

Class of Service versus Quality of Service

Class of Service (CoS) and QoS are often used interchangeably, although the industry at large generally views CoS as offering a less stringent set of capabilities than QoS. Both CoS and QoS refer to the ability for a network to offer special treatment to one class, or category, of network traffic over another.

The Asynchronous Transfer Mode (ATM) community has defined a handful of service classes. These include classes for circuit emulation and constant bit-rate video, variable bit-rate audio and video, connection-oriented data transfer, and connectionless data. In the packet world, vendors often use airline or postage analogies, referring to classes of service with terms such as *first class*, *business class*, and *bulk rate*. The IETF has defined five service classes: guaranteed load and controlled load in the Integrated Services architecture, and enhanced forwarding (EF) and assured forwarding (AF) in the Differentiated Services architecture, and best effort.

The key difference between CoS and QoS is in the technical mechanisms they employ. CoS generally relies on prioritization, congestion management, and other relatively basic mechanisms. Under a CoS scheme, similar types of traffic are lumped into a group. For example, FTP traffic may be treated as a class and given a certain priority. If you want some FTP traffic to be given higher priority over other FTP traffic, you will need a more granular way of classifying traffic, such as using flow-based schemes.

QoS is more granular than CoS. It generally refers to the collection of parameters, such as bandwidth, delay, and loss rates, being manipulated in the interest of providing differing levels of service. ATM offers the most comprehensive set of standardized QoS capabilities in the market today. In general, QoS has come to be associated with a rich set of mechanisms for controlling the flow of traffic so that it meets the desired performance levels. QoS schemes are generally designed to operate end to end and include mechanisms for coordinating resources across a network for each traffic flow or connection. In some schemes, such as ATM QoS, these resources are guaranteed to be available for the duration of the flow or connection. In the remainder of this book, we'll focus on QoS mechanisms on IP networks. This chapter cannot hope to cover all the technologies and issues surrounding QoS and is only meant as a basic introduction to QoS. For more details, see Geoff Huston, *Internet Performance Survival Guide: QoS Strategies for Multiservice Networks*, Wiley, 2000.

Quality of Service Basics

Several functions must be in place for a network to provide QoS: a method for applications to indicate their QoS requirements, a method to signal requirements across the network, a method within the network devices to handle the traffic to meet the QoS requirements. ATM has the richest support for all of these functions, but since it's not deployed in many instances as an end-to-end technology, we won't cover its features in this book. Our focus will be on the two main efforts by the IETF to provide QoS support on IP networks, the Integrated Services (IntServ) model and the Differentiated Services (DiffServ) model.

First, there must be either an explicit or implicit way for applications to indicate their QoS requirements to the network. For example, in the Windows environment, the WinSock version 2 interface provides a way for applications to explicitly discover and use the bandwidth, latency, and other QoS capabilities offered by underlying networks. Alternately, other vendors have developed host software that can identify application traffic by its IP port number and other information so that QoS mechanisms can be applied to that traffic.

Second, there must be some mechanism by which end nodes (such as servers and desktops) convey information about the application's requirements across the network so that the network can reserve the appropriate resources. As an example, the Resource Reservation Protocol (RSVP) is an IP-based signaling protocol that packet-based systems can use to communicate their QoS requirements to routers and other layer 3 devices. DiffServ, on the other hand, uses implicit signaling, in which traffic entering a DiffServ network is classified according to rules set at the edge devices.

Third, the network equipment itself must have the necessary capabilities to handle the traffic in a way that meets the application's requirements. For example, switches and routers must have adequate queuing capabilities so that different traffic flows can be isolated and queued properly. Likewise, network devices must reserve adequate bandwidth and other resources, such as buffer memory.

Finally, for QoS to work, a network needs traffic and congestion management mechanisms, including controls for admitting traffic onto the network in the first place and handling that traffic in the event of network congestion.

Traffic Management

Among the key traffic management techniques are admission control for controlling what traffic gets onto the network; policing, which keeps the traffic in line once it's admitted to the network; and traffic shaping, which includes techniques for ensuring that traffic is put on the network in accordance with its QoS contract.

Call admission schemes are essentially responsible for limiting the number of *calls* (basically, flows, sessions, or connections) allowed and for determining whether a new call can be serviced without degrading the performance of the existing sessions or connections. In principle, an admission control mechanism must understand the resources needed to fulfill a QoS request and be able to evaluate this request in light of what's happening on the network (that is, what resources are currently being consumed) and the priority of the new call in relation to existing calls.

Admission control schemes can become quite sophisticated and may support various options for handling a QoS request should there be insufficient resources to service the request. For example, an admission control scheme may support negotiation so that the QoS requester (say, a server) can reformulate its request based on parameters that the network can accommodate, such as a lower amount of bandwidth or higher latency. Alternatively, the admission control mechanism may be able to degrade existing flows or connections in order to free up the resources necessary for the request. Likewise, the admission control mechanism may deny the request.

Once a traffic flow or connection is admitted to the network, there may be mechanisms for ensuring that the traffic is well behaved. These so-called *policing methods* ensure that an information flow doesn't go beyond the agreed bounds—for example, by trying to use more bandwidth than it has asked for. Policing encompasses those actions the network can take in the event a QoS agreement is violated, such as throttling back a flow or cutting it off entirely. Policing is necessary to prevent aggressive or rogue users from consuming bandwidth and other resources to which they're not entitled, and thus degrading network performance for other users.

Another function, traffic shaping, is complementary to traffic policing. Simply speaking, *traffic shaping* is a mechanism for ensuring that traffic entering a part of the network conforms to the agreed bounds (in other words, it adheres to its traffic contract) so that it doesn't need policing. Traffic shaping can take place as the traffic leaves a host, switch, or router.

Congestion Management

Congestion management is a necessary function of a QoS scheme, but may be provided independent of full-blown QoS. For example, many routers and switches today support some form of congestion management, but may not support RSVP or 802.1p prioritization. On the other hand, many vendors combine congestion management with a prioritization scheme to create a CoS offering.

Congestion management can be either proactive or reactive. One form of proactive congestion management is random early discard (RED). Under RED, a device monitors its buffers and begins to selectively discard packets before its buffers are full to overflowing. Network managers can specify which traffic should and shouldn't be dropped. In addition, RSVP signaling can be viewed as a form of proactive congestion management since it operates on the assumption that connections will only be allowed if sufficient network resources are available.

A key example of reactive congestion management is the TCP's use of a sliding window protocol. The sliding window protocol allows TCP to vary the amount of data it sends before it receives an acknowledgment. Under this scheme, receivers can indicate how much data they can accommodate. If the receiver's buffers become full, it can indicate a window size of zero to stop all transmissions.

Quality of Service Standards

Two industry organizations are defining QoS standards that are pertinent here: the Institute of Electrical and Electronics Engineers (IEEE) and the IETF.

As part of its efforts to define virtual LAN (VLAN) standards, the IEEE has defined an eight-level priority scheme that will allow LAN switches to prioritize packets. The key specifications involved are 802.1Q and 802.1p.

The 802.1Q specification defines a tag that is appended to MAC frames to carry VLAN information. This tag accommodates two types of information: 3 bits are allocated for priority information, while 12 bits are allocated for a VLAN ID. The way in which the priority bits can be used is defined in the 802.1p specification.

Over the past several years, the IETF has had two active working groups focusing on QoS architectures, the Integrated Services Working Group and the Differentiated Services Working Group. As part of this work, the IETF has defined several classes of service—specifically, controlled load as defined in

RFC 2211 and guaranteed load as defined in RFC 2212, and Enhanced Forwarding, which is defined in RFC 2598, and Assured Forwarding, as defined in RFC 2597—and related QoS control services. (The first two are the work of the IntServ WG and the last two come from the DiffServ WG.) In addition, the IETF has defined the RSVP protocol as a means to communicate an application's requirements to network devices along the data path. RSVP can also function to convey QoS management information between network devices and the requesting application.

The Integrated Services approach is based on the use of an explicit, end-to-end setup mechanism whereby applications tell the network what type of service they need. The Resource Reservation Protocol (RSVP) is one such setup mechanism. The combination of IntServ classes of service and RSVP allows applications to signal their QoS needs and network devices along the traffic path to commit the necessary resources.

The other active IETF working group involved in defining QoS is the Differentiated Services Working Group, whose goal is to define simple, relatively coarse methods of providing differentiated classes of service for Internet traffic. This specification will focus on the use of existing bits in the IPv4 header, specifically the Type of Service field (which contains the IP Precedence bits), and the Traffic Class field within the IPv6 header. These bits will be used to mark packets so that they receive a particular forwarding treatment on a per-hop basis across a network.

The Differentiated Services approach represents a provisioned, hop-by-hop approach to QoS. With DiffServ, application traffic is first classified (either by the sending host or a network edge device), then marked in a way that tells network devices along the traffic path how to handle it. (The main IETF documents describing the Differentiated Services approach are RFCs 2474, 2475, 2597, and 2598.)

These two approaches, IntServ and DiffServ, provide for very different traffic handling within a network. IntServ using RSVP, for example, allows for more granular QoS treatment based on individual traffic flows, while DiffServ provides somewhat coarser QoS handling of combined (aggregated) flows, where a number of individual session flows are grouped and treated consistently by the network. As we explain later in this chapter, these two technologies can function in a complementary fashion so that RSVP signaling indicates the QoS needs of DiffServ aggregated traffic.

Integrated Services

The IntServ framework addresses two basic requirements. One is that there be a set of QoS service definitions and that network elements have the mechanisms, such as queuing schemes and buffering, needed to support these services. The second is that applications need a way to communicate their QoS requirements to network elements. The IETF has addressed the first requirement by defining two IntServ QoS control services: controlled load and guaranteed service.

Controlled load service essentially provides for the equivalent of best-effort services on an unloaded or lightly loaded network. Applications that request controlled load services should expect a very high percentage of their packets to be successfully delivered and delay times close to the minimum transit delay. Transit delay includes any delay inherent in the media itself plus fixed processing time in routers and other network elements along the data path.

The IETF intentionally kept the controlled load specification minimal. For example, peak rate is the only optional function in the specification. Network operators can specify a particular peak rate or set the peak rate as infinite. The controlled load service is not isochronous and does not provide any explicit information about transmission delay. Rather, the application is expected to provide any necessary timing recovery mechanisms.

Controlled load service is useful for applications that are highly sensitive to overload conditions. Examples include adaptive real-time applications, such as digitized audio and video, which require the continuous transport of data. Controlled load services may also prove useful for applications such as real-time modeling, database updates, process monitoring, and any type of push media.

Applications that wish to use controlled load services must provide the network with an estimation of the data traffic they will generate. Through admission control, the service then ensures that the intervening network elements have the necessary resources, such as adequate bandwidth, port buffer space, and packet-processing resources, to honor the service request.

In contrast to controlled load, guaranteed service actually guarantees that packets will arrive within a specified delivery time and won't be discarded due to queue overflows as long as the traffic stays within its specified traffic parameters. Guaranteed service works by controlling the maximum queuing delay; it does not control the minimum or average delay, nor does it attempt to minimize jitter or address transmission delays or other delays.

In general, guaranteed service is most useful if every network element (including routers and links) along the data path supports it. Some industry players believe it may be possible to get around this requirement by overprovisioning certain parts of the network, such as the portion of the LAN closest to the users, while applying guaranteed services to the WAN portion of the connection.

Guaranteed service is subject to admission control as well as to policing. Two forms of policing are specified for guaranteed service: simple policing and shaping. Simple policing is done at the edge of the network, where network elements ensure that the traffic conforms to the specified service parameters. The IETF recommends that nonconforming traffic receive best-effort handling. Shaping entails delaying packets or otherwise manipulating them to ensure that they conform to the specified service parameters. Shaping generally takes place inside the network, at branch and merge points from the source outward into the network.

Broadly speaking, guaranteed service is intended for applications that need a firm guarantee that a packet will arrive no later than a certain time after the source transmits it. Real-time applications, such as interactive voice and video, will benefit from guaranteed service. Telemedicine, remote control, and financial transactions are other applications that can benefit from guaranteed service. Some vendors, such as Cisco Systems, that have implemented controlled load and guaranteed service maintain that they can provide adequate levels of service for interactive traffic using the controlled load service.

Both controlled load and guaranteed service require applications to provide similar traffic parameters to the network. In particular, both allow you to specify a data rate and both rely on the use of a token bucket. A *token bucket* is a traffic specification that consists of a token rate—that is, the continually sustainable data rate—and a bucket size, which indicates the extent to which the data rate can exceed the sustainable level for short periods of time. With controlled load, you can specify the mean rate and burst size and, optionally, the peak rate. Guaranteed service lets the receiver specify the data rate and requires that you specify the peak rate. In addition, these services encompass a maximum datagram size. The key difference between controlled load and guaranteed service is that guaranteed service specifies a maximum upper bound on delay, while controlled load does not.

RSVP Overview

RSVP, currently the primary setup mechanism in the IntServ architecture, provides transport for traffic control and policy information. The IETF defined RSVP to run over both IP version 4 and version 6, and to operate transparently through non-RSVP-enabled regions of a network. Some industry players view RSVP as a network control protocol that operates at the transport level of the Open Systems Interconnection (OSI) model. Other players see RSVP as an attribute of the network layer, or even an application that runs on the network layer. However you conceptualize it, the key concept to keep in mind is that RSVP is a control protocol.

In the context of QoS, a host uses RSVP to request a specific QoS from the network on behalf of an application data flow. In RSVP, a *flow* is a sequence of packets that have the same source, destination, and QoS requirements. RSVP carries the request in the form of a flow specification through the network and attempts to make a resource reservation at each network element through which the flow will pass. Network elements, such as routers, use RSVP to deliver QoS requests to other network elements along the data path.

Originally, RSVP supported only per-flow reservations. However, extensions to the protocol enable resource reservations to apply to aggregate traffic, that is, sets of flows. This work, known as aggregated RSVP, could go a long way toward defusing one of the major criticisms of RSVP. Tracking individual flows places a burden on routers, particularly when there are a large number of flows. Consequently, it has become generally accepted that RSVP doesn't scale to work in environments, such as the Internet, with a high volume of flows. The ability to apply resource reservations to aggregated traffic flows would reduce, if not eliminate, this scaling problem. For example, aggregated RSVP signaling could be used to dynamically provision trunks through a network's core (or an entire WAN), while per-flow signaling could be used at the edges for admission control.

RSVP isn't a routing protocol. Rather, it relies on the network's underlying routing protocols to determine where it should carry reservation requests. When a route changes, RSVP adapts its reservation to new paths. RSVP's ability to adapt dynamically to network changes—and to support dynamic group membership changes—is due to the fact that the protocol establishes soft, or temporary, state in routers and hosts. Specifically, RSVP installs state on all RSVP-aware devices between the source and destination.

RSVP uses specific types of messages to create, refresh, and delete soft state. State is necessary because network elements and hosts must be aware of the QoS requirements specified in an RSVP request and must allocate the appropriate resources. In addition, RSVP state is used to police and shape traffic. RSVP periodically scans the soft state so it can build and forward appropriate messages to succeeding hops. RSVP also sends periodic messages to refresh state, which is deleted if no refresh messages arrive before a specified timeout interval. Alternately, RSVP can delete soft state in a router or host using an explicit teardown message. By checking and refreshing state, RSVP can, for example, adjust and alter the path between RSVP senders and receivers in response to router changes.

RSVP involves a fairly complex sequence of interactions. We'll first provide a high-level overview of how RSVP works, then delve into more detailed specifics of its operation later in the chapter.

With RSVP, QoS services are actually requested by the receiver in response to special messages from the sender. A sending host initiates an RSVP-based session by sending a particular type of message known as an RSVP PATH message. Once the receiving host receives the PATH message, it starts sending the appropriate reservation request messages, specifying the class of service it can support (guaranteed, controlled load, or best effort). These reservation messages are passed along to all the network elements in the reverse path until the sending host receives them.

At each RSVP-enabled network element along the path, the RSVP program applies admission control to determine whether that element can provide the requested QoS. If admission control succeeds, the RSVP program sets the appropriate parameters to achieve the desired QoS, and the sending host can begin transmitting. If admission control fails at any node, the RSVP program sends an error message to the application that originated the request. Figure 13.1 illustrates this process.

RSVP Components

Clearly, both hosts and network elements have roles to play in establishing and maintaining resource reservations. Let's examine each role.

In general, IP hosts acting as either the source or destination of a resource request will be running one or more RSVP-enabled applications and an RSVP signaling stack. By using an API such as Windows Sockets 2, applications indicate their requirements and characteristics to the RSVP software. The RSVP software is responsible for signaling as well as interacting with any traffic control components that may be on the host, including admission control, policy components, and a packet classifier and scheduler. (Not all hosts will perform traffic control functions. Rather, the host may depend on the network for some or all of these functions.) The RSVP software is also responsible for establishing and maintaining path and reservation state. Figure 13.2 illustrates the host-based RSVP components.

As we noted earlier, admission control is responsible for ensuring that the requested resources are available. Specifically, admission control tracks resource consumption on a particular interface and makes sure sufficient

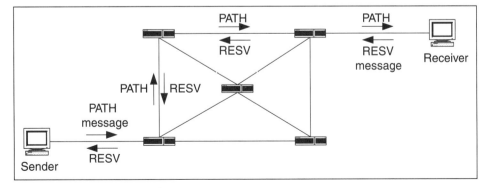

Figure 13.1 RSVP reservation process.

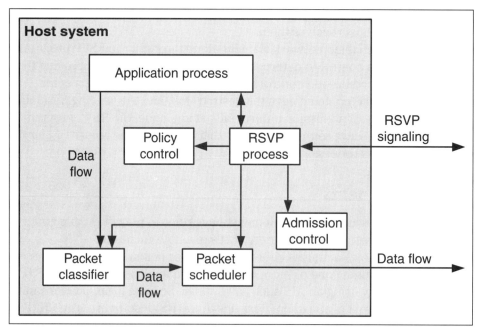

Figure 13.2 Host-based RSVP components.

resources are available to support a given resource request. If the resources are available, the admission control system allocates them. If the resources are not available, the admission control system rejects the resource request.

The policy control component controls who (users and/or applications) gets to make reservations and what kind of reservations they can make. The policy component is responsible for enforcing any policies the network manager may have defined regarding the usage of RSVP. Policy control components on the host can create policy data objects to be carried in a path or reservation message, while network elements interpret this information and apply the appropriate policies. For example, a router could use the policy information to authenticate the RSVP message as coming from a particular host or application.

As its name implies, the packet classifier is responsible for identifying the packets that correspond to a particular flow. Five fields in the IP header uniquely identify each flow: the source and destination addresses, the protocol ID, and the source and destination ports. On a router, a filter that identifies a flow is installed in the classifier after the flow has been accepted by admission control.

Once a packet has been classified, the packet scheduler does its job. On the host side, the packet scheduler ensures that the packets generated by the application are in profile with the specified QoS. For example, the packet scheduler can delay bursts of packets to make sure they conform to a specified flow rate. On the router side, the packet scheduler makes sure that the flow's QoS requirements are satisfied—for example, by forwarding the packets from a flow in a timely fashion. As with the host, the router's packet scheduler may also take steps to keep a flow's traffic in profile.

In cases where some or none of the traffic control functions are available on a host, the network equipment must perform these functions. For example, some IT managers may not be comfortable about having policy control running on hosts unless the host operating system is able to isolate user and administrative functions, making the policy tamper-proof by users.

Advances in network hardware, including new packet-processing components, make it feasible for newer network equipment to handle the packet classification function without performance degradation. However, in very large networks and for specific applications, it may still be desirable to have hosts perform these functions.

In some cases, the network won't be able to perform classification. For example, some applications use dynamically assigned port numbers, or source multiple traffic flows—each requiring a different QoS—on the same port. Likewise, use of IPSec for encryption or the Dynamic Host Configuration Protocol (DHCP) for dynamic IP address assignment can hamper classification. IPSec may encrypt IP port information, thus rendering it useless for classification purposes, while DHCP may make it difficult to consistently associate an IP address with a particular user. In these cases, the host needs to preclassify the traffic or use RSVP to indicate to the network how to identify certain traffic.

RSVP on Shared LANs

Use of RSVP on shared LAN segments poses some challenges. On a shared segment, multiple devices share a network segment and no one device controls it. This poses a problem for RSVP, which expects to apply admission control and provision resources based on individual senders. Since no one host on a shared segment has control, it's possible for the resources on that segment to become overcommitted. The IETF has addressed this problem through a technology called the Subnet Bandwidth Manager (SBM).

SBM allows for one device on a shared segment (or a layer 2 switched segment) to act as a resource broker. The devices on the segment using an election protocol select this device, which could be a host, router, or layer 2 switch. The resource broker handles admission control on behalf of all devices on the shared segment, keeping track of the resources consumed on the segment from any reservations and determining when to accept additional reservations.

Using extensions to RSVP signaling, devices on the shared segment can request resources from the resource broker. The broker has a special MAC and IP address to which devices on the shared segment address their QoS requests (PATH messages, specifically). The broker creates and maintains state and inserts itself in the RSVP signaling path. When receivers send back RESV messages, the messages are intercepted by the broker.

Differentiated Services

The IETF began work on the Differentiated Services (DiffServ) model several years ago as a simpler alternative to IntServ. Many industry players and service providers were concerned about the flow-oriented nature of IntServ and RSVP's scaling capabilities. In addition, it was clear that IntServ could not address many legacy applications since it would be difficult, if not impossible, to modify these applications so they could indicate their QoS requirements. Similarly, some applications, such as the World Wide Web, generate short-term flows, which can't be effectively addressed by IntServ.

In the DiffServ model, a host or network device at the edge of the network classifies and marks packets. Routers and other layer 3 devices act on these markings to queue the packets appropriately and to provide access to reserved bandwidth. Unlike the traditionally flow-oriented IntServ model, DiffServ allows packets to be classified into a small number of aggregated flows. In addition, DiffServ operates on a hop-by-hop basis. Both of these characteristics are key to DiffServ's scalability.

In looking for a way to mark packets, the IETF turned to the Type of Service (ToS) field in IPv4 and the Traffic Class field in IPv6. The DiffServ Working Group renamed these 8-bit fields the Differentiated Services (DS) field, and currently uses the six most significant bits for DiffServ markings. The remaining two bits are for experimental use; there is interest within the IETF in using these two bits for explicit congestion notification.

In the DiffServ architecture, edge devices (hosts or routers) play a different role from devices in the interior of a DiffServ network (see Figure 13.3). Edge nodes perform traffic conditioning functions to ensure that traffic conforms to a service provisioning policy and to prepare it for proper handling by routers in the interior of the network. DiffServ allows for top-down provisioning so network managers can determine the amount of bandwidth or latency needed for a class of traffic, or the relative priority of classes of traffic, and configure their routers accordingly.

The DiffServ Working Group has defined some procedures for how a particular device should treat a packet with specific markings. These procedures, known as per-hop behaviors (PHBs), are based on specific values in the DS field, known as DiffServ Code Points (DSCPs). Packets entering a DiffServ network are marked with a DSCP, and routers or other layer 3 devices along the forwarding path select a per-hop behavior for a packet based on its DSCP.

As the name implies, a PHB is an individual behavior applied at each router.

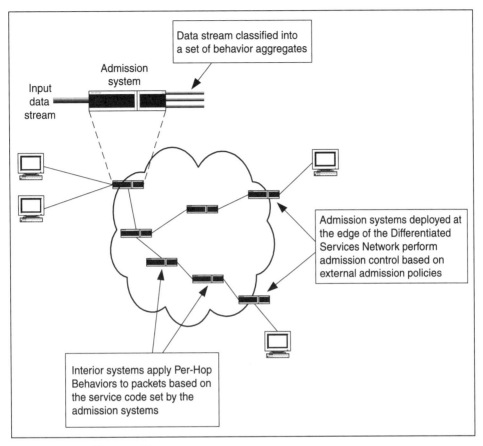

Figure 13.3 DiffServ architecture.

That is, a PHB defines how packets belonging to a particular traffic aggregate should be treated at an individual network node. PHBs can be specified in terms of their resource priority (that is, use of buffer space, bandwidth, and so on) relative to other PHBs, or in terms of their traffic characteristics (such as delay, loss, and so on). In principle, you can achieve end-to-end QoS by concatenating routers with the same PHBs. However, it may be necessary to use policy management and possibly signaling to coordinate all the parameters for the PHBs along the traffic path.

In a given network domain, there's a locally defined mapping between DSCP values and PHBs. The DiffServ Working Group has defined two standard PHBs at this time, called expedited forwarding (EF) and assured forwarding (AF), and others are being considered. Although the IETF has defined standard mapping between certain DSCPs and PHBs, network operators are free to choose other mappings. Clearly, there are no interoperability issues if these mappings are used within a given network or DiffServ domain. Interoperability issues that affect the end-to-end QoS could arise if traffic is handed off from one network or DiffServ domain to another and the respective network managers haven't agreed to honor the mappings in an equivalent fashion.

Traffic Conditioning

In the DiffServ architecture, edge nodes are responsible for traffic-conditioning functions such as classifying traffic, aggregating individual flows into macroflows, and shaping and dropping traffic to ensure that it conforms to some predefined behavior or traffic profile. Once the edge node has determined that traffic is conformant, it marks it appropriately and admits it to the DiffServ portion of the network.

Because these conditioning functions are handled at the edge of the network, devices in the interior of a DiffServ network have a relatively simple job. In general, devices in the interior of a DiffServ network simply look at the DSCP to determine the appropriate handling. However, devices in the core of the network may perform traffic shaping and dropping in order to keep aggregated traffic flows separated and in compliance with their profile.

The DiffServ architecture defines a number of traffic-conditioning elements, including classifiers, meters, markers, shapers, and droppers. A DiffServ classifier can classify traffic based solely on its DSCP or by using multiple fields within the IP header (source and destination address and port along with the protocol ID), as with RSVP. As its name implies, the meter monitors traffic based on its classification. In addition to checking to see whether the traffic conforms to its provisioned characteristics, the meter can also collect statistics on flows for accounting and billing purposes.

Markers are responsible for setting the values in the DS field so as to provide the correct PHB for a flow. A marker may also re-mark packets. Re-marking can come into play as traffic is handed off from an enterprise to a service provider or from one service provider to another. Re-marking can also be done to downgrade packets that are not adhering to their service profile.

Shapers and droppers perform actions on packets based on whether they conform to their traffic profile. For example, shapers can delay packets in a queue, or store bursts of packets and forward them at an acceptable rate. Droppers police traffic and can drop traffic that is not conformant.

The Roles of RSVP and DiffServ

Both IntServ/RSVP and DiffServ have roles to play in both LANs and WANs, and the general view in the industry is that these technologies are complementary. As a flow-oriented QoS scheme, IntServ/RSVP can be deployed at the campus level to support applications, such as IP telephony, that may need quantitative QoS or some (albeit loose) form of QoS guarantees. Although RSVP support has been available for some time in routers and in a few operating systems, there has been virtually no application-level support for it. Microsoft's delivery of Windows 2000 and a few RSVP-enabled applications has changed the situation, however.

Deployments of IP telephony to the desktop could also help drive the use of IntServ/RSVP, or other QoS mechanisms. In the case of applications such as voice and video that are latency- or bandwidth-sensitive, RSVP can play a key role in admission control. For example, if at a given point in time the network has the resources to accommodate 10 simultaneous IP telephony calls but can't handle an eleventh call, then RSVP can be used to deny the call. In this way, the user gets a busy signal or some other indication that the call can't go through, rather than having the call handled with what is likely to be an unacceptably low level of quality.

Many industry players see this type of admission control as the primary use for RSVP, both in LANs and at the WAN edge. One of RSVP's key strengths here is that it can provide feedback to applications as to whether their QoS requests can be granted. This feedback enables applications to take appropriate action, such as resubmitting their requests with a lower service level or waiting to try their requests later. RSVP also acts to coordinate QoS among disparate devices along the traffic path, allowing for a higher quality of service than would otherwise be possible.

In another scenario, hosts or edge routers may mark DSCPs or 802.1p values based on the results of RSVP signaling. This is a truly complementary use of the technologies. While RSVP provides admission control, DiffServ or 802.1p provides CoS handling for aggregate traffic flows. In this way, the overhead associated with per-flow QoS is avoided.

Microsoft, in particular, favors the use of RSVP signaling for admission control and policy enforcement and for providing classification information to a policy system. As we noted earlier, RSVP can carry policy information. When an RSVP message arrives at a policy enforcement point (specifically a router), the device can extract any policy elements from the message, along with the description of the requested service type and the traffic profile. The PEP/router would then pass the relevant information to the policy decision point for comparison with QoS/CoS policies set for that user or application. The policy decision point would return a thumbs up or down for the resource request, and could also provide the appropriate DSCP (or 802.1p value) for RSVP to carry back to the sender. Figure 13.4 illustrates this process.

Despite extensions to RSVP that allow it to work with aggregate flows, there is a consensus in the industry that IntServ/RSVP won't be used in the core of WANs. In general, service providers show little interest in the IntServ classes of service. However, they do demonstrate interest in using RSVP for

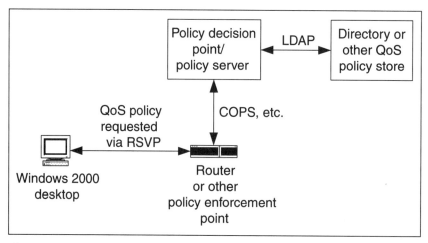

Figure 13.4 Use of RSVP for admission control.

admission control at the WAN edge, similar to its use in LANs. For example, a multimedia application could use RSVP to signal its QoS requirements to the service provider network. The router at the edge of the service provider's network would intercept the RSVP messages and mark packets with the appropriate DSCP for transmission across the DiffServ portion of the provider's network.

On the other hand, RSVP signaling could flow end to end across a WAN, simply being ignored by devices in the WAN core. For example, an edge router could pass along RSVP PATH messages, which routers in the interior of the network would ignore. However, the edge router on the egress of the network would pass the PATH message along to the enterprise network, where the router on the enterprise site could interpret it and pass it along to the appropriate receiver. Alternately, some devices within the WAN core may listen to RSVP in order to apply admission control at key points in the network.

Industry players generally agree that DiffServ is the preferred method of handling CoS for traffic in aggregate. In what many players see as a typical scenario, an enterprise customer would mark its traffic with an appropriate DSCP and then submit it to a service provider. The service provider would police the traffic on a per-customer, per-DSCP basis to verify that the traffic conforms to a predefined service level agreement (SLA).

Either the enterprise customer or the service provider might shape the traffic to ensure that it conforms to the SLA. Likewise, either the enterprise customer's egress router or the service provider's ingress router could provide admission control and any mappings from IntServ to the corresponding DiffServ service levels.

Summary

Many mission-critical applications cannot reliably run on today's networks if only best-effort forwarding of traffic is used. Some means of classifying traffic and then forwarding classes of traffic in a preferred, or differentiated, manner is required.

Two main methods have been proposed for QoS on IP networks: Integrated Services (IntServ) and Differentiated Services (DiffServ). IntServ relies on explicit signaling for requesting network resources. The primary setup mechanism for IntServ is RSVP. On the other hand, DiffServ allows packets to be classified to a small number of aggregated flows, and processes marked packets on a hop-by-hop basis. In the rest of this book, when we refer to signaled QoS, we mean IntServ/RSVP. Similarly, when we refer to provisioned QoS, we mean DiffServ.

In the next chapter, we continue our discussion of QoS by illustrating how policy-based networking can be used to control QoS.

Policies for Quality of Service

While QoS holds a great deal of promise for controlling congestion and providing improved network support for mission-critical applications, the administration of QoS can be particularly troublesome and tedious and may, in fact, delay the deployment of QoS on some networks. In the real world, the ease of managing the myriad QoS techniques will determine whether QoS succeeds or fails to meet enterprise business requirements.

The default mode for QoS administration is to separately configure each switch or router in the network using telnet, FTP, or Web-based terminal interfaces. This may be practical for small networks that need multiple service quality levels or larger networks that don't require QoS. But when it comes to administering QoS for large numbers of routers or switches, this approach falls short. With the advent of QoS features, the interaction of multiple network components cannot easily be controlled by configuring, or looking at, individual nodes. Ideally the network must be managed as a system, which leads to policy-based networking.

As vendors deliver on the promise of QoS capabilities in their switches and routers, their customers then have to figure out how to make use of this technology. In many cases, configuring the network to deliver the appropriate QoS would seem to require "rocket scientists", that is, highly skilled and trained network analysts. There are many QoS algorithms and techniques—prioritization, queuing, bandwidth management, rate control, and so on—that must be understood and their interaction may be unpredictable. It is also hard to relate these algorithms to the service experienced by the end users of the network.

Control of service quality and setting the correct policies may be a challenge for IP networks. There are many different configuration parameters to play with, each of which may change only a single network component, but which may affect the total end-to-end performance experience by many users. The problem is that there are generally no network-wide mechanisms in place to control network performance. Furthermore, there is the risk that if QoS parameters are incorrectly set, the resulting inconsistent switch and router configurations can cause the network to fail.

This is where policy-based networking can prove its value. First, a policy-based networking system can shield the network manager from having to know all the parameters for all the possible algorithms employed on the network's devices. Instead, he or she can create high-level policies for QoS and let the policy-based networking system take care of the translations to device-dependent configurations.

Second, the policy-based networking system can ensure consistent deployment of policies across the network. No longer do network managers need to worry if they've properly configured the same capabilities with the same parameter values in identical (or similar) enforcement devices on their networks.

Now let's investigate how policies can be applied to the two main frameworks for QoS, IntServ and DiffServ. Then we'll also take a look at another system in which both frameworks are used together to provide end-to-end QoS.

Policies for Signaled Quality of Service

As we pointed out in Chapter 13, "An Introduction to Quality of Service," the IntServ/RSVP framework defines a set of QoS mechanisms and how applications can communicate their QoS requirements to network devices. This approach is often called signaled QoS because the applications explicitly signal their requirements to the devices on the network.

Let's briefly review how an application interacts with network devices using RSVP before we discuss how policies can be applied to RSVP.

To start the process of reserving network resources, the originator of the session uses RSVP to send a PATH message toward the destination of the session (see Figure 14.1). Each intermediate RSVP-capable router along the delivery path intercepts the PATH message and checks it for validity. If an error is detected, the router will drop the PATH message and send a PATHERR message to inform the sender so it can take appropriate actions.

For a valid PATH message, the router will update the path state entry for the source. The router is also responsible for generating PATH messages based on

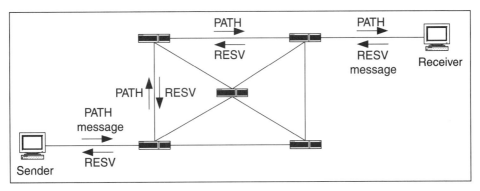

Figure 14.1   Sample RSVP setup.

the stored path state and forwarding them down the routing path until the PATH messages arrive at the intended destination for the session.

Upon receipt of the PATH message, the RSVP receiver then sends RESV messages back upstream to the sender along the same hop-by-hop path the PATH messages traversed from the sender.

A host uses RSVP to request a specific QoS from the network for a particular data stream from a data source. An elementary RSVP reservation request consists of a specification for an end-to-end desired QoS (e.g., peak/average bandwidth and delay bounds) and a definition of the set of data packets to receive the QoS.

RSVP defines a number of objects carried in its messages. Most of these objects are directly useful to RSVP-specific processing or traffic control. Some of the information in RSVP messages, such as the Session, FlowSpec, and FilterSpec, is useful for policy control in determining where a data flow is going, where it came from, and how much of the resources it is attempting to reserve. This information is contained in the appropriate objects in the RSVP message. (See Durham and Yavaktar, *Inside the Internet's Resource reSerVation Protocol*, Wiley, 1999, for more details.)

An elementary RSVP reservation request consists of a FlowSpec together with a FilterSpec; this pair is called a *flow descriptor*. The FlowSpec specifies a desired QoS. The FilterSpec, together with a session specification, defines the set of data packets—the flow—to receive the QoS defined by the FlowSpec. The FlowSpec is used to set parameters in the node's packet scheduler or other link layer mechanism, while the FilterSpec is used to set parameters in the packet classifier. Data packets that are addressed to a particular session but do not match any of the FilterSpecs for that session are handled as best-effort traffic.

The FlowSpec in a reservation request will generally include a service class and two sets of numeric parameters: (1) an Rspec (R for reserve) that defines the desired QoS and (2) a Tspec (T for traffic) that describes the data flow.

During reservation setup, an RSVP request is passed to two local decision modules, admission control and policy control. Admission control determines whether the node has sufficient available resources to supply the requested QoS. Policy control determines whether the user has administrative permission to make the reservation.

Policy control may require more information than that provided by the basic RSVP objects, so the IETF defined the RSVP Policy Data object specifically for carrying policy information. Policy data may include credentials identifying users or user classes, account numbers, limits, quotas, and so on. Like a FlowSpec, policy data is opaque to RSVP and RSVP simply passes it to policy control when required.

A single policy data object can encapsulate a number of policy attributes called policy elements, as well as a list of RSVP-defined objects. The policy elements can carry pieces of policy information. Such information can theoretically include authenticated username information, credit card information, administratively assigned tokens, or other information useful for securely identifying the credentials of an RSVP message.

Local versus Outsourced Policies

It should be obvious that RSVP events, such as those we just described, require some sort of a policy decision. For instance, someone or something has to allocate resources, deciding whether, and to what extent, resources can be allocated to an RSVP flow. And this must be done at each device along the path between sender and receiver.

The decision-making process for RSVP can actually take place in two different locations, the PEP and the PDP (see Figure 14.2). In normal practice, a network device would receive an ACL (access control list) as part of its initial configuration upon booting, and it would apply the ACL to any incoming traffic. But it's highly unlikely that the local policies defined in the device's ACL will cover all possible situations that the device will encounter. Network traffic patterns, QoS requests, and resource availability all change over time.

If the enforcement device cannot use local policies to process incoming RSVP events, it then has to request a decision from its PDP.

Under the best of circumstances, the PDP will already contain the policies it requires to forward a decision to the PEP processing the RSVP event. (Many vendors cache most, if not all, policies on the PDP to cover these situations.) If the PDP does not have the appropriate policies, it will have to request the policies from the policy repository, further adding to the latency of processing the RSVP event.

The involvement of the PDP in this process also points out how two-tier and three-tier architectures differ in their response to an RSVP event (see

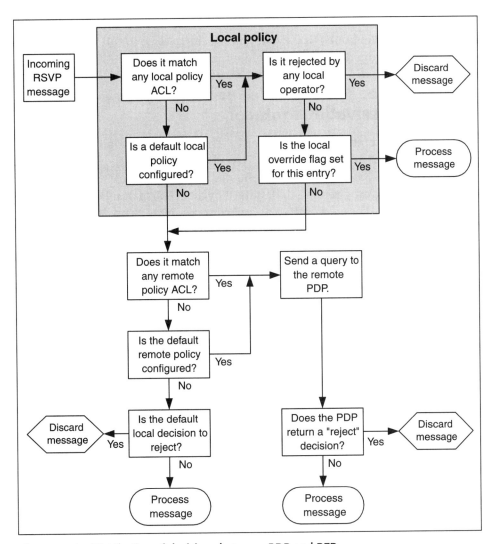

Figure 14.2   Distribution of decisions between PDP and PEP.

Chapter 4, "Architectures for Policy-Based Networking"). In a two-tier system, each RSVP enforcement point stands alone and may have to request policies directly from a policy repository when local policies are insufficient. However, by using a PDP to control multiple PEPs in a three-tiered architecture, we can gain some efficiency in processing RSVP events. The reason is that, if the PDP has to request policies from the repository to process an RSVP event for one PEP, it can then push related decisions to other PEPs along the path so they will have new local policies and will be prepared to process incoming RSVP events. In other words, the PDP can configure other PEPs in anticipation of an incoming RSVP event once that event hits the first PEP, without requesting further policies from the repository, reducing the decision-making latency.

Common Open Policy Service and Resource Reservation Protocol

We've already covered COPS in Chapter 7, "The Policy Decision Point," so we'll only recap some of its salient features here.

Recall that COPS is based on a stateful model where requests from a PEP are remembered by the remote PDP until they are explicitly deleted by the PEP. This model allows the PDP to asynchronously change its decisions while a request remains valid. For example, suppose that a message arrives at a PEP that requires a policy decision. The PEP will issue a COPS Request message to the PDP. The PDP will then process the request and return a COPS Decision message specifying what action the PEP should take. The PEP will then execute its PDP's decision, and proceed normally. After some time, the PDP can issue an unsolicited Decision message for the original PEP Request, modifying its decision (say, moving from an accept decision to a reject decision). The PEP will then use the newly dictated action.

COPS distinguishes between four different types of requests. Requests can be specific to admission control, resource allocation, forwarding events triggered on a network device, or device configuration. An admission control request asks the remote PDP what to do with an incoming message received by the PEP that requires an admission control decision. The resource allocation request queries whether local resources are to be committed locally on the device and how they should be committed when necessary. Third, the forwarding request determines if and how a signaled message is to be forwarded out of the device. Finally, COPS also provides a configuration request that allows a PEP to be configured by its PDP upon request.

Since RSVP is a signaling protocol, network devices can use COPS to outsource RSVP requests to a PDP. When a PEP receives an RSVP message, it should notify the PDP via a COPS Request message (see Figure 14.3). The type of request depends on whether the message just arrived, is about to allocate resources from the device, or is being forwarded out of the device. The PDP uses COPS to return the appropriate decision corresponding to the request. The decision may instruct the PEP to accept or reject an arriving RSVP message, allocate resources for a reservation request, or either forward or drop an outgoing message, depending on the request.

The Request message includes the context in which the request is being generated. This may be an admission control request, a resource allocation request, or a request for configuration data to be downloaded to the PEP. The request also holds the client-specific information for which a decision is being

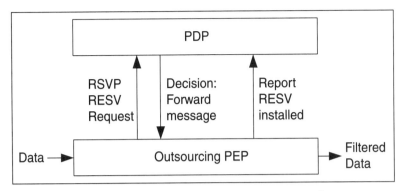

Figure 14.3 RSVP-triggered interactions between PDP and PEP.

requested. In the case of COPS support for RSVP, the Client-Specific Information (ClientSI) field of the COPS message includes all the objects in the received RSVP message, including all policy control extensions to RSVP. For each policy event that triggers a REQ message, the PEP must include all the RSVP objects in the RSVP message (incoming or outgoing) in the encapsulated ClientSI.

As RSVP messages received by a PEP result in either path or reservation states, COPS requests are maintained with respect to these states. Due to this stateful model, the PEP does not have to continuously re-request RSVP refresh messages from the PDP via COPS. Rather, the initial request is retained, and a new request is issued only when a new or updated RSVP message is received. When a path or reservation state is finally removed from the device due to a timeout situation or RSVP Tear message, a COPS Delete message is sent to the PDP notifying it of the state's removal.

COPS can return more than just a simple yes or no decision to a PEP's request. COPS can also specify that specific information be replaced in a signaled message. In the case of RSVP, for example, the PDP can use COPS to command the PEP to replace the policy data object in a forwarded RESV message. This mechanism allows PDPs to insert information into the RSVP messages and communicate with other policy servers.

One example of policy data replacement is user authentication. A border router along an ISP may receive reservations for a shared multicast session from multiple hosts within its administrative domain. These reservations may carry policy data objects with user authentication information. The border router is responsible for authenticating each of the reservations and then merging them before sending them to the peer router. The peer router may require reservations to carry a token or certificate that proves the ISP will pay for the high QoS. In this example, a PDP authenticates a user's reservation using the incoming policy data information and then produces a certificate policy data for the forwarded reservation. COPS simply specifies that the incoming policy data needs to be replaced with the new policy data before the RSVP message is forwarded across the administrative boundary (see Figure 14.4). The policy data object is simply carried opaquely by RSVP messages and is interpreted only by PDPs.

This in-band policy data mechanism offers significant benefits for policy processing as it guarantees delivery of the information along the data path, fully synchronized with the RSVP messages in which it is embedded. It is important to note that Policy Data is an RSVP (non-COPS) mechanism. Without COPS (assuming RSVP nodes include both PEP and PDP internally), it provides communications between RSVP nodes; however, when COPS is added, the policy data mechanism allows PDP-to-PDP communications.

Sample COPS/RSVP Scenario

As an example of a typical RSVP PEP and PDP exchange, consider the arrival of a unicast PATH message at a PEP, as illustrated in Figure 14.5. When the PEP receives the PATH message, it will first check whether a local policy (part of its existing ACL) can handle the request. If not, the PEP issues a COPS

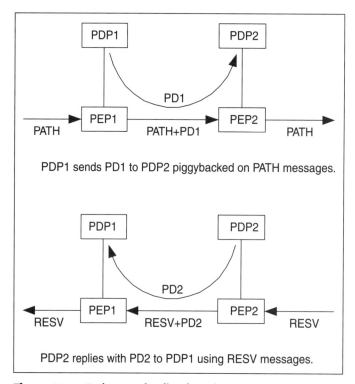

Figure 14.4 Exchange of policy data via RSVP.

Request to the PDP asking if the message can be admitted and forwarded toward its destination. Assuming the PATH is allowed, the PDP will return a positive decision to the PEP that will then set up a path state and forward the message downstream.

Next, suppose that an RESV message eventually arrives for this path state, as shown in Figure 14.5. Again the PEP will issue a request to the policy server asking whether the RESV can be admitted, whether resources should be allocated for the RESV, and whether it should forward the message on to the previous hop. Assuming the PDP responds positively, the PEP will accept the reservation and install a corresponding reservation state, reporting to the PDP whether the reservation passed capacity admission control.

Since COPS follows a stateful model, PDPs can update their decisions at any time. In this example, after some time the PDP may change its decision about the RESV from accept to reject. In this case, the PDP would send an unsolicited decision to the PEP specifying that the RESV is to be rejected. The PEP will then issue an RESV Error to the downstream hop, remove its reservation state, and, finally, send a Delete message to the PDP for the removed request.

One model of the IntServ architecture has the RSVP RESV message treated identically by all the nodes along the path from the receiver to the sender. Within this model there is no particular delineation between those RSVP nodes that lie in the interior of a network and those that lie on a boundary between one network and another. This particular model scales poorly since all routers must maintain state on each RSVP session.

It is more efficient to set policies so that the majority of the admission control is performed solely by the devices on the edge of the network, leaving the interior nodes to focus only on resource availability. If an RSVP request is passed to an interior node, then the node can assume that the policies of the network and the RSVP request are in alignment, and the network is willing to accept the request. In this case, the decision process used by the interior node is one of

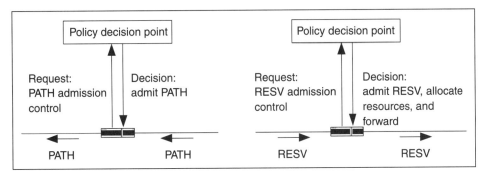

Figure 14.5 Example of PEP and PDP exchanges.

resource availability. If there are sufficient available resources to accommodate the reservation request, then the request is honored and the RESV message is passed one hop upstream to the neighboring node. But this requires that the decision-making framework on the network boundary be more involved, as the node has to compare the details of the RSVP request with the prevailing network admission policy in order to make a decision as to whether to admit the RSVP request at all.

COPS is seen as assisting the network admission points in making consistent admission decisions regarding RSVP requests. The emerging provisioning model for IntServ networks using COPS is for the RSVP request itself to provide all the information describing the request, both in terms of the details of the resource requirements and in terms of the identity of the requestor and the policy associations that may be attached to the request. The decision process then becomes one of matching the network's current state and policies to the information provided in the RSVP request.

RSVP and Other Policy Distribution Protocols

There's a good working synergy between RSVP and COPS, partly because many of the designers of RSVP have also been involved in the development of COPS. But COPS is not the only protocol that can be used by a PEP to request decisions for RSVP events.

For instance, a PEP can use LDAP to request policies directly from a policy repository for translation into decisions in response to an RSVP event. (More specifically, the device would probably be a colocated PDP-PEP in a two-tiered architecture.) The main point is that the PEP requires a protocol that supports queries back to either a repository or decision-making device. LDAP supports such query capabilities, but it does not include definitions of RSVP objects similar to those found in COPS. It's also possible to use CORBA to exchange policies for signaled QoS, using CORBA-capable device drivers on the network devices. In either case, these solutions are vendor-specific, since the protocols are not specifically designed to handle RSVP events and messages and code must be added to handle these exchanges in a manner similar to the way COPS works.

Policies for Provisioned Quality of Service

Unlike IntServ and RSVP, the DiffServ architecture depends on implicit, rather than explicit, signaling to provide QoS. This means that the information needed to process a packet is contained within the packet rather than transmitted in separate control packets, as with RSVP. This information is encoded within the Differentiated Services (DS) field of the IP header.

As we pointed out in the previous chapter, edge devices play a different role from devices in the interior of a DiffServ network. Edge devices perform traffic-conditioning functions to ensure that traffic conforms to a service provisioning policy and to prepare it for proper handling by the routers in the interior of the network. DiffServ allows for top-down provisioning so network managers can determine the amount of bandwidth or latency needed for a class of traffic, or the relative priority of classes of traffic, and configure their routers accordingly.

DiffServ also defines some procedures for how a particular device should treat a packet with specific markings. These procedures, known as per-hop behaviors (PHBs), are based on specific values in the DS field, known as Diff-Serv Code Points (DSCPs). Packets entering a DiffServ network are marked with a DSCP, and routers or other layer 3 devices along the forwarding path select a per-hop behavior for a packet based on its DSCP.

Per-hop behavior (PHB) groups define how routers deal with traffic of a given class of service. The actual forwarding behavior is controlled by the QoS mechanisms that control the queuing and dropping of packets on each router, and thus are specific to particular device manufacturers and types. However, as far as possible, the definition of PHB groups is generic. PHBs are usually divided into two groups, access PHB groups and core PHB groups. The purpose of an access PHB group is to manage the traffic going into the core network from an access router at the edge of the network. Access PHBs can provide more low-level control over queuing mechanisms. On the other hand, the purpose of a core PHB group is to maintain the prioritization of traffic, as set at the edge of the network, throughout the core network. For more details, see Geoff Huston, *Internet Performance Survival Guide: QoS Strategies for Multiservice Networks* (Wiley, 2000).

In order to process traffic, the network devices forming the DiffServ network need to know ahead of time how they're to process packets with specific DSCPs. That means that the network must be configured or provisioned beforehand in a top-down manner, which is why this approach is often called provisioned QoS.

When it comes to using DiffServ, the routers can fulfill various roles according to their location in a network. For instance, an edge router can mark traffic with no traffic management or it can mark and manage traffic. Similarly, a router may apply a bandwidth limit to the traffic on an access interface, or apply a guaranteed bandwidth to manage the traffic on the outbound interface of an access router. Some devices can perform all these functions, marking packets as well as applying a bandwidth guarantee and limit. Third, network devices can apply access rules, identifying packets by various criteria and then either denying access or explicitly permitting the traffic to proceed. Last, an interior (or core) router can use transmission rules, allowing packets that have been previously marked with a code point to be policed by their class of service. Transmission rules define the permitted bandwidth limits, including burst rate and packet destination.

Setting Policies

Just as the functions of a network device can differ according to its location in a DiffServ network, so too can its policies differ. A network manager can use a policy-based networking system to set policies for traffic classification, access, and transmission (dropping as well as re-marking packets) and see that those policies are distributed to the proper devices in the network (see Figure 14.6).

The DiffServ architecture defines a number of traffic-conditioning elements, including classifiers, meters, markers, shapers, and droppers. A DiffServ classifier can classify traffic based solely on its DSCP or by using multiple fields within the IP header (source and destination address and port along with the protocol ID), as with RSVP. As its name implies, the meter monitors traffic based on its classification. In addition to checking to see whether the traffic conforms to its provisioned characteristics, the meter can also collect statistics on flows for accounting and billing purposes.

If an edge router is also supposed to manage traffic, then added policies would be defined identifying which queuing mechanism and/or traffic-shaping algorithms would be used for traffic in a particular class of service, that is, with a specific packet marking.

If access policies are implemented, packets are identified by various criteria and then either denied access or explicitly permitted to proceed. Usually, when access policies are applied to an interface at the same time as classification policies, the access policies take effect first.

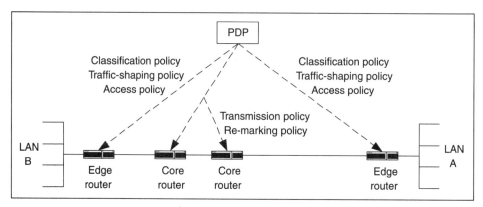

Figure 14.6   Policy distribution for provisioned QoS.

Transmission policies allow packets that have been previously marked with a DCSP to be policed by their class of service. Transmission policies define the permitted bandwidth limits, including burst rate, and optionally the packet destination. Policing PHB groups defines the action to be taken if specific network traffic conforms to or exceeds the agreed bandwidth, for example, permitting conforming traffic to proceed and dropping or re-marking nonconforming packets with a new DSCP.

Policy Distribution for DiffServ

While COPS seems a good fit for policy distribution for signaled QoS, there is no one protocol that's ideally suited for distributing policies for provisioned QoS. The leading candidates are COPS-PR (i.e., COPS with extensions for provisioning) and SNMP. It's also possible to use telnet/CLI and CORBA to provision policies; although we won't cover them in this chapter; the process of provisioning using CLI and CORBA is similar to that using SNMP.

COPS

Although COPS was originally designed with RSVP in mind, extensions have also been written that enable COPS to work with provisioned systems, such as DiffServ (see Chapter 7).

Unlike COPS for RSVP, COPS-PR is not designed to push decisions to a PEP upon request. Instead, a PDP using COPS-PR sends policy-based decisions to a PEP when the PEP first connects to the PDP (usually when starting or rebooting) and any time after that, as long as the PEP and PDP are communicating (see Figure 14.7). Thus, policy changes higher in the policy-based networking system trigger the distribution of updated admission criteria or other policies (packet marking, transmission policies, etc.) across all appropriate PEPs.

If the configuration of the device changes—a board is removed, a new board is added, or new software is installed, for example—in ways not covered by policies already known to the PEP, then the PEP sends this unsolicited new information to the PDP. On receiving this new information, the PDP sends to the PEP any additional provisioned policies now needed by the PEP.

In order to facilitate the transmission of decisions to a PEP using COPS-PR, a PEP uses a PIB (Policy Information Base) to define its capabilities to the controlling PDP. (We described the PIB in Chapter 7.) Just like COPS for RSVP, a PDP and PEP pair using COPS-PR maintain state. A PDP-PEP pair using COPS or COPS-PR also locks out any changes in configuration from other controllers, such as a telnet/CLI session or an SNMP management tool, during the length of the connection between the two devices.

The provisioning model for COPS-PR makes no assumptions of a direct one-to-one correlation between PEP events and PDP decisions. The PDP may

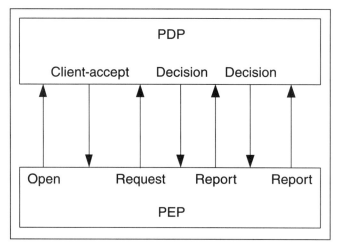

Figure 14.7 COPS command flow in provisioning.

proactively provision the PEP to react to external events (such as user input), PEP events, and any combination of these different types of events. If conditions change so that the PDP determines that changes are required in the currently provisioned policies, then the PDP sends the changes in policy to the PEP, and the PEP updates its local QoS mechanisms appropriately.

SNMP

SNMP is dominant in the areas of network status monitoring and statistics gathering. It has not been as widely used for configuration management as telnet/CLI, however. Despite SNMP's relative lack of use as a configuration protocol, proponents of SNMP have suggested that SNMP could be extended to fill many of the roles required by policy-based networking systems, including policy distribution. SNMPv3 lacks some of the features needed to fulfill these roles, such as resource locking and the use of stateful sessions for device management, but the SNMPCONF WG is working on extending some of SNMPv3's features to support policy-based networking.

When used for configuration management, SNMP deals primarily with device-local configurations. However, the IETF's SNMPCONF Working Group has defined a policy-based MIB module and technology-specific policy MIB modules that can fulfill many of the requirements of a policy-based networking system, at least for provisioning. The policy-based MIB module would be embedded in the network device and would act as a middle-level manager to assist in the configuration of specific policy MIB modules. Each technology-specific policy MIB would register with the Policy Module, informing the main module of its capabilities. The Policy Module, in turn, can then provide information to the management application of the device's capabilities (see Figure 14.8).

The Policy Module helps translate from one level of abstraction to another. It helps move from the mechanism-independent to the mechanism-dependent and helps move from the instance-independent to the instance-dependent level of abstraction.

The Policy MIB Module contains standard MIB tables that managers can populate, which tell the managed system the following:

- What policy filters to apply in order to select the instances to which a specific policy (action) should be applied

- When and how long the policy should remain in effect; for example, every Monday to Friday from 9 A.M. to 5 P.M.

- If and how to apply mechanism-specific parameters such as DiffServ

- If and how to apply instance- and implementation-independent parameters as needed to the instances that are appropriate to the local system

The mechanism-specific parameters are found in the mechanism-specific MIB modules such as the Differentiated Services Policy MIB Module (DiffServ Policy MIB).

The Policy MIB Module also provides important information to the management system. This information includes the current state of the policy and global utilization information about the resources used by a particular policy.

The DiffServ architecture defines a MIB module that operates on a device level. The DiffServ Policy MIB Module creates a coherent policy configuration

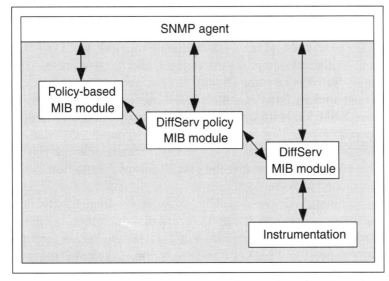

Figure 14.8 Architecture for policy-enabled SNMP-based configuration.

management view (domain-specific) as an umbrella over this mechanism-specific MIB.

Bandwidth Brokers

As service providers deploy QoS, especially using DiffServ, they will encounter another reason for using policy-based networking: the bandwidth broker. As we pointed out in Chapter 13, the primary goal of the DiffServ architecture is controlled sharing of bandwidth and router resources. As part of this goal, policies must be distributed to edge devices to perform admission control, traffic shaping, and other QoS-related functions. In the DiffServ architecture, the policy decision point is often called a bandwidth broker.

The bandwidth broker can configure devices with organizational policies as well as monitor available bandwidth, interpret service-level requests from clients, and keep track of the current allocation of marked traffic. Even more significantly, a bandwidth broker can communicate with bandwidth brokers in other DiffServ domains (another ISP, for example) to ensure the viability of end-to-end traffic agreements.

Consider the operation of the bandwidth brokers in Figure 14.9. As an illustration, the router can inform the bandwidth broker of available bandwidth for each of its links and can further specify some percentage of bandwidth available for premium (EF) service. The router can also support multiple different classes of service, each with an associated DSCP marker. The router can specify support of a traffic rate (packets per second) for each service. When a client wants to make a connection, it specifies a peak and perhaps a burst traffic rate and/or a delay tolerance and a time period (9:00 A.M. to 5:00 P.M., for example) for the connection. The edge device constructs a policy request and forwards the request to the bandwidth broker. The bandwidth broker examines the destination address and validates the user profile to ensure that the user is privileged to make the request, and the resources remain on the connection. If everything checks, the bandwidth broker sends a confirmation to the client with the specified DSCP marker to apply to the packets for the flow. The bandwidth broker then recalculates available bandwidth and queue depths for the QoS queue and uses the updated information for subsequent client requests. Additionally, at 5:00 A.M., the bandwidth broker can proactively inform the router that the DSCP marker for the flow is no longer active.

In the event the connection traverses DSCP domains, the local bandwidth broker informs the adjacent region's bandwidth broker, which then recalculates available bandwidth and network resources and configures the remote edge device with the appropriate packet flow information. Typically, the process entails a secure association between the bandwidth broker peers.

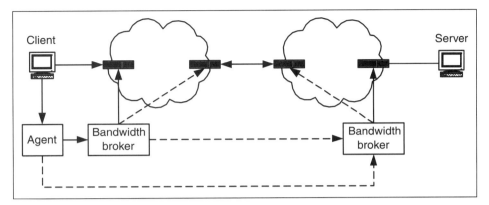

Figure 14.9   Communication between agents and bandwidth brokers.

Of course, this presumes that some bilateral agreement exists between the two DSCP domains.

Combining Signaled and Provisioned Quality of Service

While both IntServ and DiffServ have their strengths, neither approach offers comprehensive and robust solutions for supporting QoS on a multiservice network. The IntServ model, while providing a very high level of assurance of per-flow resource management, has significant scaling issues. The DiffServ model, on the other hand, scales well, but has a weak approach to resource management since network managers must anticipate traffic needs and provision bandwidth and other network resources ahead of time. Some Internet engineers have proposed combining the two models to provide end-to-end QoS.

In the case of applications such as voice and video that are latency- or bandwidth-sensitive, RSVP can play a key role in admission control. For example, if at a given point in time the network has the resources to accommodate 10 simultaneous IP telephony calls but can't handle an eleventh call, then RSVP can be used to deny the call. In this way, the user gets a busy signal or some other indication that the call can't go through, rather than having the call handled with what is likely to be an unacceptably low level of quality.

Many industry players see this type of admission control as the primary use for RSVP, both in LANs and at the WAN edge. One of RSVP's key strengths here is that it can provide feedback to applications as to whether their QoS requests can be granted. This feedback enables applications to take appropriate action, such as resubmitting their requests with a lower service level or waiting to try their requests later. RSVP also acts to coordinate QoS among disparate devices along the traffic path, allowing for a higher quality of service than would otherwise be possible.

In another scenario, hosts or edge routers may mark DSCPs or 802.1p values based on the results of RSVP signaling. This is a truly complementary use of the technologies. While RSVP provides admission control, DiffServ or 802.1p provide CoS handling for aggregate traffic flows. In this way, the overhead associated with per-flow QoS is avoided.

As we noted earlier, RSVP can carry policy information. When an RSVP message arrives at a policy enforcement point, the device can extract any policy elements from the message, along with the description of the requested service type and the traffic profile. The PEP/router would then pass the relevant information to the PDP for comparison with QoS/CoS policies set for that user or application. The PDP would return a thumbs up or down for the resource request, and could also provide the appropriate DSCP (or 802.1p value) for RSVP to carry back to the sender (see Figure 14.10).

There's also interest in using RSVP for admission control at the WAN edge, similar to its use in LANs. For example, a multimedia application could use RSVP to signal its QoS requirements to the service provider network. The router at the edge of the service provider's network would intercept the RSVP messages and mark packets with the appropriate DSCP for transmission across the DiffServ portion of the provider's network.

Managing Combined Services with PBN

The situation that we just described seems rife with difficulties, especially for the network manager. After all, he or she has to face the task of configuring all of the participating devices—subnet bandwidth managers, admission control devices (switches and routers), as well as core routers—to map traffic classifi-

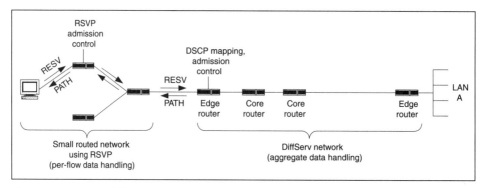

Figure 14.10 Providing QoS using RSVP and DiffServ.

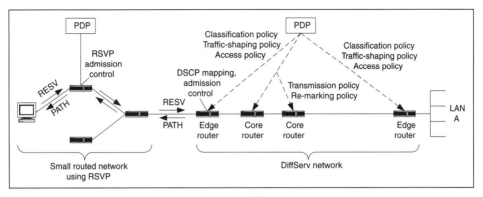

Figure 14.11 Policies for a combined RSVP-DiffServ network.

cations, allocate bandwidth, and control access. On any decent-sized network, this seems like an insurmountable task, if done manually.

Policy-based networking can be the glue that ties all this work and different QoS models together, however. Based on our discussions of policies for signaled and provisioned QoS in this chapter, it shouldn't be too hard to see how a policy-based networking system can combine the tasks of configuring RSVP and DiffServ devices. The policy-based networking system simply needs to know the role of each device—for instance, admission control, traffic classifier, or core router—to distribute the proper policies based on the high-level policies that the network manager creates for each domain.

Figure 14.11 sums this up by illustrating how these policies might be distributed to different entities in this combined network.

Summary

Now that you've finished this chapter, you should have a better idea of how policies interact with the two main models for providing QoS, the IntServ model and the DiffServ model. In the IntServ model using RSVP, the PEP proactively seeks decisions from the PDP in response to incoming RSVP messages. COPS was originally designed to support the PEP-PDP communications for RSVP traffic. On the other hand, in the DiffServ model, policy-based decisions are pushed downward to the PEPs in response to the creation of higher-level policies, prior to receipt of traffic requiring QoS treatment.

Both IntServ and DiffServ have some shortcomings when it comes to providing end-to-end QoS. It's possible to combine both RSVP and DiffServ on a network to improve the support of end-to-end QoS, as we've shown in this chapter, but this combination makes it even more important to deploy policy-based networking. Without policy-based networking, the configuration of devices in this scenario would be an overwhelmingly complicated and time-consuming task. By assigning roles to specific devices, such as traffic classifier, access control, and core DiffServ router, a network manager can use a policy-based networking system to distribute the proper configurations to each of the devices required to support QoS.

In the next chapter, we'll take a look at another application of policy-based networking, that of network security.

Policies for
Network Security

Admittedly, we've spent a lot of time discussing how policy-based networking can be used for one major service, QoS. There are two reasons for this emphasis. First, there's a major interest among vendors and users alike to use QoS on IP networks, and policy-based networking is perceived as essential to the success of QoS, since QoS can be very complicated to configure. Second, there has been more work on creating standards for the use of policy-based networking with QoS than for any other application of policy-based networking. But there's another very important application of policy-based networking, one that many organizations rate as highly as QoS, and that's security.

The word *policy* has long been associated with security. Organizations usually have an official "security policy," although this relates to how information is protected and used and isn't necessarily a list of conditions and actions such as those stored in a policy-based networking system. This type of security policy is centralized inasmuch as it's determined by management. But enforcement of the policy may not be applied consistently, since security managers often have to apply security policies to devices on a one-by-one basis, rather than distributing the appropriate policies to all devices from a central data store. That's where policy-based networking can be helpful, since it makes it easier to relate the configuration of devices to management's security policy and promotes consistent application of policies to all affected devices from a central data store.

This chapter discusses how policy-based networking can be applied to security. Before we discuss how security policies can be applied to various devices to enforce security, we'll describe the components of a security framework that should form the basis of any organization's security policy. When we discuss the application of security policies using policy-based networking, we'll focus on two major areas of security: access control and virtual private networks.

The Security Framework

Much of security enforcement evolves around the concepts of trusted and untrusted regions. The general idea is to allow communications between trusted regions and to block, or at least control, communications from an untrusted region. A framework that's applicable to securing trusted regions consists of five components:

- Perimeter security
- Access control
- Network services
- Content management
- Policy enforcement

Each component is interconnected via network media and services, as shown in Figure 15.1, resulting in a trusted network at a given site. In order to connect multiple trusted networks securely across an unsecured medium, such as the public Internet, organizations are likely to turn to a virtual private network (VPN), which we discuss later in this chapter. First, let's look at each of the components of this security framework.

Perimeter security prevents attackers from gaining access to data center systems, is most often related to physical security, and includes such seemingly mundane items as door locks, ID badges, secure wiring closets, and fire protection.

Access control focuses on the logical and physical separation between trusted and untrusted networks and services. This component usually consists of firewalls, address translation, authentication services, and circuit-control devices.

The *network services* component consists of the application services provided on the network, including the Web and other intranet-related applications, DNS, e-mail and news, and FTP. These services may be provided from a number of locations with different restrictions according to the people they're meant to serve. For instance, an organization might have internal FTP servers

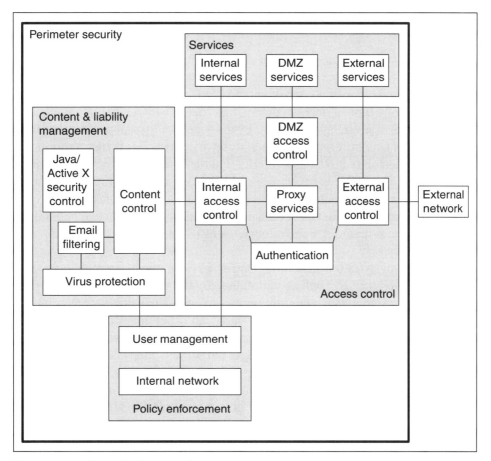

Figure 15.1   A security framework.

for the use of its employees, but also maintain a public FTP server in a demilitarized zone (DMZ) for the exchange of files between the public and the organization.

Content management ensures data and network integrity. This component usually includes virus scanning, for instance.

The *policy enforcement* component consists of the internal usage guidelines for the Internet, intranet, and extranets and their enforcement via user management and logging utilities.

While all of these components are essential for maintaining the security of your organization's network and information, we'll focus on the component that has been impacted the most by policy-based networking, access control. Then we'll discuss how policy-based networking is applied to virtual private networks, which provide the links between sites.

Access Control

We already touched on the subject of access control in Chapter 14, "Policies for Quality of Service." In that chapter, a policy-based networking system configured routers with access control lists (ACLs) to control admission to a network. This is one type of access control, one that can be further supplemented by other forms of access control, usually associated with a network operating system (NOS). One difference between the two approaches is that a router enforces admission control based on the IP address of the source or destination, while a NOS enforces access control based on an authenticated user's ID. Furthermore, a router controls access to a network or a subnet, which can consist of a number of hosts, servers, and other network devices, while the NOS can be more granular, controlling a user's access to specific servers, printers, and so on.

In many cases, NOS-based access control services won't actually be a part of a policy repository, but will be maintained by the resources themselves. File services, for example, may maintain their own access control, determining who can read, write, delete, append, or carry out other operations on files and folders, while a database service may maintain its own separate access control, determining who can query or update databases, tables, indexes, fields, or records.

In most systems, access control is maintained via access control lists, or ACLs, which are lists of users and their access rights. A file service ACL, for example, contains the lists of users and what each user is allowed to do within the file service. ACLs often contain lists of lists. A user group list, for example, can usually be put in a service ACL, thereby granting a common set of rights to all member users of the group and saving the administrator from having to physically enter the name of each user.

In the past, these types of access control policies were often set as ACLs at each enforcement point individually. One reason for this approach was that each server might have its own list of permitted users and users rarely needed

AUTHENTICATION

Authenticating a user establishes the user's identity but doesn't in itself grant the user any rights to access network resources. The network must provide access control mechanisms that determine which resources on the network a given user can access. Users can be authenticated by simple username-password combinations, public and private crypto keys, shared secrets, Kerberos tickets, or biometric devices, such as fingerprint or voiceprint recognition.

access to all available servers. But now, with the advent of the Web and the increased interaction between users and large numbers of servers, the same access rights have to be distributed to more devices. NOSs often fulfill this need, but only for servers, printers, and related resources supported by a particular NOS.

Policy-based networking systems can serve as a bridge between these two types of access control—network-based and NOS-based. In Chapter 8, "Policy Enforcement Points," we pointed out that policy-based networking systems often rely on user-to-address mapping, partly to allow network managers to create policies for users and groups of users without referring to fixed or dynamically assigned IP addresses. (The policy-based networking system takes care of translating user IDs into IP addresses for the manager when it's time to distribute and enforce the policies to routers and firewalls.) Since a policy-based networking system can either store or point to both user IDs and IP addresses, a network manager can use policies to control access at both routers and NOS-based enforcement points (servers, for example) from a single system.

What sort of policies might a network manager set for access control? And how might they be distributed? Securing access starts at a very basic level: either users have access to a resource or they don't. So access control policies are usually simple permit/deny policies for a resource. As we pointed out earlier, this policy would be applied against an IP address, by a router or firewall, for instance, or against a username or similar user ID, by a server, for example.

Policy Distribution for Access Control

Besides routers, there are two other points controlling network access that should be included in the security framework: firewalls and remote access servers (see Figure 15.2). Both of these can be controlled via policy-based networking systems.

Firewalls help prevent unauthorized access between network segments. Managing a single firewall is relatively easy. But it's common these days to have several sites, each with its own firewall, connected to the Internet. You could manage such firewalls locally, but that requires a lot of time and staff. Furthermore, you'd have no guarantee of consistent security policies across your organization. Enforcing a unified security policy is complex.

Many products offer the ability to log in to separate firewalls from a single management station, but this still forces administrators to manage each firewall on a one-by-one basis. Few products allow for a global view, which is where policy-based networking systems can be of use. Managing your multiple firewalls centrally is crucial to maintaining a secure network.

Just like routers enforcing admission control, firewalls are devices that should be provisioned with policies—they do not proactively request policy

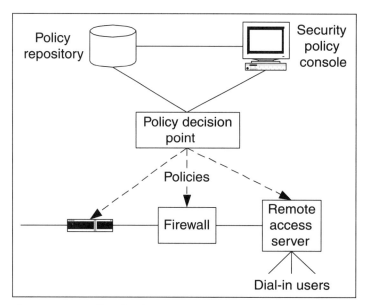

Figure 15.2   Policy distribution.

decisions from a PDP, for example. Thus, a policy-based networking system for security would distribute access control policies or policy-derived ACLs to routers and firewalls using any of the common protocols for configuring devices, such as telnet/CLI and SNMP.

When it comes to NOS-based access control of resources, few policy-based networking products actually control the NOS's ACLs. Some NOSs, such as Novell Netware and Microsoft Windows 2000, look to utilize their expanded directory services (NDS and Active Directory, respectively) to control not only the traditional NOS resources, such as servers and printers, but also to include policy control of network devices. These NOSs usually use a series of plug-in modules for their management console to add control of network devices.

Another point of admission control on a network is the remote access server (RAS), which we described in Chapter 8. However, unlike routers and firewalls, a RAS requests decisions regarding authentication and access control whenever a user attempts to establish a remote session. But this request for a decision, in current architectures, is generated by the RADIUS client running on the RAS to the RADIUS server. The RADIUS server could be provisioned from a policy-based networking system's repository and policy management tool and thus act as a PEP for the remote access server (see Figure 15.3).

Despite the popularity of RADIUS for control of remote access, the changing demands of authentication and authorization for remote users along with the increasing variety of mobile devices is leading to new efforts to refine network access servers and their authentication services. For example, the Net-

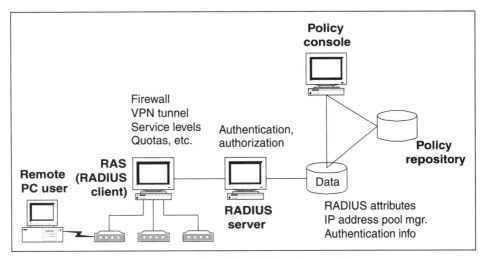

Figure 15.3   Remote access, RADIUS, and policy-based networking.

work Access Server Requirements (NASREQ) Working Group of the IETF has been defining the requirements for network access servers, including support for authentication and authorization as well as other services. Some of the requirements for limiting operational access and restricting usage authorization include time-of-day restrictions, port locations, concurrent login limits, session expirations and idle timeouts, packet filters, and QoS parameters. In addition, the Authentication, Authorization, and Accounting (AAA) Working Group has been working on a successor protocol to RADIUS that meets the needs of IPv6, explicit proxies, as well as mobile IP.

Since RADIUS (and any of its likely successors) has proven valuable as an integrator of authentication services from network operating systems and other sources of authentication data, it should fit into the scheme of policy-based networking. In some ways, RADIUS servers already enforce policies for remote access, but they're not integrated into policy-based networking products. The LDAP support that some RADIUS products include also makes exchange of user data with other repositories easier, but policy-based control of RADIUS servers hasn't yet appeared.

Virtual Private Networks

Enterprises rarely are the isolated secure islands of information that we just described. Most organizations are composed of multiple islands of security, perhaps one for each building on a campus or one for each geographic site. Pulling together all these islands into a single enterprise-wide network requires secure connections between them, using leased lines, frame relay virtual circuits, or IP-based VPNs. In this book, we're interested in how enterprises can manage the security of IP-based VPNs.

There are many ways to create virtual private networks (VPNs). Three protocols—Point-to-Point Protocol (PPTP), Layer 2 Tunneling Protocol (L2TP), and IP Security (IPSec)—can be used to create VPN tunnels across the Internet by encapsulating IP traffic within other packets. IPSec offers the best security for IP-VPN tunnels, since it can be configured to protect the encapsulated packets either by authenticating the packet's contents, encrypting the contents, or both. But this added security comes with a price, that of added complexity. IPSec depends on cryptographic key exchanges between VPN gateway protecting sites, or between a remote user and a VPN gateway. The Internet Key Exchange (IKE) protocol was developed to manage these key exchanges.

Using IPSec with the Internet Key Exchange (IKE), a system can set up security associations (SAs) which include information on the algorithms for authenticating and encrypting messages, the lifetime of the keys employed, the key lengths, and so on. Each pair of communicating computers will use a specific set of SAs to set up a VPN tunnel.

Among other information, a security association specifies the authentication algorithm used in AH, ESP authentication, and encryption algorithms, and the keys used, how often keys are changed, and the source address.

Consider a situation in which two sites are protected by a VPN gateway. Host A at site 1 (protected by security gateway 1, SG1) wants to send secure traffic to host B at site 2 (protected by security gateway 2, SG2). Depending on the individual policies involved, any combination of these SAs may have to be established by host A (see also Figure 15.4):

SA between host A and host B

SA between host A and SG1

SA between host A and SG2

SA between SG1 and SG2

SA between SG1 and host B

SA between SG2 and host B

Given any significant number of hosts communicating over a VPN, it's easy to see that the number of SAs that need to be negotiated for a VPN session can be numerous. While the negotiation of cryptographic and other security parameters for IPSec SAs is supported by key management protocols, the IPSec key management layer does not provide a scheme for managing, negotiating, and enforcing the security policies under which SAs operate.

Control of VPNs using policy-based networking is thus not as well developed as that for QoS. The IETF IP Security Policy (IPSP) Working Group has

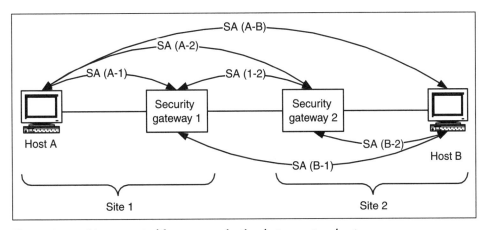

Figure 15.4 SAs generated for communication between two hosts.

been working to define the policy architecture for IPSec VPNs and to develop a language for describing packet filters and SA policies for use with VPNs, along with a management scheme for IPSec credentials.

Their requirements for VPN policy include the following:

A policy model

Gateway discovery mechanism

A policy language for nodes

Policy distribution mechanism

Policy discovery protocol

Method for resolving SA parameters

Semantics for compliance checking SA parameters and gateway against each node's policy

Using policy-based networking built on IPSP's work, network managers can create policies governing the specification of an SA's contents according to the endpoints of the tunnel. For instance, an SA could be created to use triple DES (3DES) to encrypt data transferred between offices in the United States, but a different SA specifying only DES encryption would be used to create a tunnel involving an office in a country where export restrictions apply.

Policy-Based Exchange of VPN Information

The IPSP Working Group's development of the Security Policy Protocol (SPP) shows how hosts and gateways can share policy information regarding VPN parameters. Let's take a look at a typical exchange between two sites, as shown in Figure 15.5.

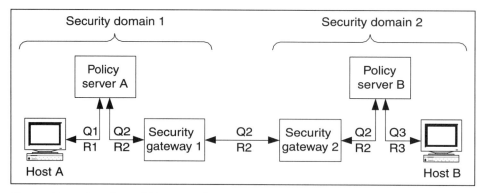

Figure 15.5 Overview of SPP operation.

Host A, wanting to communicate with host B, invokes its policy client. Host A's client sends a query (Q1) to its configured local policy server, policy server A. Policy server A looks in its cache for a policy record that matches the query. If it doesn't find one, it sends a query (Q2) containing the same policy request information to host B. Q2 is sent to host B since policy server A may not know about the existence of security gateway B (SGB) or policy server B. This message includes a digital signature that validates the authenticity and integrity of the query's content. Q2 is intercepted by security gateway B. SGB forwards the message (Q2) to policy server B. Policy server B verifies that it can accept queries from policy server A and validates the signature in Q2. It searches its database for the appropriate policy information after verifying that it is authoritative over host B.

Policy server B merges its local policy with the policy information in Q2 and it sends a reply (R2) to policy server A. The reply includes the original query information and all policy information needed to allow policy client A to establish a secure communication with host B. Policy server B also attaches additional information to the reply asserting its authority over host B.

When policy server A receives the reply (R2) from policy server B, it validates the signature in R2 and cryptographically verifies that policy server B is authoritative over host B. It then merges its local policy with the policy information in R2 and sends a reply (R1) to host A. Policy server A caches the merged policy to use when answering future queries. Host A may then use this information to establish necessary security associations with host B.

If, however, policy server B is not authoritative over host B, it would query host B for its policy with respect to this particular communication. Policy server B would generate a third query (Q3). Host B would respond with its policy in R3. Policy server B merges its policy for this communication and the policy in R3 before replying to policy server A. Policy server A processes the reply as it did in the preceding.

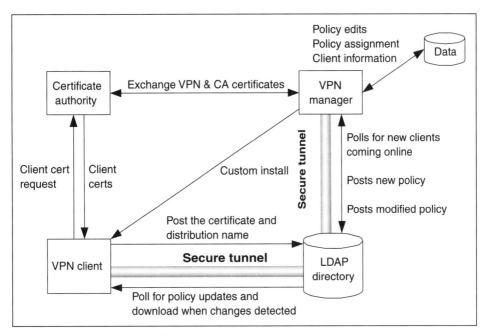

Figure 15.6 VPN client configuration.

Configuring VPN Remote Clients

Some enterprises have tried to simplify the configuration of their VPN security gateways by pre-sharing secret keys, rather than having multiple keys and SAs generated dynamically. But, at the same time, these organizations may face an even larger configuration task, that of supporting remote VPN users. Policy-based networking can be applied to remote users in much the same way as we described for communications between security gateways.

But some VPN vendors have chosen to implement what they call policy-based systems for the management of remote VPN clients. In their products, the network manager creates policy files for the clients, and these policy files—in effect, VPN configurations—can be distributed to the users by CD or downloaded from the Web (see Figure 15.6). Also, each client can periodically poll the configuration server at regular intervals to check for a new or modified security policy.

Summary

Although policy has long been associated with security, developers of security products have followed the path of point-based configuration. They've only recently turned to the centralized management of security devices via policy-based networking, partly because the number of security devices and clients has increased significantly and security operations have become more distributed. The security market is still somewhat fragmented, with many vendors offering policy-based management of a single class of security device such as firewalls or VPN gateways. Only a few products can claim to control and configure multiple classes of security devices.

NOS-based access control of servers and printers can be integrated with network-based admission control in some products, and we expect these ties to get stronger over the next few years. At the same time, policy-based management of VPNs will improve as standards evolve and more VPN vendors support them in their management products. This will improve the management of security associations for VPN sessions as well as the configuration of remote clients for VPNs.

This is the last chapter detailing specific applications of policy-based networking. In the following section of the book, we turn our attention to advice on how enterprises and service providers can deploy policy-based networking, including tips from some case studies.

CHAPTER 16

Policy-Based Networking
for Enterprises

Now that we've picked apart the components of policy-based networking and covered some of the main applications, it's time to close the loop and discuss how policy-based networking can be used on particular types of networks. In this chapter, we'll discuss some of the ways that enterprises have used policy-based networking for their networks, pointing out some of the questions you should answer as you plan your own deployment of policy-based networking.

First, we start out by reviewing the reasons why you might choose to deploy policy-based networking, and then we discuss some of the common challenges you may face during deployment. The next section of this chapter covers many of the major considerations you'll face during deployment of a policy-based system. We close the chapter by using two case studies to illustrate how some of the early adopters of policy-based networking have accomplished their goals and what they've learned.

Motivation for Deployment

As we mentioned in the opening chapters of this book, there are a number of possible reasons why an organization might choose to deploy policy-based networking. These include automation of device configuration, control of

QoS, consistent application of security, configuring large numbers of clients, dealing with shortages of experienced networking personnel, and even inventorying devices.

Device Configuration

Most device configuration today is done manually by a network manager who is occasionally assisted by some scripting software. For those situations in which scripts aren't used or maintained on a regular basis, configuration of network devices can be error-prone and time-consuming. In addition, it's difficult to keep track of the parameters each device requires for its configuration when different versions of operating systems are used and the same type of device fulfills different roles according to its location in the network.

Even when it comes to something as straightforward as a router, many organizations do not store configurations in a centralized fashion. (Many ISPs and large organizations do store copies of router configurations centrally, however.) That makes it difficult to refer to a backup configuration file if the device must be rebooted or replaced. It may also be difficult to replace personnel who have left the organization if there's little documentation of what steps an individual followed to configure a router.

Policy-based networking not only offers a central repository for storing device configurations, but it also ties the configuration of network devices to business rules and the services considered essential to the business. Furthermore, the policy-based approach helps ensure a consistency of configuration that is not ensured when you configure the network box by box. Also, policy-based networking can shield network managers from learning all the complicated details of a device's configuration, converting the rules they create into appropriate configurations for them.

Quality of Service

While QoS features are useful, enterprises still have to figure out how to apply all of these capabilities in their networks. In particular, network managers have to determine which QoS features should be turned on in each network node, so that the resulting flow of traffic meets enterprise needs.

Network managers need policy control over bandwidth-hungry applications, which consume bandwidth at the expense of performance and drive up the cost of expensive wide-area resources. The network manager also needs to be able to map business requirements into specific policies that link the business needs with the desired network behavior. For example, if an organization is running an enterprise resource planning (ERP) application for strategic competitive advantage, the network manager can create a policy that guarantees a minimum fraction of the network's bandwidth for ERP traffic. The business policy is automatically translated into network behavior, such as QoS mechanisms, to provide the guaranteed bandwidth for ERP traffic.

Policy-based networking systems are needed because QoS capabilities, while desirable, are often too difficult to implement, especially if you want to ensure network-wide consistency. Some of the issues include the complex and difficult learning curves for switches and routers; the workload associated with configuring QoS parameters and a large enterprise network; and the lack of the system-wide view. Some of the ways policy-based networking helps network managers deal with these problems is by providing the following features: centralized network configuration; management of the network as a system; nontechnical definitions of policy; and ease of use to shield the network manager from all the QoS parameters for each network device.

Security

As enterprise networks open up for external access and more business-critical resources become available on the network, security becomes a more critical component of daily operations. Administrators must not only control who has what level of access to what resources, but must also audit the network to guarantee that security policy enforcement. Security management includes not only configuring firewalls and servers, but also managing VPN gateways and a public key infrastructure, each of which has its own parameters and complexity.

But enforcement of the policy may not be applied consistently, since security managers often have to apply security policies to devices on a one-by-one basis, rather than distributing the appropriate policies to all devices from a central data store. Rather than force the network manager to set security policies for individual devices, policy-based management systems can consolidate and synchronize access control lists and related policy information to promote a consistent security policy across the enterprise, regardless of the types or number of devices involved.

Client Management

Another factor driving the need for policy-based networking and automatic configuration of both network devices and session setup is the proliferation of more types of mobile devices, such as laptop PCs, cellular phones, and personal digital assistants (PDAs). Now, with a business network supporting all of these different types of devices, the type and quality of the data being transmitted to the user depends on the type of device he or she is using. And it's highly likely that any single user will use more than one type of device, which means that the network has to be smart enough to maintain multiple user profiles for each user and react based on the type of device that the user is using.

The proliferation of different client types among users makes it more difficult to manually apply policies to users, either for security or bandwidth management. For instance, a mobile user with a laptop may require different access rights and encryption policies if he or she is on the road in the United States versus traveling abroad. Similarly, different rules for content delivery may be applied if someone's using a computer or a PDA.

Obviously, a network manager cannot manually configure the policies for each of these sessions, especially if users keep getting new devices, travel to new customer sites, or start telecommuting with a new computer or a different connection (using DSL instead of a dial-up modem, for example). But you can define user profiles that include conditions for different types of network conditions and user devices and then tie policies to these profiles in a policy-based networking system. This will enable the network to enforce policies in a dynamic fashion that's tailored to the users, their location, and the equipment they're using.

Staffing Problems

Networks don't run on their own; they must always be monitored and tweaked, which requires skilled personnel. Finding experienced personnel to manage IP networks is a difficult enough task these days, but the difficulty is also compounded by the fact that many of the services supported by new network devices and software are so new that it's difficult for network staff to gain experience in the short time since the devices were introduced. By translating policies into device configuration, policy-based networking allows network managers to specify policies describing the proper operation of their networks at a high level of abstraction, shielding them from setting the myriad number of configuration parameters themselves. This, in turn, simplifies the task of deploying new services for less-experienced network managers, who can work at this higher level of policy abstraction without concerning themselves with the details of each device's possible settings.

Device Inventories

While it may seem like a mundane task, policy-based networking can help with inventorying hardware and software in an organization. This is not strictly an application of policy-based networking, but rather it uses the same data repositories as the policy-based networking system. Tracking system information in a central data store simplifies the task of planing upgrades for both hardware and software, for instance, and is one of the aims of the DMTF and its Web-based Enterprise Management (WBEM) initiative.

Also, information that's stored as part of this inventory might help in the configuration of network devices, where it's important to know each device's network interfaces, version of the operating system, and so on.

Common Challenges

Whatever the reason for using policy-based networking, organizations face a number of common challenges in deploying policy-based networking.

First and foremost, there's the business justification for using policy-based networking. Policy-based networking can be a cost saver for IT departments, especially if a large number of complicated devices need to be configured (such as for QoS) and the pool of experienced network managers is limited. But keep in mind that installation of a policy-based networking system does not guarantee a reduced demand on network managers. After all, someone has to take on the responsibility of creating the policies that the policy-based networking system enforces. And that can be an onerous task in itself.

The number and type of applications planned for policy-based networking will affect your business justification and system deployment. The more applications you can tie to policy-based networking, the easier it should be to justify the system to management. But beware of hidden costs. If you need to tie custom applications to a policy-based networking product, you may find it difficult to justify the added programming resources. And try ensuring that the vendor's information model is flexible enough to meet the needs of your applications, or that customization of the schema is possible. As we've mentioned previously, most organizations are interested in using policy-based networking first for QoS and security, and other applications such as device inventory and client management may follow later.

The dissemination of network policies to enforcement points sounds as though it's mainly a technical issue, but policy-based networking is also a strongly political issue. Who in your company has the authority to determine which applications and users get the highest quality of service, for instance? You'll probably find that it's necessary to form a committee to define network policies at the higher levels of your organization. You might also have to formulate some procedure (keep it simple, though) so that users or departments can request changes in the policies affecting their application traffic.

A big issue, one centered on politics, is that of data ownership. As network managers look to use existing information in the organization that others create and maintain, they may have to struggle to obtain permission to use that information. You may also have to consider how you'll coordinate the updates of that information to ensure that it's up-to-date. For instance, you don't want your system to continue allowing access by an employee who was laid off weeks, or even days, ago. (We'll discuss more of the issues of and possible solutions to information ownership in the next section on deployment.)

Since a network manager has to create and validate network policies within the context of the state of the network and user requirements, policy-based management systems may need to factor in data from these other sources. Furthermore, since it's unlikely that storage of these other types of information will change significantly in the near future, policy-based management systems need to link to them in their current form. Nor should you expect that all the pertinent data would be stored in a single directory or database.

Solving the system and service management challenges of today's networks demands a new generation of network management systems featuring a tighter linkage between network, system, and application-level management information. Effective allocation of network resources requires that network elements understand the profiles governing the performance and business-critical nature of the applications and users on the network. Management information for computing and network elements and resources, whether for configuration, troubleshooting, or performance management, resides in enterprise management applications that should be able to share this information.

However, information describing users and binding them to application services and computing resources is more often the province of enterprise directory systems, not network management systems. Since directories already hold some of this data because of the role that they play in locating systems, mailboxes, Web pages, and application processes, it's become more important than ever to integrate directory, policy and lower-level network and systems resource data.

Deployment Considerations

When you're planning to deploy a policy-based networking system for your enterprise, there are eight things to consider:

Which applications will you use policy-based networking for?

What types of domains and how many domains will you create?

How will you integrate policy-based networking with other management systems?

What will be your enforcement points?

How will you handle non-policy-aware devices?

How granular will your policies be?

Who owns the information the system uses?

How will you determine whether your policies are effective?

Let's take a look at each of these issues in more detail.

First, you'll need to decide what the primary applications of policy are. Security and QoS certainly come to mind, and they're the leading reasons for using policy-based networking in many companies. Furthermore, most policy-based networking products are written for these two applications. A few vendors have also turned their attention to client management for VPNs.

Second, and this is related to the first issue, you should determine how you'll assign responsibility for creating and managing policies. Many organizations treat network management and security management as two separate areas of responsibility, with two different managers handling them. That's still possible with policy-based networking, since the policies can be stored centrally in the policy repository, but each manager can use his or her own console, one customized to the particular policy domain—security versus QoS, for instance.

As part of your domain structure, you'll need to decide how many managers are involved and how flat their organizations should be. Many organizations can probably get by with a single manager for each policy domain at each major site. But large networks may require a hierarchy of managers, especially for larger sites. In such cases, one manager at the top of the hierarchy could create initial policies, and the other managers, perhaps for certain departments, would have the responsibility (and authority) to modify or create policies to meet the special needs of their users. But, on the whole, keep the structure as simple as possible.

Then there's the issue of integrating policy-based networking with your other management systems. Some vendors have integrated network management functions with policy-based networking, and more are working on that type of system integration. The increasing use of such technologies as XML will ease the exchange of information between management systems.

Fourth, you'll also need to decide where the enforcement points will be located on your network. That depends on what kinds of policies you want to enforce and what parts of the network they affect. For instance, a primary application of policy might be to control WAN traffic, so you may need to make all your edge routers enforcement points. But if you're encrypting traffic on the LAN, hosts may need to enforce classification and marking policies. As another example, you may need to prioritize traffic and control bandwidth on some departmental subnets, which means the routers serving those subnets will have to become enforcement points.

Fifth, an added concern about enforcement points is the capabilities of your current equipment. Are they all policy-aware? Or can they be handled by policy-based configuration provisioned via a policy proxy? It may prove beneficial to upgrade some of your critical devices so they are policy-aware (using COPS or SNMP Policy MIBS, for example) and have the requisite processing power to handle the policies without hindering other functions. The policy capabilities of each device vary according to its functionality. For instance, firewalls are more capable at handling large ACLs than are routers. Also keep in mind the possibility of using servers and hosts as enforcement points. While this distributes the processing of policies, it also requires a more scalable policy distribution system than when only a few enforcement points are used.

Sixth, it's worth making a few suggestions about getting started with policies. The best principle is KISS—keep it simple, stupid. Keep the number of policies to a minimum. Let most situations be handled by default policies and then create special policies for the exceptions as necessary.

In order to keep your policy structure as simple as possible, you'll need to determine how granular you need to make your policies. For example, many early adopters of policy-based networking have focused on specifying only a few QoS classes—usually only two to four—for application traffic and have not chosen to write policies for specific users. On the other hand, they usually create more user- or group-related policies for security. Increasing the granularity of security policies can become more important if you're supporting an extranet and your partners need different levels of access to resources on your network.

We cannot emphasize policy granularity enough. Most early adopters of policy-based networking have found that the fewer policies, the better. Furthermore, they've been able to achieve their desired results by focusing on application traffic rather than further subdividing the traffic classifications according to users. If you must set up some policies for users, try to do it for groups of users rather than individuals. And keep in mind that user-based policies require user-to-address mapping, so pick a policy-based networking system that can link to existing DHCP services.

DHCP is only one example of the link between policy-based networking and other data sources. Policy-based networking systems need to link a variety of data sources, such as DNS and DHCP servers, NOS directories, and HR databases, among others. To a network or security manager, policy-based networking may be the central control point for using all this information, but they don't have actual control of this information. The question of information ownership will undoubtedly come up as you attempt to integrate all this ancillary information. Who gets to modify it? Who maintains the directories and databases? Departments such as HR will be reluctant to let non-HR personnel modify their databases, but you may need the latest information on an employee's status to set security and access policies. In most companies, integration of all this data is far from a done deal. If anything, it's a major challenge of this decade. Look to meta-directories as a possible solution.

Network managers, therefore, may be faced with helping to build a meta-directory (or using an existing meta-directory) to access the data the policy-based system needs, or linking their policy repository to a number of other sources by means of a variety of protocols.

Keep in mind that you need to determine whether your policies are, in fact, producing the desired results. This means that you need to rely on some means of monitoring your network, and these systems are usually independent of your policy-based networking system. Some monitoring tools may already exist in your organization. For instance, your firewalls already generate audit and event logs that you can use to assess security policies. For QoS, you might use traffic monitors on your network or have agents that can monitor end-to-end responses on servers and/or hosts.

Like the installation of any major system, deploying policy-based networking takes some planning. One thing you should keep in mind is that the concepts of policy and particularly policy-based networking will be new to many of the people involved in policy-based networking's deployment. Many parts of this book should serve as a good starting point to acquaint them with many of policy's concepts and fine points. But some additional training of IT managers may be required to get the most out of a policy-based networking system.

Keep in mind that the vendors of policy-based networking products are quite willing to help you properly deploy their products. Many of the vendors that we've spoken with admit that policy-based networking is as much of a learning experience for them as for their customers. They're interested in working alongside you to see that their system provides the proper results on your network.

Case Studies

Let's take a look at some real-life case studies to see how enterprises have used policy-based networking. We'll cover two cases in detail: one is a major global bank that needed to provide improved quality of service for its mission-critical applications, and the second is a university that needed to control Napster-related traffic as well as provide sufficient bandwidth for distance training to a community college.

The Global Bank

This major bank, whose operations include branch offices in more than 50 countries, wanted to ensure the timely operation of its two mission-critical applications, both of which require real-time responses. One application is for currency trading and the other is a market data stream, similar to a stock ticker. On the original network (see Figure 16.1), which consisted of 2-Mbps links in the core network and 64-Kbps links to the branch offices, the two applications suffered from erratic performance.

The bank considered two solutions before trying policy-based networking.

First, it considered overprovisioning the links to branch offices. But this suggestion was disapproved for three reasons: The cost of the upgrade was prohibi-

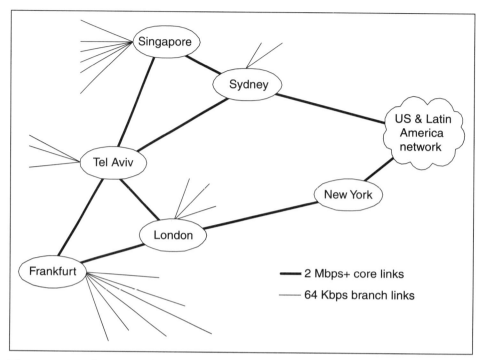

Figure 16.1 Schematic of bank's network.

tive in many countries and was thought to be more than the profit margins in those offices; it would take too long to install all the upgrades; and the bank didn't have the right people to go out into the field and oversee all the upgrades.

The second possibility was to optimize the network's performance manually by configuring the routers to use an appropriate QoS technique. The company decided to try this approach, configuring its Cisco routers with the simplest QoS technique, priority queuing, giving the trading application top priority. However, the results were less than optimal. Traffic from the two main real-time applications swamped the bandwidth on the 64-Kbps links, in effect starving all other applications of bandwidth.

At this point, although the company considered trying a slightly more complicated QoS technique, custom queuing, it decided to try a policy-based networking system. The deployment followed four stages:

Business profiling. Determine which applications should get priority.

Application profiling. Determine the bandwidth requirements, including average data rates and amounts and frequency of data bursts, for the application.

Implementation. Determine the appropriate QoS technique to use.

Monitoring and review. Determine what results were achieved.

Business profiling is the primary business-related decision a company has to make about its applications and their use of the network. This is where your business managers must determine how important each application is to the company's operations. In the case of the bank we're describing here, it focused on the five major applications running on its network—a currency trading application, a market data feed app, database operations, FTP file transfers, and e-mail. The most important applications are the trading application and the data feed application; these two were classified as real-time applications and the remaining applications were lumped together as "other traffic." The real-time applications deserved the highest priority.

Next came the task of profiling the applications, that is, determining their behavior on the network. For example, the trading application was described as an interactive, inquiry-based application using TCP with small packet sizes and requiring low latency. For each action in the application, the user sends out 100 bytes and receives 2,000 bytes as a response. Plus, five traders use the application concurrently at any branch office, performing a transaction every 10 seconds, on the average. Although it's possible to monitor an application's network traffic with the right tools, the bank used a modeling approach to profile the trading application using the information we just outlined.

It modeled two different scenarios, one where the applications has 5 Kbps of dedicated bandwidth, and one where 10 Kbps was allocated to the application. In the first case, their model predicted an average response time of 3 seconds and a worst-case response of 5 seconds. For the second case, the model yielded an average response of 2 seconds and a worst-case response time of 3 seconds. Based on these results, the bank chose to reserve 10 Kbps of bandwidth for the trading application.

Its second important application, the market data feed, was treated differently. It's an application that provides constant data in one direction, from the server to the clients, although it is latency sensitive. Plus, the application uses UDP. Since transactions aren't involved, the application wasn't modeled and the IT department simply decided to dedicate 32 Kbps to this application's traffic.

Now we come to the configuration of the network using the policy-based networking system. First, the bank had to create classes of service and assign applications to those classes. It defined three classes of service: mission-critical, real-time, and best-effort. The mission-critical class consisted only of traffic from the trading application, while only the data feed application's traffic was assigned to the real-time class. Traffic from all remaining applications, database, FTP, and e-mail, was part of the best-effort class.

The classification rules for each application's traffic was set in a straightforward manner. The trading application uses a well-defined range of IP port numbers, so those port numbers were defined in a policy assigning traffic to the mission-critical class. (The system, in turn, converts this policy into an

ACL for the routers at each branch office.) Similarly, the IP address of the server for the market data feed is a static, well-known address, so a second policy was created to assign traffic sent from this address to the real-time class. All other traffic was treated as best-effort. When the policies were deployed to the routers acting as enforcement points, packets traversing a router were marked with the IP Precedence bits using a simple scheme of 1 = mission-critical, 2 = real-time, and 3 = best-effort.

In addition to the classification rules, a policy had to be defined telling the routers what queuing algorithm to use for the three types of traffic. The bank chose to configure the routers using Cisco's custom queuing algorithm, assigning 15 percent of the link's bandwidth to class 1, 50 percent to class 2, and the remaining 35 percent to class 3 traffic (see Figure 16.2).

All traffic on a branch office's LAN is treated equally, and QoS (classification and queuing) is only applied at the router for the 64-Kbps WAN link.

Although we weren't able to gain access to actual traffic statistics that showed the effects of applying the policies, the bank's IT department produced some traffic models of the trading application's response before and after implementation of the policies. Almost all transactions take place in 1 second or less in the policy-driven network, while other applications (which are more delay tolerant) did not significantly increase in response times. This is a reversal of the original situation, where the FTP and database traffic usually had a response of less than 1 second, while many of the trading application transactions took more than 2 seconds.

Once the first set of routers was configured using policy, it was a relatively simple matter to deploy copies of those policies to other branch offices around the world. Distributing the four policies (three for defining the classes, one for the router's queuing behavior) took about 5 seconds per site.

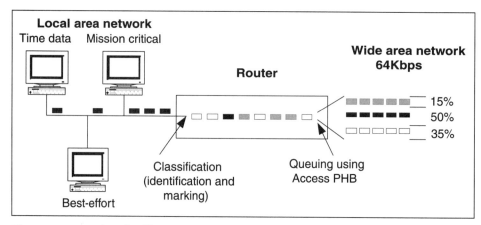

Figure 16.2 Packet classification and queuing.

A University Network

Our second case study is that of a state university that not only handles its campus network but serves as a local service provider for some public sector clients. In addition, the university has been pursuing arrangements with a local community college to offer distance training by video over its network.

The university's network has an OC-3 (155-Mbps) WAN link to a service provider's gigaPOP and has a gigabit core network on the campus with 1000-Mbps pipes to each dormitory. (See Figure 16.3.)

One of the problems the university's campus networking staff faced was high utilization of both its core campus network and its Internet link to the gigaPOP. At the time this work was started, the OC-3 link was provisioned to allow only 35 Mbps of bandwidth to the Internet. Since the core was originally thought to be sufficiently overprovisioned, the university did not actively implement any performance management. When network engineers reviewed typical SNMP MIB-II performance data, they found that links were 99 percent utilized whenever users complained about poor performance. The engineers identified traffic from Napster and similar peer-to-peer applications as the major reason for such high utilization. The university therefore wanted to limit Napster traffic but not completely shut it down.

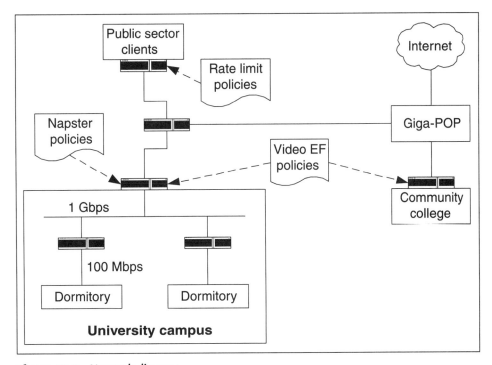

Figure 16.3 Network diagram.

The university installed a Packeteer 4500 traffic shaper as a front end to the OC-3 link. Since Napster uses some well-known ports but can also use other ports, the traffic shaper was used to discover and profile the Napster traffic based on an application signature (conceptually like a virus signature used in intrusion detection systems, but using network protocols).

Once the application profile was determined, the following policy was deployed to the traffic shaper:

If application Traffic == Napster, then Committed Rate = 1 Mbps

This policy was translated to a bandwidth partition policy and implemented on the traffic shaper, limiting the amount of Napster traffic, which appears to have done the trick of reducing utilization of the core network and the gigaPOP link. (Unfortunately, we were unable to get any real traffic data before this book went to press.)

The university also plans to use the same approach to support video-based distance learning in conjunction with the community college. In this case, however, the traffic shaper will be configured to provide a minimum bandwidth for the video broadcasts.

Summary

While there are many different reasons for deploying policy-based management, such as QoS, security, and client management, there are a number of challenges that are common to all deployments. These include justifying the new system, determining appropriate policies, and data ownership.

When you're planning your own policy-based networking system, you should consider at least the following issues:

Which applications will you use policy-based networking for?

What types of domains and how many domains will you create?

How will you integrate policy-based networking with other management systems?

What will your enforcement points be?

How will you handle non-policy-aware devices?

How granular will your policies be?

Who owns the information the system uses?

How will you determine whether your policies are effective?

The case studies that we included in this chapter should give some concrete examples of how other organizations have addressed these questions and put policy-based networking to work.

CHAPTER 17

Policy-Based Networking for Service Providers

Enterprises are not the only organizations that can benefit from policy-based networking. Another significant market consists of Internet Service Providers (ISPs), Network Service Providers (NSPs), and Application Service Providers (ASPs). These organizations have many of the same problems as enterprises do, but often on a larger scale than many enterprises. For instance, ISPs and NSPs may have tens or even hundreds of thousands of routers or switches to manage.

In this chapter, we talk about some of the reasons service providers (SPs) use policy-based networking and point out some of the unique problems they face on their networks. We also discuss some of the deployment issues they have to take into account, and close with a few case studies that show what ISPs are already doing with policy-based networking.

Reasons for Deployment

Service providers face a dilemma. Demand for IP networks and associated services is increasing. Yet competition among service providers is forcing the prices of standard IP connectivity down, cutting into the providers' profit margins. The demand is being driven by the cost-effectiveness of using the IP networks for data communications, either between corporate sites using an intranet, or among business partners by means of an extranet. The increased interest in e-commerce, both business-to-business and business-to-individual, has led to standardization on IP networks and the Web for many communications tasks.

In addition, when IP connectivity is sold as a commodity, there's a great deal of churn, forcing service providers to look for new ways to keep their customers. Thus, service providers are looking for ways to deploy value-added services to gain a competitive edge. But these value-added services are expensive to configure and maintain if the old methods of point-based configuration and management are used.

Enterprise customers looking for advanced IP services are faced with making expensive capital and networking investments, limiting their deployment of these IP services. Rather than build the networks themselves, many enterprises may prefer to outsource these new services to an ISP or NSP. However, this trend toward outsourcing network service is constrained somewhat by the flexibility of the service providers, concerns over service quality and security, and expensive network access arrangements. Enterprise customers want the flexibility to purchase and consume advanced IP services when required, without an expensive IT and networking infrastructure.

In order to provide new value-added services to their customers, service providers need more than just high-density edge devices, low-cost bandwidth, and fast routing switches in the core. Many existing network devices lack the intelligence required to switch users' sessions across a diverse array of applications and services. To solve this problem, NSPs are looking to deploy a service layer in IP networks that is located above the transport layer (see Figure 17.1). This service layer provides user-oriented, session-aware processing and switching of traffic flows to support a wide range of applications and services. And much of the control of this service layer comes from policy-based networking systems.

There are other, equally important reasons for the development of policy-based networking systems on service provider networks. These include a need to simplify increasingly complex networks, the availability of new services, business prioritization of applications, and the increasing need for network security. The service providers face many of the same problems as enterprises do, as we detailed in the previous chapter.

Both the number of network devices and the complexity of these devices have been increasing for the past few years. As enterprises and service providers add more services to their networks, such as multicasting, differentiated service levels, IP telephony, and virtual private networks (VPNs), the number of parameters that the network manager must set in each router or multilayer switch increases, as does the possibility of configuration errors. When you add to this the increasing number of edge devices at each site that's connecting to a wide-area network (WAN), coupled with the number of ven-

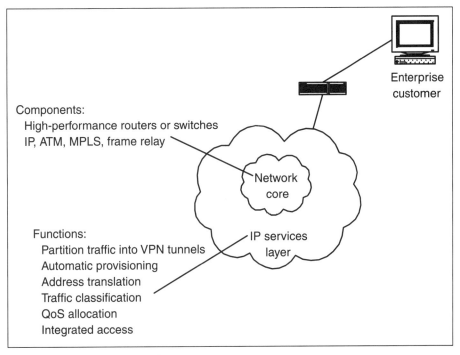

Figure 17.1   The IP services layer.

dors offering these devices, custom configuration of all the devices connected to the WAN becomes an almost impossible task.

Bandwidth-intensive applications are also increasing in number and usage, adding to the load on networks. The cost of adding bandwidth in the WAN, while declining, is still prohibitive and provides no guarantee that mission-critical applications will receive priority service. As an alternative to overprovisioning, enterprises and service providers are employing QoS mechanisms to provide acceptable network resources for mission-critical applications, particularly for their WAN links.

Nevertheless, the number of devices and parameters that have to be managed to provide end-to-end QoS makes a solution based on the configuration of individual devices practically impossible, as we've pointed out frequently throughout this book. In addition, as new applications emerge, network managers often want to be able to specify the priorities of these applications relative to other applications. With policy-based network management tools, a service provider can configure both core and customer premise equipment (CPE)-based routers to handle different classes of traffic based on criteria such as classes of users and applications and on changing network conditions.

One approach to providing these services in a manner that's cost-effective for the service provider is to automate as much of the device configuration as possible and perform configuration remotely. This method leads to the use of policy-based network management to handle the configuration tasks. The use of policy-based network management also makes it possible for service providers to centrally define new policies for customers and distribute the policies across the service provider's networks as needed.

Service providers are continually faced with the task of engineering their networks for optimal use. Employing QoS is only part of the solution, covering the needs of the customer by providing differential responses for various types of traffic. The need for differentiated services arises from localized congestion conditions that impact application performance. Looked at this way, QoS differentiation is managed damage control in response to congestion. An alternative is to avoid the congestion condition in the first place. One possible solution is overprovisioning, that is, adding more bandwidth than required for the current (or expected) load on that network segment. Another is to use traffic engineering to mitigate the effects of congestion, and in doing so prevent the need for engineering differentiated responses to congestion.

A protocol often connected with traffic engineering is Multiprotocol Layer Switching (MPLS) which involves mapping traffic to Forwarding Equivalence Classes (FECs), mapping FECs to Label Switched Paths (LSPs), and mapping LSPs to physical topology (see sidebar). Typically, information about bindings of labels to FECs is distributed by a label distribution protocol. Policy-based networking can be used to provide high-level descriptions of the mappings, shielding the network manager from point-by-point configuration of devices supporting MPLS, simplifying the process of label distribution (at least from the viewpoint of the network manager). An important aim is to provide high-level means for mapping traffic that matches a specific traffic filter onto an LSP with specific QoS characteristics. Such high-level policies could be used with DiffServ over MPLS, for instance.

As service providers deploy QoS, they need methods for controlling resource allocations within their own domains. They will also need methods for negotiating resource allocations with other domains (other ISPs) to ensure end-to-end consistency of service for their customers. The bandwidth broker, which we described in the context of DiffServ in Chapter 14, "Policies for Quality of Service," aims to solve these issues for service providers. As we pointed out in Chapter 13, "An Introduction to Quality of Service," the primary goal of the DiffServ architecture is controlled sharing of bandwidth and router resources. As part of this goal, policies must be distributed to edge devices to perform admission control, traffic shaping, and other QoS-related functions. In the DiffServ architecture, the policy decision point is called a bandwidth broker.

The bandwidth broker can configure devices with organizational policies as well as monitor available bandwidth, interpret service-level requests from

TRAFFIC ENGINEERING AND MPLS

Traffic engineering is the process of selecting paths for network traffic with the goal of balancing the load on various links, routers, and switches in the network. The benefits of traffic engineering include the ability to route primary paths around known bottlenecks or points of congestion and to provide more efficient use of available bandwidth.

Traffic engineering can also help network operators enhance a network's performance by minimizing packet loss or periods of congestion, and maximizing throughput. In addition, traffic engineering is key to supporting a mix of data, voice, and video traffic in that it can be used to statistically bound performance characteristics such as loss ratio, delay variation, and transfer delay.

One approach is to spread the load using an overlay switching model, such as Multiprotocol Layer Switching (MPLS). MPLS is a combination of switched forwarding with network layer routing. The added value of MPLS is provided by a better price/performance ratio of network layer routing, improved scalability in the network layer, and greater flexibility in the delivery of routing services. These advantages are achieved by label switching: a packet is assigned to a Forwarding Equivalence Class (FEC) when it enters the MPLS network. The FEC is encoded as a label in the packet so that it can then be used at subsequent hops between ingress and egress nodes to determine the forwarding treatment by indexing into a table. All packets belonging to a particular FEC travel the same path through the network. For more details on MPLS, see Paul Izzo, *Gigabit Networks*, Wiley, 2000.

Current routing techniques offer limited traffic engineering capabilities, consisting primarily of load balancing, which operators configure by adjusting the metrics associated with network links. In contrast, MPLS promises to provide IP-based traffic engineering similar to that of Asynchronous Transfer Mode (ATM). With MPLS, labels make certain capabilities, such as explicit routing and load sharing, more efficient.

Explicit routes enable both traffic engineering and policy routing. For example, since MPLS enables network operators to individually identify streams of data from any ingress node to any egress node, they can explicitly route that stream over a preferred path. Explicit routes can be based on administrative policies, enabling network operators to select routes with an eye to traffic management, including the loading of the bandwidth through the nodes and links in the network.

clients, and keep track of the current allocation of marked traffic. Even more significantly, a bandwidth broker can communicate with bandwidth brokers in other DiffServ domains (another ISP, for example) to ensure the viability of end-to-end traffic agreements.

Application Service Providers

The use of ASPs by enterprises is another part of the outsourcing trend we mentioned earlier, although ASPs are concerned with business applications and data rather than the networks themselves, which is the purview of the ISPs and NSPs. Many ASPs provide economic benefits to their customers by sharing the costs of expensive data center mainframes, databases, and infrastructure across many customers. However, expensive dedicated networking arrangements are typically required in order to meet service-level guarantees to each customer site.

While ASPs are achieving success in offering services over expensive private networks or via existing best-effort Internet networks, the ASP industry can grow tremendously when quality guarantees are offered across the Internet. These quality guarantees must be offered across the complete network connection, from ASP to the business customer's LAN. While ASPs typically offer service level agreements (SLAs) within their areas of control (that is, the data center) and NSPs typically offer SLAs between the edges of their core networks, what business consumers require is guaranteed QoS from the ASP data center to the business location.

The ASPs therefore need to insure that their customers' traffic receives the proper priority treatment on any network that it crosses. But they don't want to get involved in the installation and management of network hardware at customer sites. Nor do the ASPs want to place special requirements on what network hardware their customers can use, or they might lose business. ASPs therefore find themselves in the position of either negotiating arrangements with NSPs to provide the appropriate service levels necessary for their application traffic, or trying to set up policy-based network management so that they can manage not only the necessary network devices, but also the backend services, including directories, user authentication, and so on. But this is new ground for the ASPs as well. If ASPs plan to offer service-level guarantees that cross NSPs' domains, they may have to deploy policy-based network management systems on their own.

A Model for Service Management

ISPs and NSPs are faced with a number of possible services they can offer to their customers, starting with simple connectivity to the Internet and domain name services to managed security services, multicasting, virtual private networks, and so on. But each one of the services has to be managed by the service provider.

The service providers that started out as telecommunications carriers have legacy operations support systems (OSSs) that they use to manage their networks and handle customer services. But the architecture of these OSSs, which includes large numbers of APIs and custom applications, makes it difficult to maintain consistency of data across disparate systems, increases the cost of adding new technology and services, and slows the development of new applications. While the functions of these legacy OSSs still need to be supported, the trend is to roll out new systems that improve the speed of delivering new systems, support intelligent applications and services, and provide improved customer interfaces to services.

The service provider industry has its own model and specifications for managing its operations. These stem mainly from the work of the International Telecommunications Union (ITU), which developed the Telecommunication Management Network (TMN, see Figure 17.2). Historically, TMN was born of the necessity to extend the private and proprietary—but well-developed—network management systems and make them interoperable. Despite efforts in other standards bodies to create a management system, TMN became the only

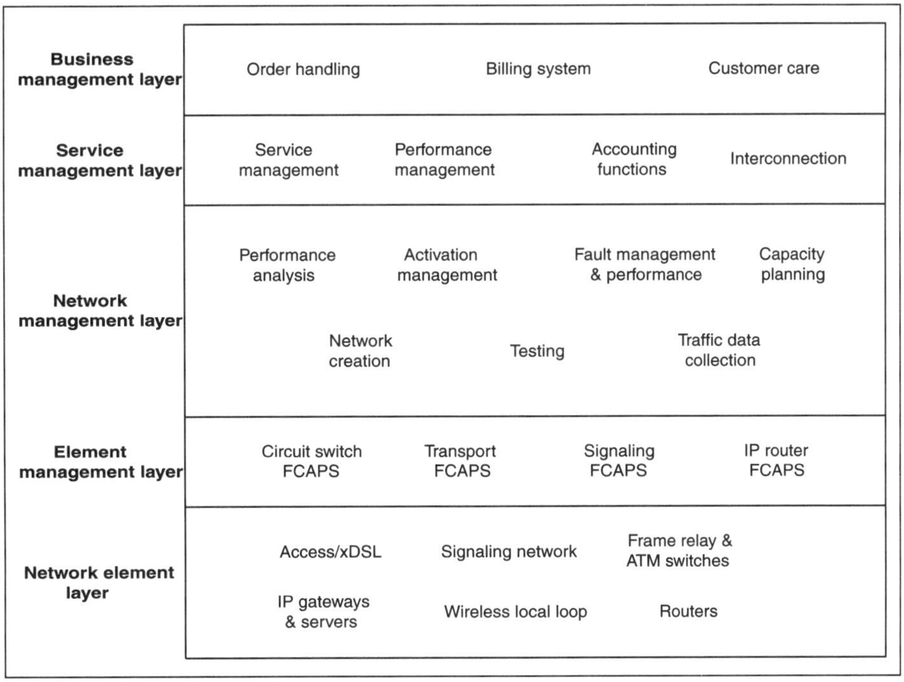

Business management layer	Order handling	Billing system		Customer care
Service management layer	Service management	Performance management	Accounting functions	Interconnection
Network management layer	Performance analysis	Activation management	Fault management & performance	Capacity planning
	Network creation	Testing	Traffic data collection	
Element management layer	Circuit switch FCAPS	Transport FCAPS	Signaling FCAPS	IP router FCAPS
Network element layer	Access/xDSL	Signaling network	Frame relay & ATM switches	
	IP gateways & servers	Wireless local loop	Routers	

Figure 17.2 The TMN model.

framework that addressed not only the management of network elements, but also the management of networks, services, and business.

TMN is a management system framework, architecture, and set of specifications that support the management needs of network and service providers. TMN provides an organized architecture that enables various types of OSSs and telecommunications equipment to work together to exchange management information.

TMN fills the business requirement to automate business processes for network and service management. This automation facilitates the rapid development and deployment of high-quality services in a cost-effective manner.

TMN categorizes network management into five functional areas: fault, configuration, accounting, performance, and security management (FCAPS).

Fault management involves the detection, isolation, correction, reporting of faults in the network, and service. In addition, fault management tracks the correlation of related services, including reliability, availability, survivability, quality assurance, alarm surveillance and alarm management, fault localization, fault correction, testing, and trouble administration.

Configuration management covers the configuration and control of network elements and services, the identification of resources, the collection of information about the resources, and the management of connections between network elements. Configuration management deals not only with the state of network elements, but also with the provisioning of resources and services. Generally, configuration management involves network planning, installation, service planning and negotiation, service provisioning, equipment provisioning, status and control, and network topology.

Accounting management is the collection of data that measures network and service usage; it also enables billing for usage. In addition, it controls the flow of funds within the enterprise including tariffing/pricing, usage measurement, collection and finance, and enterprise control.

Performance management involves the gathering and reporting of the behavior of network elements, the network, and services, including performance quality assurance, performance monitoring, performance management control, and performance analysis.

Security management involves the prevention and detection of any improper use of network resources and services and recovery from security violations, including security, administration, prevention, detection, and containment and recovery.

Management tasks within these functional areas are separated into layers that reflect the business level impacted, ranging from tasks that affect specific network elements to those that apply across the entire business enterprise. These layers usually include business, service, network, and element management, and a base layer that represents the elements themselves. Each layer provides an abstraction of the functional characteristics of its layer and hides the details associated with other layers. The levels of abstraction simplify management at each layer.

The lowest architectural layer represents the elements that are being managed. Network elements include transmission equipment, networking equipment, computing resources, and so on.

The *element management layer* encompasses functionality to manage and monitor a set of similar network elements, such as WAN Asynchronous Transfer Mode (ATM) switches, and presents an abstraction to the network management layer. Element management layer entities hide the physical network element details from upper layers and are typically vendor and technology specific. But they also lack complete knowledge of the network and its topology and are primarily concerned with interacting directly with the agents that represent the network elements.

The *network management layer* contains end-to-end knowledge of the entire network and is responsible for managing all the network elements as presented by the element management layer. The network management layer provides the abstraction of a network and network services to the service management layer. It manages and monitors the network as a whole. Functions such as end-to-end connection management consequently reside at this layer. The network management layer coordinates activities across the network via the element management layer in support of services located at the service management layer.

The *service management layer* is responsible for the contractual aspects of services provided by a carrier to its customers. This layer assumes access to network management layer functionality to manage and monitor network resources in support of the services offered. Examples of services are virtual private networks (VPNs), Internet telephony, electronic commerce services, and ATM or frame relay private virtual circuits (PVCs) and switched virtual circuits (SVCs).

The *business management layer* is responsible for the total enterprise; agreements between operators are made at this layer, which is part of the overall management of the enterprise and interacts with other management systems.

When combined, the functional areas and management layers create a complex matrix for defining and describing the management capabilities offered by any OSS in any TMN. Since most service providers today accept the functional separations that describe the structure of TMN, and the abstractions that each layer provides, policy-based networking systems should integrate with this model.

So where does policy-based networking fit into the TMN architecture? Policy-based networking actually spans the element management, network management, and service management layers of the TMN architecture. Policy-based networking systems can not only automate the configuration of network elements—the task of the element management layer—but also link element configuration to service definitions, which is part of the network management layer's tasks, as well as relate network performance and policies to service-level agreements, a task delegated to the service management layer. By tying together users, services, service-level agreements, policies, and network elements in a single management system, policy-based networking simplifies some of the tasks operations managers face in provisioning new services for customers.

For example, a service might include specifics such as the application, per-flow bandwidth requirements, maximum number of simultaneous connections, and maximum aggregate bandwidth for all services within that policy. The policy-based networking system allows the operations manager to create service plans that include such specifications or can be derived by combining more than one service. While the detailed network actions and element configurations are defined and handled by the policy-based networking system, the resulting plans would be offered to the customer through the provider's billing system.

When a customer orders a new service, the billing system authorizes the service and sends a service activation request to the policy-based networking system. The policy-based system then converts the service request into the appropriate policies for distribution to the relevant policy enforcement points on the provider's network.

Deployment Considerations

Service providers face many of the same concerns in deploying policy-based networking as their enterprise counterparts (see Chapter 16). In addition, they must also be concerned about the scalability of the system, since they typically maintain larger networks than enterprises do, and they need to integrate any policy-based networking system with their billing and accounting systems.

Many service providers manage networks that consist of tens or hundreds of thousands of switches and routers. These networks are larger than those of most enterprises. The first issue of scalability thus becomes whether a policy-based networking system can handle all of these devices and how much equipment (policy decisions points, for instance) must be installed within the service provider's network. There is one more scalability concern, however. The service provider also has to consider the scalability of the management interface itself. In other words, how many people does it take to run the policy-based system for a network as large as the service provider's? If, in the long run, the operation of the policy-based system takes more effort and money than the previous way of doing things, it makes little economic sense to install and use the system.

Service providers already have some type of accounting and billing system in place; after all, charging for services is central to their operation. Only a few vendors of policy-based network management systems provide links between their systems and existing accounting and billing systems. Some of the larger vendors link their policy-based networking products with their own service management systems, while others have provided APIs that other vendors can use to exchange data to handle billing and accounting tasks.

Although enterprise network managers can configure policy-based network management systems to control traffic at core and edge network devices as well as at desktop computers, service providers face another choice in how they set up their network infrastructure to provide new IP-based services.

Currently, service providers offering additional IP services, such as VPNs, do so by installing and managing routers or similar devices at the customer's site (the CPE-based approach). However, this is an expensive approach to offering such services, with added costs coming from the premises-based devices and the expenses associated with their management. This is one instance in which policy-based network management can reduce the cost for NSPs. Policy-based network management systems can significantly decrease the cost of managing the devices, although NSPs still must deal with the installation of CPE hardware at each customer's site.

Another option, which uses newer equipment called service switches, allows the service provider to install minimal equipment at each customer's site (usually just a router) and concentrate the intelligence at the central office or point of presence (POP). This reduces the number of devices that a service provider has to manage, since most of the service functions are installed and controlled at the service switch, which serves multiple customers (see Figure 17.3) and reduces the number of "truck rolls" a provider must make to set up a new service for a customer. And these service switches can be configured by policy-based networking systems in much the same manner as the CPE devices we described earlier—there just are fewer of them.

Case Studies

Let's take a look at some real-life case studies to see how service providers have used policy-based networking. We'll cover two cases in detail: one is a global ISP that uses policy-based networking to control multicast traffic between customers, and the second is a video services ASP.

Note: Service providers are notoriously reluctant to give out detailed information on the technologies they employ because these technologies often give them a competitive advantage, which they want to maintain. Some details may be missing from these case studies; what you see is all we could get from the service providers.

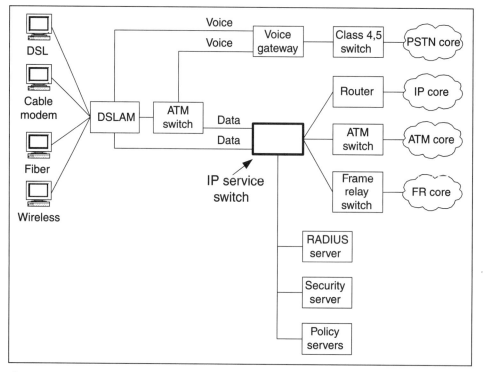

Figure 17.3 Location of service switch in service provider's network.

Global Internet Service Provider

This major service provider, with operations in all 50 states in the United States and 30 other countries around the world, deployed a policy-based networking system for a rather unique application: to control IP multicasting services on its network. These multicasting services are offered as a special value-added service to the service provider's customers.

Aside from the installation of the policy-based networking system, very little else had to be done to the network to prepare it for the multicasting services. The first policy distributed to all edge routers on the service provider's network was to block *all* multicast traffic. The service provider then created a policy for all edge routers to admit multicast traffic from a certified multicast address. The provider also set that group address for filtering and marking packets, assigning an EF DiffServ Code Point at the edge for preferred forwarding.

As a pilot project, the service provider configured its routers so that staff members visiting customer locations could use multicasting for training and internal meetings. The multicasting applications were developed and tested internally, and internal operations staff assigned group addresses for any of the off-site uses.

Since the pilot project was successful, the service provider rolled out a similar service to its customers. In order for a customer to transmit multicast traffic on the ISP's network, the customer first has to submit its multicast application for testing and certification. If the application is well behaved according to the service provider's tests, the ISP provides a certified multicast group address for that application's traffic. (See sidebar for more on multicast addresses.)

When a customer's application is approved and the group address is assigned to the customer, new policies are created for a particular group address in the policy-based networking system. These policies take care of configuring all edge routers to pass the customer's multicast traffic and, if necessary, provide preferred forwarding of the traffic.

Furthermore, since the provider can track traffic by the group address, it can perform a very basic level of accounting on the multicast traffic, although that hasn't been integrated with the actual billing software.

Video Application Service Provider

Our second case study in this chapter is that of a service provider that was looking to provide telephony, cable TV, and ISP services to residential customers over a converged network. One of its first steps along this path was to offer video on demand over its network, so we'll call them a video ASP for the time being.

The SP has its own regional network infrastructure and focuses on providing fiber-optic feeds to multiunit dwellings and new housing developments. It also installs structured wiring in these dwellings and developments, installing two to three 10/100 Mbps CAT 5 drops in each unit (see Figure 17.4). The resident can then plug in either a set-top box for cable TV, an IP phone for tele-

---

MULTICAST ADDRESSES

A major difference between IP multicasting and unicast data is the host group model. A host group consists of a set of networks sharing a common identifying multicast address; they all receive any data packets addressed to this multicast address. In IPv4, the class D address is used for controlling multicast sessions. Class D addresses start with 1110 as their high-order bits, which covers the range of host addresses from 224.0.0.0 to 239.255.255.255. For more details, see my book, *IP Multicasting: The Complete Guide to Interactive Corporate Networks*, Wiley, 1998.

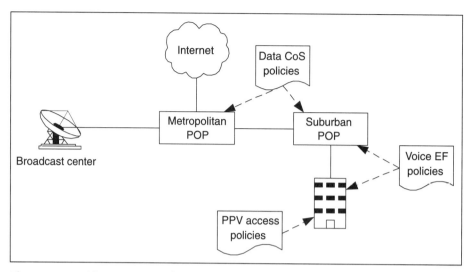

Figure 17.4 Video ASP network.

phony, or a computer for ISP services. The network is a multivendor network, using one vendor's switches and routers in the core, and a different vendor's switches at the network edge, that is, at the multiunit dwellings.

As we said, the service provider was initially interested in controlling the delivery of video, in this case by means of IP multicasting. The access control point to the multicast traffic was set at the edge switch port.

Originally, the service provider planned to use the scheduling functions (i.e., time-based policies) available in the policy-based networking system to take care of blackout periods and access control for video on demand and use basic access control policies to support basic TV, cable, and premium channels. However, the content providers were concerned that customers could substitute a PC for the set-top box and record the broadcast specials. To deal with the issues of the content providers, the service provider decided to encrypt the content before multicasting it, so that only the set-top box can decrypt the video stream and map the IP multicast traffic to an analog channel for viewing. The set-top box talks to a channel server in the provider's network to get the mapping of the IP multicast to an analog channel and the decryption key for each channel.

The ASP was also looking to let the customer subscribe to content as easily as possible (self-provision, as it were), either over the phone or via the Web. As part of this effort, the ASP used the API provided by the vendor of the policy-based networking product to add a customer care interface to the policy system. The customer can now use this system to purchase tiered services for Internet access as well.

Summary

Service providers—ISPs, NSPs, and ASPs—can benefit from the use of policy-based networking. In many cases, they have even greater issues of scale to deal with than their enterprise counterparts. The Telecommunication Management Network (TMN) model that many service providers use to maintain their network operations forms a good basis for compartmentalizing operational functions, but it still does not offer many of the benefits of policy-based networking. Policy-based networking should not be considered as a substitute for TMN-based systems, but as an adjunct that should integrate with existing systems. As the case studies show, some service providers have already started to use policy-based networking to offer new services to their customers.

Deploying Policy-Based Networking Systems

In this book, we aimed to introduce you to many of the details surrounding policy-based networking. This includes not only the reasons for deploying policy-based networking systems in your own networks, but also the functions of each component of a policy-based system and how the components perform those functions.

Since policy-based networking is an evolving technology, one that involves the use of many technologies themselves that are also evolving, it's impossible to always say that there's only one right way of doing things. We hope that this book has left you with a sense of some of the possibilities, giving you an idea of what questions to ask vendors and engineers when you shop for a policy-based networking system of your own.

Now it's time to draw this book to a close. In this, the book's final chapter, we recap the important steps to deploying policy-based networking.

Guidelines for Deploying Policy-Based Networking

In a nutshell, here are the steps we recommend that you follow in the development of your policy-based networking system:

1. State clear objectives.
2. Take the measure of your infrastructure.
3. Define mission-critical applications.
4. Define service classes.
5. Categorize devices.
6. Create policies.
7. Deploy policies in a pilot project.
8. Roll out larger implementations.
9. Monitor, refine, and do it all over again.

As we describe these guidelines in the following paragraphs, keep in mind that some of the specifics are aimed at QoS, since that's the service to which most organizations have applied policy-based networking. However, the general guidelines apply to any application of policy-based networking.

State Clear Objectives

As we've seen in the past few chapters, an organization can have a variety of reasons for installing policy-based networking. To ensure the success of your project, you should be as clear as possible on the objectives for policy-based networking. Stating clear objectives up front not only makes it easier to present a business case to management for the use of this new technology, but it also makes it easier to measure the success of your project.

Take the Measure of Your Infrastructure

You probably already have some idea of the capabilities of your network and what its problems are. That's why you've decided to turn to policy-based networking. But it's crucial to learn the capabilities of your network devices with respect to policy and any other supplemental technologies you may employ (such as traffic classification and load balancing, for instance). Assess the ability of your network devices to support a policy-based networking system. For instance, can a network device support resource assignment and forwarding policies? If so, it can be a policy enforcement point; if not, it cannot play a role unless it is upgraded or replaced.

It's also important to baseline the behavior of your network. We saw from the case studies that some network managers had a vague idea of the applications causing problems on their networks when they first thought about deploying QoS and policy-based networking, but they had to refine their view of their network traffic in order to create service classes and appropriate policies. Detailed knowledge of networked applications and services, access requirements for individuals or groups, and current service quality are essential for creating realistic policies.

As you study your network, you'll need data that answers questions such as the following:

What does the network support today?

Which applications consume the most resources?

How do traffic patterns change with time of day and day of the week (or even day of the month)?

Are there applications that should not be using network resources at all?

What are the choke points?

Take a look at Chapter 9, "Monitoring Network Behavior and Policies," to see some of the ways that you can monitor an application's traffic and create a profile of your applications. When you create an application profile, keep in mind that it should include at least the following information to help with policy planning:

- Availability of servers and applications
- Response times of each application or service
- Transaction rates of the application
- Packet distributions, bandwidth utilization, and burstiness
- Port numbers, server addresses used
- Latency and jitter requirements
- User/group access requirements
- How an application can be classified (IP address, port number, host name, URL, etc.)

Define Mission-Critical Applications

For many, it may be a simple matter to select those applications that are critical to the continued health of your business. But it may be more difficult to rate them in their relative importance. Usually there are no more than a few applications that deserve the best performance possible.

As you attempt to rate your applications, it may be necessary to take into account their application profiles. While such issues as response times and user access requirements won't necessarily make one application more mission-critical than another, the profiles may help you decide the relative importance of some applications; see the bank's case study in Chapter 16, "Policy-Based Networking for Enterprises," as an example.

Define Service Classes

With your list of mission-critical applications and their corresponding application profiles in hand, you should be able to define service classes and match the applications to them. As we've said before, keep it simple—don't make a separate service class for each application. The case studies we've discussed, and other information obtained from network managers we've spoken to, indicate that two to four service classes are enough to handle most situations.

As you define your service classes, keep in mind what parameters are the distinguishing characteristics of each class. For instance, a service class defined for voice over data (IP telephony) may impose stringent requirements on jitter, but none of the applications in your other service classes may care about jitter. Keeping track of the distinguishing parameters of each service class will be important if you decide that some policies will have to be implementation-specific, such as requiring DiffServ. Furthermore, the parameters of each service class may help you decide between techniques when there's more than one way to meet the requirements of a class.

Keep in mind that policy-based networking systems are not infallible. They need guidance from network managers and network designers to enforce policies properly. While policy-based networking systems may shield you from the need to know and set all the parameters for QoS techniques, you still need to know what approaches are appropriate for your devices and traffic. This is one area in which the vendors of the systems can help you select techniques appropriate to your situation.

Your network infrastructure may also place limits on your service class definitions. There's a limit on how many service classes some technologies can support. For instance, there are only eight priority levels within a switched LAN using the IEEE 802.1p tagging standard. On the other hand, routers supporting DiffServ or MPLS can recognize a larger number of flows.

When it comes to QoS, you're trying to allocate your network resources for the preferential treatment of some traffic. That means that each service class must include a method for assigning resources whenever a new connection is initiated. For example, you can easily map traffic priorities into each class. The class with the most demanding QoS/business value combination receives the highest forwarding priority, and so forth, proceeding toward best effort. Some classes may also require guaranteed bandwidth to meet the business goals.

Categorize Devices

We'd already touched on the ability of your network infrastructure to support policy. Now's the time for you to assess the policy roles of your devices based on their capabilities. You need to at least identify which resources will be used for policy enforcement. For instance, will your requirements be met by marking packets and enforcing policies at the LAN-WAN boundary, as we saw in many of the case studies? Or will you have to deploy policies to servers and end-user hosts to classify and mark traffic, with edge routers handling traffic shaping and other QoS enforcement mechanisms?

Create Policies

Once again, keep it simple. (Have we said that enough times?) The high-level policies should be few in number. Let most situations be handled by default policies and then create special policies for the exceptions as needed.

As you design your policies, think about how you'll provision your bandwidth. Some amount must be set aside for best effort; the remainder is used as service policies dictate. (Review the case studies we covered in Chapter 16, "Policy-Based Networking for Enterprises," and Chapter 17, "Policy-Based Networking for Service Providers.") Select a maximum amount of bandwidth that can be committed, in aggregate or for each category. Bandwidth reservation policies should consider these boundary conditions. For example, what should happen when the maximum bandwidth has been allocated and another user wants a service? Some choices are as follows:

- Block any new service activities until bandwidth is released from this class at a later time.

- Allow the activity at a lower priority or bandwidth allocation—a better best effort. Each organization will have its own approach; there is no correct solution for all.

Also, keep in mind how the policies will be enforced. There are several options to consider, including identifying each flow, reserving bandwidth (using IEEE 802.1p, ToS, CoS, DiffServ, MPLS, for example), controlling queues, admission control, and traffic shaping. Refer to Chapter 13, "An Introduction to Quality of Service," for the basics on QoS mechanisms and see Geoff Huston, *Internet Performance Survival Guide: QoS Strategies for Multiservice Networks*, Wiley, 2000, for more details.

Deploy Policies in a Pilot Project

If you have complete faith in your understanding of the network, your newly defined policies, and the ability of the policy-based system to configure all the appropriate network devices properly, then you could just load and deploy your new policies in the network and walk away. But we doubt that any of you would have that much faith in the system the first time you use it (and maybe not even after the nth time...).

It's always a good practice to start small. You could start by setting up a lab with a few routers and switches that are similar to the ones on your production network. Or you could select a restricted part of your network to test the effects of the policies you've created. In Chapter 16, the bank started out testing its policies with a local branch before propagating policies to other branches around the world. The video ASP in Chapter 17 started testing its policies with a few multiunit dwellings first.

Roll Out Larger Implementations

Once you're satisfied that your restricted tests of policy are achieving the desired results, then and only then are you ready to deploy policies to larger portions of your network.

Don't forget that deployment to larger networks may strain the scalability of your policy system, so you need to consider installing more PDPs and perhaps more policy repositories to meet the needs of your network. Also, you may

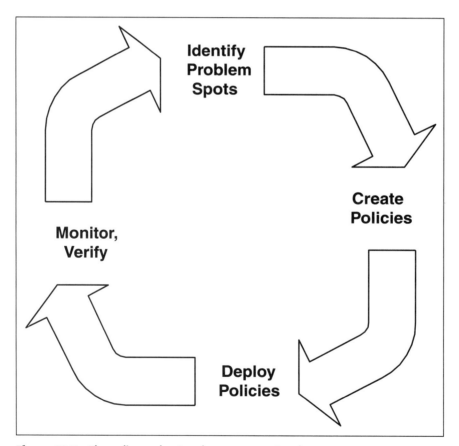

Figure 18.1   The policy and network management cycle.

have to set up a hierarchy of policy managers with different creation and editing rights for policies so they can handle localized policies, such as those for a remote site or a particular department.

Monitor, Refine, and Do It All over Again

Even though policy-based networking automates many of the functions of device configuration and dealing with the network as a whole, networks are too dynamic for you to simply walk away and let the policy-based system run everything for you. For one thing, today's policy-based networking systems are not capable of doing everything for you.

Monitoring is essential to determine the efficacy of your policies. We reviewed many monitoring procedures in Chapter 9. You should use at least a few of those techniques regularly to determine the state of your network. And don't forget to check with your end users; after all, they're the final say as to whether the applications are running properly.

Network traffic has the habit of changing frequently as new users and new applications are added, so you'll need your monitoring results to tell you when and if you should refine your policies (see Figure 18.1).

Here's to your success with policy-based networking!

References

Books

Bumpus, Winston, John W. Sweitzer, Patrick Thompson, Andrea R. Westerinen, Raymond C. Williams. 2000. *Common Information Model*. New York: John Wiley & Sons, Inc.

Durham, David, and Raj Yavatkar. 1999. *Inside the Internet's Resource Reservation Protocol*. New York: John Wiley & Sons, Inc.

Huston, Geoff. 2000. *Internet Performance Survival Guide: QoS Strategies for Multiservice Networks*. New York: John Wiley & Sons, Inc.

Izzo, Paul. 2000. *Gigabit Networks*. New York: John Wiley & Sons, Inc.

Kosiur, David. 1998. *Building and Managing Virtual Private Networks*. New York: John Wiley & Sons, Inc.

McDysan, David. 2000. *VPN Applications Guide: Real Solutions for Enterprise Networks*. New York: John Wiley & Sons, Inc.

Strassner, John. 1999. *Directory Enabled Networks*. Indianapolis, IN: Macmillan Technical Publishing.

Zeltserman, David. 1999. *A Practical Guide to SNMPv3 and Network Management*. Upper Saddle River, NJ: Prentice-Hall PTR.

Internet Drafts

Authentication, Authorization, and Accounting Working Group

Durham, D., H. Khosravi, W. Weiss, and A. Doria. 2000. "COPS Usage for AAA" (June 6). <draft-durham-aaa-cops-ext-00.txt>

Ekstein, R., Y. T'Joens, B. Sales, and O. Paridaens. "AAA Protocols: Comparison between RADIUS, DIAMETER and COPS" (April 6). <draft-ekstein-aaa-protcomp-00.txt>

Khosravi, H., D. Durham, and J. Walker. "Comparison of COPS against AAA Network Access Requirements" (June 1). <draft-durham-aaa-cops-reqments-00.txt>

Diameter

Calhoun, P. R., G. Zorn, P. Pan, and H. Akhtar. 2000. "DIAMETER Framework Document" (June 16). <draft-calhoun-diameter-framework-08.txt>

Authentication, Authorization, and Accounting Architecture Working Group

Carle, G., S. Zander, and T. Zseby. 2000. "Policy-Based Accounting" (July 21). <draft-irtf-aaaarch-pol-acct-00.txt>

de Laat, C., G. Gross, L. Gommans, J. Vollbrecht, and D. Spence. 2000. "Generic AAA Architecture" (April 19). <draft-irtf-aaaarch-generic-01.txt>

DiffServ Working Group

Baker, F., K. Chan, and A. Smith. 2000. "Management Information Base for the Differentiated Services Architecture" (July 19). <draft-ietf-diffserv-mib-04.txt>

Bernet, Y., S. Blake, D. Grossman, and A. Smith. 2000. "An Informal Management Model for DiffServ Routers" (July 19). <draft-ietf-diffserv-model-04.txt>

Fine, M., K. McCloghrie, J. Seligson, K. Chan, S. Hahn, A. Smith, and F. Reichmeyer. 2000. "Differentiated Services Quality of Service Policy Information Base" (July 21). <draft-ietf-diffserv-pib-01.txt>

Radhakrishna, C. 2000. "Use of RSVP for Differentiated Services Signaling and Admission Control" (July 6). <draft-rk-diffserv-rsvp-sig-00.txt>

Integrated Services over Specific Link Layers Working Group

Baker, F., C. Iturralde, F. Le Faucheur, and B. Davie. 2000. "RSVP Reservations Aggregation" (March 13). <draft-ietf-issll-rsvp-aggr-02.txt>

Bernet, Y. 1999. "Format of the RSVP DCLASS Object" (October 27). <draft-ietf-issll-dclass-01.txt>

Bernet, Y., R. Yavatkar, P. Ford, F. Baker, L. Zhang, M. Speer, R. Braden, B. Davie, J. Wroclawski, and E. Felstaine. 2000. "A Framework for Integrated Services Operation over DiffServ Networks" (May 24). <draft-ietf-issll-diffserv-rsvp-05.txt>

Wroclawski, J., and A. Charny. 2000. "Integrated Service Mappings for Differentiated Services Networks" (March 15) <draft-ietf-issll-ds-map-00.txt>

Internet Protocol Security Policy Working Group

Blaze, M., A. Keromytis, M. Richardson, and L. Sanchez. 2000. "IPsec Policy Architecture" (July 18). <draft-ietf-ipsp-arch-00.txt>

Blaze, M., A. Keromytis, M. Richardson, and L. Sanchez. 2000. "IPSP Requirements" (July 20). <draft-ietf-ipsp-requirements-00.txt>

Blaze, M., J. Ioannidis, A., and D. Keromytis. 2000. "Compliance Checking and IPSEC Policy Management" (March 15). <draft-blaze-ipsp-trustmgt-00.txt>

Condell, M., C. Lynn, and J. Zao. 2000. "Security Policy Specification Language" (March 9). <draft-ietf-ipsp-spsl-00.txt>

Cuervo, F., and A. Rayhan. 2000. "IPSEC Policy Architecture" (July 21). <draft-cuervo-ipsp-arch-00.txt>

Iyer, M., R. Kale, L. Apsani, and S. Iyer. 2000. "IP VPN Policy Information Model" (July 24). <draft-iyer-policy-ipvpn-info-model-00.txt>

Jason, J. 2000. "IPsec Configuration Policy Model" (July 12). <draft-ietf-ipsp-config-policy-model-01.txt>

Li, M., D. Arneson, A. Doria, and J. Jason. 2000. "IPSec Policy Information Base" (July 21). <draft-ietf-ipsp-ipsecpib-00.txt>

Sanchez, L. A., and M. N. Condell. 2000. "Security Policy Protocol" (July 12). <draft-ietf-ipsp-spp-00.txt>

LDAP Extensions Working Group and Related Topics

Merrells, J., E. Reed, and U. Srinivasan. 2000. "LDAP Replication Architecture" (July 10). <draft-ietf-ldup-model-04.txt>

Reed, E. 2000. "LDUP Replication Information Model" (March 16). <draft-ietf-ldup-infomod-01.txt>

Smith, M., G. Good, R. Weltman, and T. Howes. 2000. "Persistent Search: A Simple LDAP Change Notification Mechanism" (March 7). <draft-ietf-ldapext-psearch-02.txt>

Stokes, E., D. Byrne, and B. Blakley. 2000. "Access Control Model for LDAP" (July 19). <draft-ietf-ldapext-acl-model-06.txt>

Stokes, E., and G. Good. 2000. "The LDUP Replication Update Protocol" (July 20). <draft-ietf-ldup-protocol-02.txt>

Weiser, R. F., and E. Stokes. 2000. "LDAP V3 Replication Requirements" (August 7). <draft-ietf-ldup-replica-req-03.txt>

Multiprotocol Layer Switching Working Group and Related Topics

Chadha, R., and H. -A. Lin. 2000. "Policy Information Model for MPLS Traffic Engineering" (July 18). <draft-chadha-policy-mpls-te-00.txt>

Le Faucheur, F., L. Wu, B. Davie, S. Davari, P. Vaananen, R. Krishnan, P. Cheval, and J. Heinanen. 2000. "MPLS Support of Differentiated Services" (July 14). <draft-ietf-mpls-diff-ext-06.txt>

Isoyama, K., M. Yoshida, M. Brunner, A. Kind, and J. Quittek. 2000. "Policy Framework QoS Information Model for MPLS" (July 12). <draft-isoyama-policy-mpls-info-model-00.txt>

Nadeau, T. D., C. Srinivasan, and A. Viswanathan. 2000. "Multiprotocol Label Switching Packet Classification Management Information Base Using SMIv2" (July 21). <draft-nadeau-mpls-packet-classifier-mib-01.txt>

Reichmeyer, F., S. Wright, and M. Gibson. 2000. "COPS Usage for MPLS/Traffic Engineering" (July 18). <draft-franr-mpls-cops-00.txt>

Rosen, E. C., A. Viswanatha, and R. Callon. 2000. "Multiprotocol Label Switching Architecture" (July). <draft-ietf-mpls-arch-07.txt>

Srinivasan, C., and A. Viswanathan. 2000. "MPLS Traffic Engineering Management Information Base Using SMIv2" (July 21). <draft-ietf-mpls-te-mib-04.txt>

Policy Working Group

Mahon, H., Y. Bernet, S. Herzog, and J. Schnizlein. "Requirements for a Policy Management System" <draft-ietf-policy-req-02.txt>

Moore, B., E. Ellesson, and J. Strassner. 2000. "Policy Core Information Model—Version 1 Specification" (July 20). <draft-ietf-policy-core-info-model-07.txt>

Owens, K., V. Jadhwani, and H. Mahon. 2000. "Policy Management Scalability" (March 10). <draft-owens-policy-scalability-00.txt>

Snir, Y., Y. Ramberg, J. Strassner, and R. Cohen. 2000. "Policy Framework QoS Information Model" (May 1). <draft-ietf-policy-qos-info-model-01.txt>

Snir, Y., Y. Ramberg, J. Strassner, and R.Cohen. 2000. "QoS Policy Schema" (May 1). <draft-ietf-policy-qos-schema-01.txt>

Strassner, J., E. Ellesson, B. Moore, and Ryan Moats. 2000. "Policy Framework LDAP Core Schema" (July 20). <draft-ietf-policy-core-schema-07.txt>

Strassner, J., W. Weiss, D. Durham, and A. Westerinen. 2000. "Information Model for Describing Network Device QoS Mechanisms" (July 24). <draft-ietf-policy-qos-device-info-model-01.txt>

Westerinen, A., J. Schnizlein, J. Strassner, M. Scherling, B. Quinn, J. Perry, S. Herzog, A.-N. Huynh, and M. Carlson. 2000. "Policy Terminology" (July 19). <draft-ietf-policy-terminology-00.txt>

Wright, S., S. Herzog, F. Reichmeyer, and R. Jaeger. 2000. "Requirements for Policy Enabled MPLS" (March 9). <draft-wright-policy-mpls-00.txt>

Resource Allocation Protocol Working Group (COPS and Related Work)

Chan, K. H., D. Durham, S. Gai, S. Herzog, K. McCloghrie, F. Reichmeyer, J. Seligson, A. Smith, and R. Yavatkar. 2000. "COPS Usage for Policy Provisioning" (August 24). <draft-ietf-rap-pr-04.txt>

Chan, K., J. Seligson, K. McCloghrie, M. Fine, S. Hahn, A. Smith, and F. Reichmeyer. 2000. "The Policy Device Auxiliary MIB" (July 19). <draft-ietf-rap-pol-aux-mib-00.txt>

Chan, K., J. Seligson, K. McCloghrie, M. Fine, S. Hahn, A. Smith, and F. Reichmeyer. 2000. "The Policy Device Auxiliary MIB" (July 19). <draft-kzm-rap-pol-aux-mib-01.txt>

Fine, M., K. McCloghrie, J. Seligson, K. Chan, S. Hahn, A. Smith, and F. Reichmeyer. 2000. "Framework Policy Information Base" (July 21). <draft-ietf-rap-frameworkpib-01.txt>

Herzog, S. 2000. "Signaled Preemption Priority Policy Element" (July 18). <draft-ietf-rap-signaled-priority-v2-00.txt>

McCloghrie, K., M. Fine, J. Seligson, K. Chan, S. Chan, A. Smith, and F. Reichmeyer. 2000. "Structure of Policy Provisioning Information (SPPI)" (July 20). <draft-ietf-rap-sppi-01.txt>

Rawlins, D., A. Kulkarni, K. H. Chan, and D. Dutt. 2000. "Framework of COPS-PR Policy Information Base for Accounting Usage" (July 21). <draft-rawlins-acct-fr-pib-00.txt>

Smith, A., D. Partain, and J. Seligson. 2000. "Definitions of Managed Objects for Common Open Policy Service (COPS) Protocol Clients" (June 9). <draft-ietf-rap-cops-client-mib-03.txt>

Yadav, S., R. Yavatkar, R. Pabbati, P. Ford, T. Moore, and S. Herzog. 2000. "Identity Representation for RSVP" (June 19). <draft-ietf-rap-rsvp-newidentity-00.txt>

SNMP Configuration Working Group

Hazewinkel, H., and D. Partain. 2000. "The DiffServ Policy MIB" (July 6). <draft-ietf-snmpconf-diffpolicy-02.txt>

MacFaden, M., and J. Saperia. 2000. "Configuring Networks and Devices with SNMP" (July 13). <draft-ietf-snmpconf-bcp-02.txt>

Saperia, J. 2000. "Policy Configuration with SNMP" (July 10). <draft-saperia-policysnmp-00.txt>

Waldbusser, S., J. Saperia, and T. Hongal. 2000. "Policy-Based Management MIB" (July 21). <draft-ietf-snmpconf-pm-02.txt>

RFCs

2906 AAA Authorization Requirements, S. Farrell, J. Vollbrecht, P. Calhoun, L. Gommans, G. Gross, B. de Bruijn, C. de Laat, M. Holdrege, and D. Spence, August 2000. (Status: Informational)

2905 AAA Authorization Application Examples, J. Vollbrecht, P. Calhoun, S. Farrell, L. Gommans, G. Gross, B. de Bruijn, C. de Laat, M. Holdrege, and D. Spence, August 2000. (Status: Informational)

2904 AAA Authorization Framework, J. Vollbrecht, P. Calhoun, S. Farrell, L. Gommans, G. Gross, B. de Bruijn, C. de Laat, M. Holdrege, and D. Spence, August 2000. (Status: Informational)

2872 Application and Sub Application Identity Policy Element for Use with RSVP. Y. Bernet and R. Pabbati. June 2000. (Status: Proposed Standard)

2865 Remote Authentication Dial-In User Service (RADIUS). C. Rigney, S. Willens, A. Rubens, and W. Simpson. June 2000. (Status: Draft Standard)

2836 Per Hop Behavior Identification Codes. S. Brim, B. Carpenter, and F. Le Faucheur. May 2000. (Status: Proposed Standard)

2829 Authentication Methods for LDAP. M. Wahl, H. Alvestrand, J. Hodges, and R. Morgan. May 2000. (Status: Proposed Standard)

2820 Access Control Requirements for LDAP. E. Stokes, D. Byrne, B. Blakley, and P. Behera. May 2000. (Status: Informational)

2814 SBM (Subnet Bandwidth Manager): A Protocol for RSVP-based Admission Control over IEEE 802-style networks. R. Yavatkar, D. Hoffman, Y. Bernet, F. Baker, and M. Speer. May 2000. (Status: Proposed Standard)

2768 Network Policy and Services: A Report of a Workshop on Middleware. B. Aiken, J. Strassner, B. Carpenter, I. Foster, C. Lynch, J. Mambretti, R. Moore, and B. Teitelbaum. February 2000. (Status: Informational)

2753 A Framework for Policy-Based Admission Control. R. Yavatkar, D. Pendarakis, and R. Guerin. January 2000. (Status: Informational)

2750 RSVP Extensions for Policy Control. S. Herzog. January 2000. (Status: Proposed Standard)

2749 COPS Usage for RSVP. J. Boyle, R. Cohen, D. Durham, S. Herzog, R. Rajan, and A. Sastry. January 2000. (Status: Proposed Standard)

2748 The COPS (Common Open Policy Service) Protocol. J. Boyle, R. Cohen, D. Durham, S. Herzog, R. Rajan, and A. Sastry. January 2000. (Status: Proposed Standard)

2722 Traffic Flow Measurement: Architecture. N. Brownlee, C. Mills, and G. Ruth. October 1999. (Status: Informational)

2720 Traffic Flow Measurement: Meter MIB. N. Brownlee. October 1999. (Status: Proposed Standard)

2704 The KeyNote Trust-Management System Version 2. M. Blaze, J. Feigenbaum, J. Ioannidis, and A. Keromytis. September 1999. (Status: Informational)

2678 IPPM Metrics for Measuring Connectivity. J. Mahdavi and V. Paxson. September 1999. (Status: Proposed Standard)

2576 Coexistence between Version 1, Version 2, and Version 3 of the Internet-Standard Network Management Framework. R. Frye, D. Levi, S. Routhier, and B. Wijnen. March 2000. (Status: Proposed Standard)

2575 View-based Access Control Model (VACM) for the Simple Network Management Protocol (SNMP). B. Wijnen, R. Presuhn, and K. McCloghrie. April 1999. (Status: Draft Standard)

2574 User-based Security Model (USM) for Version 3 of the Simple Network Management Protocol (SNMPv3). U. Blumenthal and B. Wijnen. April 1999. (Status: Draft Standard)

2573 SNMP Applications. D. Levi, P. Meyer, and B. Stewart. April 1999. (Status: Draft Standard)

2572 Message Processing and Dispatching for the Simple Network Management Protocol (SNMP). J. Case, D. Harrington, R. Presuhn, and B. Wijnen. April 1999. (Status: Draft Standard)

2571 An Architecture for Describing SNMP Management Frameworks. B. Wijnen, D. Harrington, and R. Presuhn. April 1999. (Status: Draft Standard)

2570 Introduction to Version 3 of the Internet-standard Network Management Framework. J. Case, R. Mundy, D. Partain, and B. Stewart. April 1999. (Status: Informational)

Vendors and Products

3Com Corporation
  5400 Bayfront Plaza
  Santa Clara, CA 95052
  (408) 764-5000 or
  (800) NET-3COM
  www.3com.com

Abatis
  (now part of Redback Networks)
  Redback Networks, Inc.
  1195 Borregas Avenue
  Sunnyvale, CA 94089
  (408) 571-5200
  www.abatis.com
  www.redback.com/abatis/
    Virtual Enterprise Manager

Alcatel Internetworking
  26801 West Agoura Road
  Calabasas, CA 91301
  (818) 880-3500 or
  (800) 995-2612
  www.ind.alcatel.com

Switched Network Services (SNS),
  PolicyViewAllot
  292 E. Main Street
  Los Gatos, CA 95030
  (408) 399-3154
  www.allot.com

Aprisma Management Technologies
  121 Technology Drive
  Durham, NH 03824
  (603) 337-7000
    SPECTRUM

Avaya Communications
  (formerly Lucent)
  www.lucent.com
    RealNetRules

Centricity, Inc.
  4900 SW Meadows Road
  Suite 400
  Lake Oswego, OR 97035
  (503) 675-1200 or
  (888) 675-3090
  www.centricitysoftware.com

CenterwiseCisco Systems, Inc.
170 West Tasman Drive
San Jose, CA 95134
(408) 526-4000 or
(800) 533-6387
www.cisco.com
CiscoAssure
Cisco QPM
Cisco SPM

Deterministic Networks, Inc.
(now part of Starband
Communications Inc.)
1760 Old Meadow Road
McLean, VA 22102

Hewlett-Packard Co.
OpenView Network Management
Division
Ft. Collins, CO
www.hp.com/openview/
OpenView PolicyXpert

IBM Corporation
3039 Cornwallis Road
Triangle Park, NC 27709
SecureWay Policy Director

Internet Dynamics, Inc.
3717 East Thousand Oaks Blvd.
Westlake Village, CA 91362
(805) 370-2200
www.conclave.com
Conclave Policy Server

IP Highway, Inc.
55 New York Avenue
Framingham, MA 01701
(508) 620-1141
www.iphighway.com
Open Policy System (OPS)

Marconi Communications
North American Headquarters
1000 Fore Drive
Warrendale, PA 15086
(724) 742-4444 or
(888) 404-0444
Firewall Switching Agent
PrioriSynch

NetResource Guard
Authentifirst Agent

Nortel Networks
4401 Great America Parkway
Santa Clara, CA 95054
(800) 822-9638
www.nortelnetworks.com
Optivity Policy Services
Preside Policy Services

Novell Inc.
Provo, UT
(801) 861-5588 or
(800) 638-9273
www.novell.com
ZENworks for Networks

Orchestream Ltd.
Glen House
125 Old Brompton Road
London, England SW7 3RP
+44 (0)20 7598 7555
Orchestream Enterprise Edition
Orchestream MNS Edition
Orchestream Provider Edition

Packeteer, Inc.
(408) 873-4400 or
(800) 697-2253
www.packeteer.com
PolicyCenter

Ponte Communications
3 Waters Park, Suite 225
San Mateo, CA 94403
(650) 372-5200
www.pontecom.com

SafeNet
8029 Corporate Drive
Baltimore, MD 21236
(410) 931-7500
www.ire.com
SafeNet/VPN Policy Manager

SOLSoft, Inc.
2685 Marine Way, Suite 1320
Mountain View, CA 94043
(650) 428-2800
www.solsoft.com
NetPartitioner

Glossary

Access control   The management of rights to use resources.

Access control list (ACL)   In a router, a collection of permit and deny conditions that apply to IP addresses.

Action   An operation governed by a policy rule. When a rule evaluates TRUE, then the action is triggered. For QoS and security policies, that action is usually to provide a networking service (e.g., provision bandwidth, configure a class of service, allow access or usage).

Active networking monitoring   Measuring network performance using either special devices in the network whose sole job is to periodically test the network and report results or software agents residing on servers and end-user hosts.

Application-level monitoring   Measuring the performance of a networked application at the highest layer of the OSI stack, the application layer.

Application proxy firewall   A firewall system in which transmission service is provided by processes that maintain complete TCP connection state and sequencing for applications enabled to flow through the firewall.

Authentication   A process to determine the identity of a party, system, or application, securely and uniquely.

Bandwidth   The range of signal frequencies that can be carried by a communications channel subject to specified conditions of signal loss or distortion. A measure of a circuit's information or transmission capacity, expressed in either bits per second (bps) or hertz (Hz).

Best effort   The standard means of handling traffic on a TCP/IP network without managing the bandwidth or assigning priority. The network tries to send all traffic and accepts that some packets may be delayed due to congestion, but does not influence which packets these will be.

Class of Service (CoS)   A method of dividing traffic into separate classes to provide differentiated service to each class within the network.

Common Information Model (CIM)   An object-oriented information model published by the Distributed Management Task Force (DMTF). It consists of a specification detailing the abstract modeling constructs and principles of the information model, and a language definition to represent the model. CIM includes a set of files, written in the language specified in the specification. These are known as the core and common models, and they define an information model addressing systems, devices, users, software distribution, the physical environment, networks, and policy.

Common Object Resource Broker Architecture (CORBA)   A software architecture defined by the Open Management Group (OMG) that enables software objects to interact with each other despite their location, type of host computer, or programming language.

Common Open Policy Service (COPS)   A simple query and response TCP-based protocol that can be used to exchange policy information between a policy decision point (PDP) and its clients (policy enforcement points, PEPs).

Command Line Interface (CLI)   A user interface to a computer's operating system or an application in which the user responds to a visual prompt by typing in a command on a specified line, receives a response from the system, and then enters another command, and so forth.

Condition   An expression of a condition type and its value(s) used to specify a constraint within a policy rule. A given condition can be negated using the NOT operator.

Configuration   The set of parameters in network elements and other systems that determine their function and operation. Some parameters are static, such as packet queue assignment, and can be predefined and downloaded to a network element. Others are more dynamic, such as the actions taken by a network device upon the occurrence of some event.

Congestion avoidance   A QoS method that proactively monitors network traffic loads in an effort to anticipate and avoid congestion at common network bottleneck points. Some examples include available bit rate (ABR) and weighted random early detection (WRED).

Congestion management   A QoS method that uses queuing algorithms to sort traffic and determine a method of priority to schedule traffic onto output links. Some examples include first in, first out (FIFO), priority queuing, custom queuing, and weighted fair queuing (WFQ).

Customer premise equipment (CPE)   The equipment deployed on the customer's site when the customer subscribes (or simply connects) to a carrier's service.

Device-dependent policy   A policy that describes the conditions and actions to be taken by a specific device using terms that are particular to a given implementation.

Device-independent policy   A policy that is expressed in terms of rules that describe conditions and actions to be taken by a device in a generic or implementation-independent fashion.

Differentiated Services (DiffServ)   A service architecture in which some network traffic is treated better than the rest by applying a per-hop service response to a packet based on the marking of the Differentiated Services field of the IP packet header.

Differentiated Services (DS) field   An 8-bit field of the IP header used to specify the requested per-hop service within the scope of the Differentiated Services architecture. This field was originally specified as the Type of Service (TOS) field.

DiffServ Code Point (DSCP)   The value used to mark packets in order to provide differentiated services. Up to 64 DiffServ codepoints can be set up, each one corresponding to bits set in the DiffServ Codepoint/IP Precedence section of the header of an IP packet.

Directory   A special type of database used to store information about objects such as network users, devices, and applications and the relationships between those objects. The information in a directory is stored within a structure that helps make the information easy to retrieve. The directory and its structure are often referred to as the namespace.

Directory Services Markup Language (DSML)   A language developed cooperatively by vendors with the aim of creating a mapping between LDAP content and the Extensible Markup Language (XML).

Distinguished name (DN)   A hierarchical name in the LDAP/X.500 information model, consisting of a relative distinguished name (RDN) plus the RDNs of all its parent entries.

Distributed Management Task Force (DMTF)   A group of vendors responsible for developing the Common Information Model (CIM), Web-Based Enterprise Management (WBEM), and associated LDAP mappings and APIs for the management of networked personal computers, network devices, and services. Formerly the Desktop Management Task Force.

Domain Name Service (DNS)   The network service responsible for converting numeric IP addresses into text-based names.

Drop precedence   An externally defined value that determines which packets will be discarded when the local average queue load exceeds a predefined proportion of the available resources.

Dynamic Host Configuration Protocol (DHCP)   A protocol that enables an address server to dynamically assign IP addresses to clients on an "as required" basis using administrator-assigned address ranges.

Element monitoring   Measuring the performance of individual network devices or individual interfaces within a network device.

Extensible Markup Language (XML)   A markup language designed for application-to-application communications based on the Standardized General Markup Language (SGML) used to represent structured data in textual form. An XML Document Type Definition (DTD) defines the information schema. XML documents contain the actual information. XML tools validate the XML documents against the DTD.

Firewall   A device acting as a network filter to restrict access to a private network from the outside, implementing access controls based on the contents of the packets of data that are transmitted between two parties or devices on the network.

Global policy conflict   A policy conflict based on the properties of the policy and not the specific devices (or their interfaces) to which the policy might apply.

Information model   An abstraction and representation of the entities in a managed environment, their properties, attributes and operations, and the way that they relate to each other. It is independent of any specific repository, application, protocol, or platform.

Inheritance   A property of an object class that enables it to inherit some of the characteristics of a higher-level class from which it was derived.

Integrated Services (IntServ)   The Integrated Services architecture consists of five key components: QoS requirements, resource-sharing requirements, allowances for packet dropping, provisions for usage feedback, and a resource-reservation model (RSVP).

Internet Engineering Task Force (IETF)   A worldwide organization that develops new technology and standards for the Internet.

Internet Key Exchange (IKE)   The key management protocol used in conjunction with IPsec. Defined in RFCs 2407–2409.

IP Precedence   A three-bit field within the IP TOS byte of the IP packet header that designates the relative priority with which the packet should be handled (eight possible values). The treatment of IP packets can be prioritized based on the IP precedence value, or mark, given to each packet. IP Precedence bit settings were defined in the IETF standard RFC 791. This standard was updated by IETF standard RFC 2474, which defines the 6-bit DiffServ codepoint setting, designed to be backward compatible with IP Precedence.

IP Security (IPSec)   The network cryptographic protocols for protecting IP packets. Defined in RFCs 2401–2406, 2410, and 2411.

Jitter   The distortion of a signal as it is propagated through the network; the signal varies from its original reference timing. In packet-switched networks, jitter is a distortion of the interpacket arrival times compared to the interpacket times of the original signal transmission. Also known as delay variance.

Latency The amount of time it takes for a data packet to traverse the network from its source to its destination. Also referred to as delay.

Layer 2 Tunneling Protocol (L2TP) A mechanism whereby discrete virtual tunnels can be created for each dial-up client in the network, each of which may terminate at different points upstream from the access server. Defined in RFC 2661.

Lightweight Directory Access Protocol (LDAP) An IP-based protocol that governs how information within X.500 format directories can be obtained.

Local policy conflict A policy conflict based on the properties of the specific devices (or their interfaces) to which the policy might apply.

Management Information Base (MIB) A database of network-management information used by the network-management Simple Network Management Protocol (SNMP). Network-managed objects implement relevant MIBs to allow remote-management operations.

Meta-directory A directory service for integrating information from disparate sources. Includes the ability to join information about people who are scattered throughout multiple directory systems, synchronize passwords, or automatically create accounts in multiple applications or systems when administrators add a person to the directory.

Multiprotocol Label Switching (MPLS) Integrates a label-swapping framework with network layer routing. The basic idea involves assigning short fixed-length labels to packets at the ingress to an MPLS cloud. Throughout the interior of the MPLS domain, the labels attached to packets are used to make forwarding decisions (usually without recourse to the original packet headers). Defined in RFC 2702.

Outsourced policy An execution model where a policy enforcement device issues a query to delegate a decision for a specific policy event to another component, external to it. For example, in RSVP, the arrival of a new RSVP message to a PEP requires a fast policy decision (not to delay the end-to-end setup). The PEP may use COPS to send a query to the PDP, asking for a policy decision. *Outsourced policy* is contrasted with *provisioned policy*, but they are not mutually exclusive and operational systems may combine the two.

Per-hop behavior (PHB) The forwarding behavior applied at a DiffServ-compliant node within a network.

Point-to-Point Protocol (PPP) An Internet data-link protocol used to frame data packets on point-to-point links, such as modem links.

Policy A representation of a business objective to be implemented in the management domain by means of policy agents or policy enforcement points. A policy defines one or more rules. Each rule binds one or more actions to sets of conditions that describe by whom (users), for what (systems, applications), and in which circumstances (time, day of week, date) the actions may be triggered.

Policy action   See *Action*.

Policy-based configuration   The set of parameters in network elements and other systems that determine their function and operation, derived from one or more policies in a policy-based networking system.

Policy condition   See *Condition*.

Policy conflict   Occurs when the actions of two rules (that are both satisfied simultaneously) contradict each other. The entity implementing the policy would not be able to determine which action to perform. The implementers of policy systems must provide conflict detection and avoidance or resolution mechanisms to prevent this situation.

Policy console   The component of a policy-based networking system that provides a user interface to construct policies and monitor status of the policy-managed environment.

Policy decision point (PDP)   The core component of a policy-based networking system; it persists policy information in a policy repository, supports one or more policy consoles for the construction of policies, and utilizes one or more policy agents to enforce policies. A policy server provides storage, decision-making, distribution, and monitoring services for the system. Also known as a policy server.

Policy domain   The logical area for which network managers want to define network policy, that is, all or part of a physical network. Note that this is not necessarily the same as an NT domain or a DNS domain.

Policy enforcement point (PEP)   An agent running on or within a resource that enforces a policy decision and/or makes a configuration change.

Policy Information Base (PIB)   In COPS-PR, a collection of related policy rule classes, defined as a module.

Policy management tool   The component of a policy-based networking system that assists the policy console in the tasks of constructing policies, deploying policies, and monitoring status of the policy-managed environment. Serves as an intermediary between the console and the policy repository, as well as to policy decision points.

Policy proxy   A software process that represents one or more resources by receiving policy information on their behalf. The proxy uses this information to configure resources such that they will enforce the policy. It then uses some protocol (standard or proprietary) to communicate with the resources.

Policy repository   A specific data store that holds policy rules, their conditions and actions, and related policy data. A directory is an example of such a store.

Policy server   The central component of the system, which coordinates the creation and provisioning of policy throughout the network. It coordinates access to other system components, communicates with the database, calculates the effective policy, and passes it to the proxy agent for transmission to the routers where the policy is enforced.

Policy translation   The transformation of a policy from a representation or level of abstraction, to another representation or level of abstraction. For example, it may be necessary to convert PIB data to a command-line format. This is also known as *policy conversion*.

Provisioned policy   An execution model where network elements are pre-configured, based on policy, prior to processing events. Configuration is pushed to the network device, for example, based on time of day or at initial booting of the device. The focus of this model is on the distribution of configuration information and is exemplified by Differentiated Services. Based on events received, devices use downloaded (preprovisioned) mechanisms to implement policy. *Provisioned policy* is contrasted with *outsourced policy*.

Provisioned QoS   Methods of establishing quality of service that statically configure QoS resources. For example, defining classes of service via priority queues through the use of a policy proxy agent. See also *signaled QoS*.

Quality of service (QoS)   A set of specific measures, characteristics, and properties that defines how well a network is performing, as experienced by particular traffic across the network.

Remote access server (RAS)   A device that enables remote users to dial in to a network to access resources such as files and print and application servers.

Remote Authentication Dial-In User Service (RADIUS)   A protocol that uses a client-server model to securely authenticate and administer remote network connection users and sessions. It can support various types of user authentication, including PAP and CHAP.

Remote Monitoring (RMON and RMON2)   A protocol for measuring and reporting network statistics, history, alarms, filters, packet capture, and events.

Resource Reservation Protocol (RSVP)   An IP-based protocol used for communicating application QoS requirements to intermediate transit nodes in a network. RSVP uses a soft-state mechanism to maintain path and reservation state in each node in the reservation path.

Role   In SNMPCONF, an abstract characteristic assigned to a network element that expresses a notion, such as a political, financial, legal, geographical, or architectural attribute, typically not directly derivable from information stored on the system. In the IETF's Policy Core Information

Model, a string characterizing a particular function of a network element or interface that can be used to identify particular behaviors associated with that element. It is a selector for policy rules, to determine the applicability of the rule to a particular network element. *Roles* abstract the capabilities and/or use of network devices and resources.

Role combination   An unordered set of roles. Two interpretations of *role combination* currently exist. In COPS-PR, the set of roles in a role combination must be identical to the set of roles of the network element or interface. In the Policy Core Information Model, the selection process for a role combination chooses policies associated with the combination itself, policies associated with each of its subcombinations, and policies associated with each of the individual roles in the combination.

Rule   A component of policy that binds an action to the conditions that govern whether the action is performed. When controlling network resources, the action is usually to provide a service. A simplified expression for a rule is as follows:

if (conditions)
then action

Schema   A collection of data models which are each bound to the same type of repository.

Security association (SA)   In IPsec, an agreement between two communicating parties on which authentication and encryption algorithms will be used, along with related data, such as key lifetimes.

Security Policy Specification Language (SPSL)   A language designed to express security policies, security domains, and the entities that manage those policies and domains. It supports policies for packet filtering, IPSec, and IKE exchanges, but may be extended to express other types of policies.

Service-level agreement (SLA)   The documented result of a negotiation between a customer/consumer and a provider of a service that specifies the levels of availability, serviceability, performance, operation, or other attributes of the service. Violations of an SLA by a service provider may result in a prorated service rate for the next billing period for the subscriber, as compensation for the service provider not meeting the terms of the SLA.

Service-level objective (SLO)   Partitions an SLA into individual metrics and operational information to enforce and/or monitor the SLA. Service-level objectives may be defined as part of an SLA, or in a separate document. The actions of enforcing and reporting monitored compliance can be implemented as one or more policies.

Signaled QoS   A method of dynamically requesting an explicit class of service or an explicit amount of bandwidth. For example, using RSVP, an application signals a network element requesting it to allocate and reserve 100 Kbps of bandwidth. See also *provisioned QoS*.

Simple Network Management Protocol (SNMP) A UDP-based network management protocol used predominantly in TCP/IP networks. SNMP can be used to monitor, poll, and control network devices. SNMP traditionally is used to manage device configurations, gather statistics, and monitor performance thresholds.

Structure of Management Information (SMI) An adapted subset of OSI's Abstract Syntax Notation One, ASN.1 (1988), used to encode collections of related objects as SNMP Management Information Base (MIB) modules.

Structure of Policy Provisioning Information (SPPI) An adapted subset of SNMP's Structure of Management Information (SMIv2) that is used to encode collections of related Policy Rule Classes as a PIB.

Subnet In local area networking, the portion of a network that is partitioned from the remainder of the network by a router or another device.

Subnet Bandwidth Manager (SBM) A proposal of the IETF for handling resource reservations on shared and switched IEEE 802-style local area media.

Telnet A TCP-based terminal-emulation protocol used in TCP/IP networks predominantly for connecting to and logging in to remote systems.

Traffic shaper A device used to modify bursty communications traffic characteristics to match a desired traffic contract.

Traffic shaping A QoS method that manages traffic and congestion when there are different available bandwidths in two different domains, such as in the LAN versus the WAN. Some examples include Frame Relay Traffic Shaping (FRTS) and Committed Access Rate (CAR).

Type of Service (ToS) field A bit field in the IP packet header designed to contain values that indicate how each packet should be handled in the network.

Virtual private network (VPN) A private network built atop a public network, such as the Internet, in which secure connections are set up dynamically between a source and destination.

Web-Based Enterprise Management (WBEM) A DMTF initiative to promote the use of Internet technologies for the management of desktop computers, servers, and other devices.

X.500 A set of recommendations adopted by the International Telecommunications Union and the International Standards Organization for standardizing directory protocols used in both public-access and private computer networks.

Index